Positive Discipline for Preschoolers

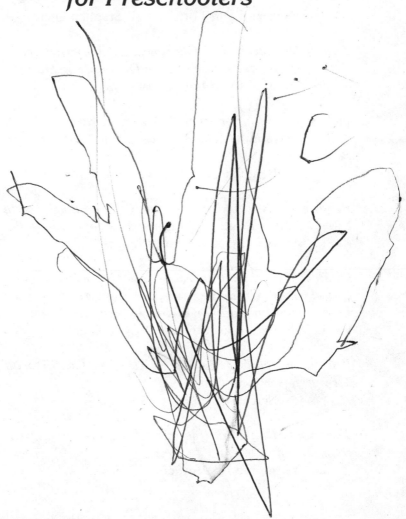

Other Books in the Developing Capable People Series

Positive Discipline for Preschoolers

For the Early Years— Raising Children Who Are Responsible, Respectful, and Resourceful

Jane Nelsen
Cheryl Erwin
Roslyn Duffy

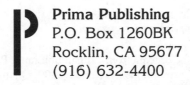

Prima Publishing
P.O. Box 1260BK
Rocklin, CA 95677
(916) 632-4400

Cover design by The Dunlavey Studio, Sacramento
Cover Photograph by Craig Hammell
Composition by Archetype Book Composition
Copyediting by Ruth Letner
Production by Andi Reese Brady
Interior design by Paula Goldstein

Lyrics from "Flowers Are Red" on pages 73–74
© 1978 FIVE J'S SONGS.
Used by permission.

Library of Congress Cataloging-in-Publication Data

Nelsen, Jane.
    Positive discipline for preschoolers: for the early years—raising children who are responsible, respectful, and resourceful / Jane Nelsen, Cheryl Erwin, Roslyn Duffy.
        p.   cm.
    Includes index.
    1-55958-497-1
    1. Preschool children. 2. Toddlers. 3. Child rearing. 4. Discipline of children. 5. Parent and child. I. Erwin, Cheryl. II. Duffy, Roslyn. III. Title.
    HQ774.5.N45 1994
    649´.123—dc20   94-27682
                                                        CIP

96 97 98 RRD 10 9 8 7 6 5 4 3 2

Printed in the United States of America

How to Order:

Single copies may be ordered from Prima Publishing, P.O. Box 1260BK, Rocklin, CA 95677; telephone (916) 632-4400. Quantity discounts are also available. On your letterhead, include information concerning the intended use of the books and the number of books you wish to purchase.

To my twelve grandchildren,
Josua, Amber, Trey, Kenny, Drew
and the preschoolers,
Woody, Kristina, Mac, Scotty, Kelsie, Katie, Riley,
and those to come.

—JANE

To all the children—our world's best hope—and to
Philip, who teaches me day by day what it means to
be a mom.

—CHERYL

With all my love to Vinnie and our children,
Blue, Manus, Rose, and Bridget
Thank you for making me a mom;
And to Lynn, Jane, and Laurie
For your friendship on my journey to rainbows.

—ROSLYN

Contents

Acknowledgments

Karen Blanco, Editorial and Marketing Coordinator for Prima Publishing, said, "Why don't you write a book on preschoolers?" After much moaning and groaning, we started thinking about how many important concepts have not been covered in our other books. Thank you, Karen. It is always a delight and pleasure to work with you!

We are grateful to Steven P. Cunningham and Lynn Lott for their help with the chapter on priorities. Steven actually wrote part of the chapter and spent many hours on the phone consulting and giving examples. Lynn has spent many years working with the Lifestyle Priorities (which she calls "Top Card") in her therapy and workshops. She made sure the Pleasing Priority didn't sound too much like Superiority.

Thanks to Professor Philip C. DiMare for reading the chapters on the emotional development of trust versus mistrust, autonomy versus doubt and shame, and initiative versus guilt. Professor DiMare is extremely knowledgeable regarding the work of Erik Erikson and offered many suggestions.

Finally, we appreciate the time that Dr. John Taylor took in consulting with us on our chapter about children with ADHD. We have been fortunate to have the expertise of so many wonderful people.

Prologue

by the Children

"I'm James. I just turned two in December. I want to do everything myself. I don't want any help. I like to do things my own way, even if it takes longer, and if you try to help we have to start all over. If you try putting on my sock, I have to pull it off and do it myself. That is much more important to me than whether I got it backwards. I keep wishing everybody 'happy birthday.' Sometimes I scream. I can't talk too well—I have a hard time getting everything out. But I've learned one word that's very powerful: NO!"

"My name is Susan and I am 3 1/2 years old. I am discovering the power of words. I am upset when people won't read me the same book over and over again, or when they try to leave out a part. My favorite question is 'why?' I like to dress up and try on all kinds of different characters. I like to have stories told to me all the time. I like to have someone to play with me all the time, too. And I don't like to have my playtime interrupted."

"I am Jeffrey F. Fraser. The 'F' stands for Frank, like my Grandpa. I am very sociable. I like talking to people. Yesterday I turned five years old. We can be friends and I will invite you to my birthday party. When I pick what I want to do, I pay attention really good. I have a little brother. He will do for a playmate if there's nobody better. I think this tooth is getting loose. Do you want to hear me count? I can sing a song for you. Do you want to play with me? Okay, you be the bad guy and I'll be the good guy . . . "

"Me is Billy. Me like dinos. Big loud dinos. Move their heads. Rex is meanest. Me 18 months. Mine Mommy. Mine brother. Me walk. Me drink. Me fast. Me want it now!"

"I am six months old. My name is Steve. I like to listen to people and make lots of faces. I like to watch faces, and see my own hands. I cry when I am hungry or tired. I sit up by myself. I like to grab things with my hands and put them in my mouth. I smile when I feel good. I nurse a lot. I eat food, too. But I don't like squash!"

"I'm four years old. I'm Cyndy. I have sparkly shoes. Do you know what kind of underwear I have on? They have the days on them. See how sparkly my shoes are when I twirl? I'm too big to be taking naps. If you read me a story, I'll be happier. I am really not tired. Do you want to see my shoes? I am going to marry Chad. Do you know Chad? He has a Batman cape. Can you read me a story now?"

This is a book about us—the children. Each one of us is different. Not all two year olds or three year olds will be like us, but you will probably find a little bit of us in the children you know. This book will help you get to know us and find out what the world is like for us. It will give you lots of ideas about how to help us grow, and how to encourage and teach us. Jeffrey calls this "possible discipline." We are alike and we are different. We all want to be loved; this book is for the people who love us.

CHAPTER 1

Setting the Stage for Raising Your Child

Close your eyes for just a moment and remember the first time you saw your child's face. That newborn infant may have been red, bald, and wrinkled, but chances are you felt you'd never seen anything more beautiful, nor heard anything sweeter than your baby's first cries. Writers and painters have often tried to capture the magic of those first moments of life, but words and pictures are rarely powerful enough to convey what happens between parent and child.

For most parents, the months leading up to that miraculous moment of birth are filled with plans, dreams, and a few worries. In reflective moments, we wonder whether we'll be good parents, whether we'll know what to do, whether the baby will be "all right." We talk endlessly about the relative merits of cloth and paper diapers, about nursing or formula feeding. We discuss names for hours, saying them aloud to see how they fit.

We buy and are given impossibly tiny garments and mysterious articles with odd names like "receiving blanket." We wonder if we'll somehow know what to do with them when the time comes. And we purchase and ponder over the fascinating gadgetry of babyhood: car seats, swings, carriers, cribs, pacifiers, bottles, breast pumps. Our homes overflow with stuffed animals, mobiles, and hand-knitted blankets and booties. It is a time for endless dreaming, a time for hope and wonder.

Fantasy Versus Reality

Sometimes, though, when we carry that helpless little scrap of humanity home from the hospital, the dreams fade a bit in the harsh light of reality. The baby cries, sometimes for hours without ceasing, and it's up to us to figure out why. The little darling sleeps all day then gurgles happily all night, much to the dismay of his sleep-deprived parents. The baby spits up when we're dressed to go out, has twelve bowel movements in a single night, refuses all known varieties of food, and cries angrily when handed to eager relatives.

And from those first moments, parenting young children can become an avalanche of questions and frustrations. The very real love and tenderness remain, but as that precious baby grows, develops, and changes, life becomes an apparently endless stream of new decisions to be made, new ideas to be tested. People look at our beloved child in public places, smile knowingly, and talk about the "terrible twos." Many a young parent feels hopelessly overwhelmed and completely at the mercy of the adorable little tyrant their baby has become.

How Will I Know What to Do?

None of us is born knowing how to be a parent. We learn by watching our own parents, and by trial and error. And we worry that those errors may cost more than we can afford. We have so many questions: Do I spank a child or not? How do I get children to listen? How do I communicate with an infant who doesn't understand words? How do I handle a defiant toddler, or a discouraged preschooler? How do I decide what's really important? How can I build my children's self-esteem, teach them responsibility and honesty and kindness? Get them to share and play nicely? How can I give them the tools to succeed on their own in a difficult and challenging world?

Advice is usually in plentiful supply—grandparents, uncles and aunts, and the lady behind you in line at the grocery store will have lots of it—but whose advice is right? It is our hope as authors—and as parents—that you will find some of the answers in this book, as well as clues to help you use your own wisdom, creativity, and knowledge of your child (or the children entrusted to your care) to go beyond what can be written in words.

This book is designed to be of use to both parents and their frequent partners in child-rearing, day care workers and preschool teachers. Examples will be given throughout the book of both home and preschool situations to show how the principles of positive discipline can be applied to all aspects of a young child's life. Developmental information will be included wherever appropriate. Because it can be immensely helpful for all the adults who shape a child's life to have the same understanding, you may want to share this book with your day care center, preschool, or other members of your family.

Your Family Is Your Family

It can help to remind yourself that all families, like all children, are different. Not all babies are born into two-parent families with a home in the suburbs, two cars, and a family dog. Your family may indeed look like that, or it may take a different shape altogether. You may be a single parent, through divorce or death or because you never married; you and your spouse may have brought children from previous marriages and added those you have together; you may have live-in grandparents or other relatives; or you may share a home with friends and their children.

A family, it has been said, is a circle of people who love each other. Whatever the form your family takes, remember that it will be whatever you have the courage to make it. With wisdom, patience, and love, you can create a place where your children can feel safe, secure, and free to grow and learn, and where they can become responsible, respectful, and resourceful people.

The Importance of Long-Range Parenting

Life with an active toddler can make us feel like we're aboard a runaway train if we let it. The days rush by, each one filled with new discoveries, new words, new crises. Parents often have to scurry to keep up with their young offspring and sometimes have little time available for thoughtful planning. But think for a moment: wouldn't it be helpful, as you set out on the journey of parenting, to know your final destination?

Perhaps one of the wisest things you can do right now is to take a moment to ask yourself a very important question: What it is that I really want for my children? When your baby, your toddler, or your preschooler has grown into an adult (as impossible as that may seem now), what qualities and characteristics do you want that adult to have?

You may decide that you want your child to develop responsibility, honesty, compassion, self-reliance, courage, and gratitude—each parent's list will be a little different. What truly matters is this: From your child's earliest moments of life, the decisions you make as a parent will shape his or her future. Each and every action we take—whether or not we slap our child's hand as she reaches for a delicate object, how we deal with food thrown across the kitchen—should nurture those qualities we want to encourage.

This thought feels overwhelming to most parents. You may be wondering, "What if I make mistakes?" "How will I know what to do?" Isn't it wonderful to realize that mistakes are not insurmountable failures, but valuable opportunities to learn? Both you and your child will make many mistakes along the way, but they needn't cause irreparable damage if you're willing to learn from them together. The most valuable parenting tools are those you already possess: your love for your child, and your own inner wisdom and common sense. Learning to trust them will carry you far along the road to successful parenting.

Remember, too, that children, especially very young children, learn by watching and imitating those around them. Your little one will not only want to push the vacuum or wash the dishes like mom and dad, he'll imitate the values you live by, such things as honesty, kindness, and justice. Remember that for children, an action is a far more effective teacher (for positive or negative) than a thousand words. Let your actions as a parent teach your child that he or she is loved and respected, that choices have consequences, and that home is a safe and wonderful place to be.

A Word About Love

Many things are done to children—or withheld from children—in the name of "love." "I spank my children because I love them," we might say. Or "I rescue and overprotect my children because I love them." "I love my children so I don't help them much—they need to learn it's a tough world out there." "I push my children—in toilet training, or early reading, or sports activities, or academic excellence—because I love them." "I work long hours because I love my children and I want them to have everything money can buy." "I decide things for my children because I love them too much to risk letting them make wrong choices." These things may be done in the name of love, but they are not the best way to show love if you want your children to be responsible, respectful, and resourceful.

Actually, whether we love our children is not the question. The real issue is whether we can show that love in a way that nurtures accountability and self-esteem, a way that helps our children blossom into their full potential as happy, contributing members of society.

How much *should* we give our children? Is it harmful to let a child have her own way? Should we push our children, or let them wander along at their own pace? All parents occasionally have questions and concerns. Fortunately, parent education and training is finally gaining wide acceptance and credibility. Society has never questioned the need for education and training in occupational fields, be it bricklaying or nursing. But somewhere along the line the notion got planted that parenting should come "naturally" and that attending a parenting class or reading a book on parenting was an admission of inadequacy.

These days parents are reading books and attending parenting classes in droves, and they testify that what they learn helps them enjoy the important job of parenting as their children learn more self-discipline, responsibility, cooperation, and problem-solving skills.

We highly encourage you to seek out and get involved with a parenting group in your community—or to start one yourself (in your free time, of course!) Reading books and attending classes will not make you a perfect parent—there is no such thing. But you will have more awareness of what works and what doesn't work for the long-range benefit of your children. When you make mistakes, you will know how to correct them—and you will be able to teach your children that mistakes provide wonderful opportunities to learn. (We can't say it often enough!)

A Word About Dads

The world of infants and very young children often seems to be a very "female" place. After all, giving birth, caring for, and nurturing the very young has traditionally been a woman's job. But times are changing; it is often a child's father who can calm him down, coax a smile, or spoon in the strained peas. And we would encourage fathers not to stop with being mere playmates; children can learn so very much from their fathers.

Dads truly are just as good as moms at changing diapers, rocking, singing, bathing, dressing, and teaching—if they choose to be. And a young child feels a wonderful sense of belonging and security when *both* of her parents, mom and dad, take an active role in raising her. The world is a busy place, and these days both mom and dad are likely to be working—which is all the more reason for parents to share as much as possible in the joys and duties of parenting.

Raising your young child can be more enjoyable and less frustrating when both parents can spell each other, share ideas, and work together to solve the inevitable problems. If you are a single mother or father you *can* raise a happy, healthy child alone (pick up a copy of *Positive Discipline for Single Parents* to learn more), but if you're lucky enough to be part of a loving parenting team, make the most of it. Your child will benefit from what both of you have to give.

Parenting from the Heart

Parenting groups are great places to learn new skills and ideas, and to get a little moral support along the way. But when all is said and done, parenting is essentially a matter of the heart and spirit as well as training and knowledge. Perhaps the greatest parenting skill of all is the ability to feel an unbreakable bond of love and warmth for your children, and to be able to listen to the voice of love and wisdom even when your patience has been stretched to the breaking point.

The best parenting translates love from word into action—and that is often easier said than done. No matter how often we say the words, it's all too easy to lose sight of love when we're confronted with the incredible variety of new misbehaviors our children can invent.

There is a popular children's book by Robert Munsch entitled *Love You Forever.* In this little gem, a mother watches her infant sleep and croons to him, "I'll love you forever, I'll like you for always. As long as I'm living, my baby you'll be." And as that child grows from baby to terrible toddler to awkward adolescent, the mother creeps into her son's room at night to watch him sleep and to croon that same little song.

The day comes at last when the mother lies ill and dying, and the son sits by her bedside to sing the old song to her. When he returns home, he shares the song—and the bond of love—with his newborn baby daughter. And that feeling—that indescribable tenderness and warmth that a parent feels for a sleeping child—is the heart of parenting.

The next time you tuck your little one in at night, let your gaze rest on that sleeping face; print it firmly in your memory. There are so many things in life that can shake a parent's confidence. We make mistakes; our children make mistakes. We're all learning to be people as we go along, experimenting on each other, blundering occasionally, doing the best we can.

But the next time you're confronted with a hysterical infant, a defiant toddler, or an angry preschooler—and there will be many such times as the years roll by—close your eyes for just a moment and look in your memory for the face of a sleeping child. Then let that love and tenderness give you the wisdom to deal with the crisis at hand.

Parenting is rarely a simple matter, and no one can challenge or stretch a parent like a very young child who is learning and exploring his world one piece at a time. There will be ample room in the chapters ahead for information, tips, and techniques, but remember that it is always the relationship between parent and child that matters most. If that relationship is based on unconditional love and trust—if your children know from their earliest days that you love them *no matter what*—you'll probably do just fine. Taking the time now to build the proper foundation by entering your child's world and understanding how he or she feels and thinks, and by talking, laughing, playing, and just being together, may be the best investment you will ever make in the future of your family.

No one ever said it would be easy to be a parent; it is undoubtedly one of life's most demanding, time-consuming, and unappreciated jobs. But it isn't always easy to be a child these days either. Have patience; work toward trust and closeness. A little love and understanding coupled with some solid skills and ideas will help you find your way to being the best parent you can be: one who parents from the heart.

CHAPTER 2

Who Is This Person Anyway? Getting to Know Your Child

Martha Richards had a story to tell. She collapsed into a chair and waited impatiently for the other members of her parenting group to stop their friendly chatter and settle down.

. The group's leader noticed Martha's exasperation and smiled. "Martha, it looks like you came prepared with something to share. Why don't you start us out?"

Martha sighed and shook her head. "I just don't know what to do," she moaned, the frustration in her voice obvious. "My two-year-old, Daniel, is driving me crazy. He insists on touching things in stores even though I must have told him a dozen times not to touch. He gets angry when I won't read to him or play with him right away—he just can't seem to wait patiently for even five minutes. He's always yanking his hand out of mine when we walk together, and I worry that he'll get away from me or run into the street."

The rest of the group smiled sympathetically, and a few heads nodded as Martha told her tale of woe. Other parents had shared such experiences and understood this mom's feelings. "This morning was the last straw, though." Martha paused dramatically then continued, her voice tight. "This morning Daniel deliberately lied to me. I've told him I won't tolerate lying, but he fibbed right to my face."

The leader met Martha's eyes and nodded. "I can see you're really upset. What did Daniel say?"

"Well," Martha said, "he told me he saw a lion in the backyard. Isn't that ridiculous? There couldn't possibly be a lion in our backyard! And if Daniel starts lying now, what will happen as he grows up?"

Another woman spoke up. "I worry, too. Are the things my child does now signs of how she will turn out as an adult?" Other members of the group nodded.

The concern and confusion these parents are feeling is easy to understand; most parents have similar moments of frustration and disappointment. But there's a good chance that young Daniel isn't intentionally driving his mother to distraction; it's very likely, as Martha's parenting group leader will undoubtedly explain, that Daniel is simply being himself: an active, curious two-year-old who is learning about his world in the only way he knows.

Getting into Your Child's World

One of the best ways of becoming an effective parent—or, for that matter, an effective human being—is to understand the perceptions of other people, to be able to "get into their world." This is especially true for parents of very young children—after all, their world is so different from ours!

A newborn infant arrives in this world from a place where he's been cradled in warmth and safety beside his mother's heart, his every need immediately met. Suddenly, after a convulsive and tiring journey out of his mother's body, he finds himself in a world of heat and cold, loud noises, moving objects, and bright lights. Faces come and go, voices come from all directions, and this new world runs on a schedule he doesn't yet understand. The instant nourishment and comfort are gone; now he must wail loudly to satisfy his hunger or to find comfort. Sleeping, eating, simply functioning—all must adapt to the new world. It wouldn't be surprising if we somehow found scientific evidence that infants long to return to the womb!

From the moment of birth onward, a child's early months and years are a voyage of discovery. And one of the first things a child must discover is himself! An infant's control of himself moves from the center outward. At first he is helpless, doing for himself only the most basic bodily functions, unable even to lift his head or to turn over without help.

But as time passes, his control increases. He learns to really see ("Is *that* Mom?") and to track objects with his gaze. One day he realizes that those things that flap in front of his face occasionally are his hands and feet; he can make them move, grab them, and even—oh, bliss!—stuff them into his mouth. Later he learns that he can grab other things with them and stuff those into his mouth as well.

The other developmental milestones follow in due time. A baby learns to turn over, scoot, crawl, pull herself up on the furniture, and, eventually, walk. Running and getting into mischief come next. Toilet training happens eventually (more about that later). The last things to be mastered are the delicate ones, things like balance and fine motor control, which explains why a five- or even a six-year-old may have such a difficult time mastering the art of tying shoes. Part of becoming an effective and loving parent or teacher means understanding the world of the little ones you're working with, and making every effort to get inside it.

Understanding Your Child's World

It's an old question: nature versus nurture, genes versus the environment. What shapes the personality of a human being? Why are our children the people they are? Why is one three-year-old peaceful and compliant, eager to please and easy to get along with, while the three-year-old next door seems bent on challenging every rule, pushing every limit, and breaking everything in sight? We will spend more time discussing these things in the chapters to follow, but there are a few ideas to keep in mind for now.

Children are a product of their parents' genes (nature), and they are undoubtedly influenced by the environment and ideas around them (nurture); we don't know the exact balance. Perhaps it is more important to realize that while children are shaped by both the raw material they inherit and the forces around them, they also bring to the world something uniquely their own: their own spirit, identity, and personality. Have you ever noticed that, despite having the same parents and the same home, children in the same family can be incredibly different? Each of us is unique. Parents need to take time to get to know—and to accept—their children for exactly who they are.

Remember Martha and two-year-old Daniel? We will examine these ideas in more detail in later chapters, but let's take just a quick look. What might explain the behavior this mom finds so frustrating?

1. A child learns about the world by doing. A child who is "playing" is actually hard at work, trying on new roles and ideas, tasting, touching, smelling, and experimenting with life. Learning is a hands-on experience, filled with the enthusiastic joy of discovery. It takes a while (and some parental patience) before children learn where the boundaries lie.

Children need secure, loving boundaries in order to feel safe, just as adults need a house with strong walls and a roof to feel protected from the weather, but any self-respecting child will feel obliged to cruise up to the boundaries you've set and test them occasionally, just to make sure they're firmly in place. He's not deliberately trying to drive you insane; he's either exploring or learning about consistency and making sure Mom and Dad mean what they say (another version of trust).

Is all of this testing annoying? Of course! Frustrating? Absolutely! And there are ways to understand and cope with misbehavior, which we'll discuss later. But children are rarely as intentionally naughty as their parents think—they're just acting their age.

2. A child's physical size and abilities have a strong influence on her behavior.   Take a moment sometime soon and get down on your child's level. Put your face on the same level as hers—what do you see? The world looks a lot different from down here! Seeing an adult's face requires tilting your head backward—an uncomfortable position if held too long. Most of the time young children gaze out at a world of knees, shins, and feet, and the only reliable way to catch an adult's attention is to pull on his hands or legs! And just imagine how frightening a yelling, pointing parent would look from down here.

A child's point of view can actually add a unique perspective to the family's life together, if we let it. On one fine Saturday afternoon, the Douglas family went out for a walk together. Mom, Dad, and the two older children were all busy admiring the brilliant colors of the autumn leaves, watching the birds in flight, and commenting on the shapes of the clouds. It was three-year-old Melissa, whose vantage point was considerably lower, who noticed the tiny frog beneath the bushes. Without Melissa's excited exclamations, the family would not only have missed seeing the tiny creature, they might have accidentally stepped on it!

Are you still down on the floor? If another adult is handy, reach up and take his hand for a moment. Imagine going for a nice long walk through the nearest shopping mall in this position. What parents often believe is defiant yanking away may simply be a child trying to get some circulation back in her hand and arm! In addition, adults have much longer legs than their little ones; children almost always have to run to keep up. No wonder they lag behind us.

It can be frustrating to be a small person whose hands won't quite do the tasks they're expected to. Often children want very much to help, to dress themselves, and to do other tasks around the house, but the sheer mechanics are beyond them. The result is often a frustrated, angry child—and a frustrated, angry parent.

3. A child's concepts of reality and fantasy are different than an adult's.

Did you know that when you walk out of your baby's line of sight, you have ceased to exist? That the toy accidentally dropped on the floor has disappeared forever? No wonder babies cry when separated from people or things they want—the concept that objects are permanent hasn't developed yet.

In the same way, a young child experiments with his imagination to explore and learn. Our young friend Daniel may not have seen a lion in his backyard, but he may have seen the neighbor's cat. Or he may have watched a cartoon about lions in the jungle. Or his picture book may have included lions and their cubs. Daniel's lion wasn't a "lie," but the product of a vivid imagination and a great deal of curiosity.

Children often have difficulty understanding that what they see on television and movie screens may not be real. For instance, even children as old as seven or eight usually believe the claims of television commercials; after all, if Michael Jordan says it, it must be true!

When Kate and Bill Jackson learned that the Disney classic "Snow White and the Seven Dwarfs" was coming to their local theatre, they were excited about the opportunity to share the movie with their three-year-old son, Philip. Philip was a bright, articulate child, and his parents explained to him carefully that the movie was fun, but it did have some scary parts.

"It isn't real," Kate told her small son. "You don't need to be afraid." Philip grinned and bounced up and down, too excited about seeing his first movie to pay much attention to his mother's warning.

Everything went well until the scene where the wicked queen drinks the potion that will turn her into a withered old hag. Suddenly, with a shriek like a tea kettle boiling over, Philip leaped from his own seat into his mother's lap, where he huddled shaking. He stubbornly refused to return to his own seat for the rest of the movie, even though the fright eventually died away.

"Hey, kiddo, didn't we tell you the movie wasn't real?" Bill asked his small son on the way out to the car.

Philip looked up at his dad in amazement. "But Dad," he said slowly, "it *was* real. I *saw* it!"

Philip recovered quickly enough, learned the names of all seven dwarfs, and enthusiastically sang "Hi ho, hi ho" for the rest of the summer. But his parents learned that the best lectures in the world don't change the fact that a child's definition of reality is far broader than an adult's.

Fantasy may also be a child's way of getting in touch with feelings for which he doesn't yet have words, a way of exploring his own inner being. Careful listening (more about that later) and acceptance by his parents will help him to understand his feelings and find healthy ways of dealing with them.

4. Patience is a virtue far beyond the reach of most young children.   Think back for a moment to when you were a child. Remember how long it took for Christmas to come? Have you noticed how quickly the entire process speeded up as you grew older? (These days it seems like Christmas comes every six months; we're either putting up the decorations or taking them down!)

Time moves far more slowly for an eager child than it does for an adult. Five minutes can seem like an eternity, and adults take far too long to do everything. Yes, children need to learn patience; but parents need to be patient enough to let them learn.

Adults also need to learn that units of time simply don't have the same meaning for children. Jimmy was an extremely bright two-year-old. His parents took him to a drive-in theatre one night. It didn't take long before Jimmy was fast asleep— just as his parents had planned. A week later the family drove past the drive-in and Jimmy said excitedly, "Look, we went there last night!" His father spanked Jimmy for lying. But Jimmy wasn't lying; his father didn't understand child development and didn't realize that Jimmy simply hadn't mastered the concept of time yet. With more understanding his father would have been delighted at Jimmy's developing memory instead of concerned about his "untruthfulness."

With a little thought and consideration, it isn't hard to see that simply getting into your child's world can provide many solutions to the mysteries of behavior. Your child is a marvelous, unique being; getting to know him and understanding his perceptions of the world around him can be an exciting and enjoyable adventure for parents and children alike.

CHAPTER 3

The First Year of Life— Can I Count on You?

The first six years of a child's life are critically important, and the experiences parents provide or fail to provide can make a profound difference in their children's emotional, intellectual, and physical development. We will explore these years in detail in the chapters ahead, but let's take a quick look at the concepts your child must somehow learn and absorb during this busy period.

Children learn about their own worth and value during their early years. They observe the members of their family and their interactions with one another. They watch their peers and teachers at day care. And they constantly make internal decisions about what it all means. Usually, by the age of five a child has decided whether or not she is loved and wanted, whether she's smart or dumb, cute or homely, a joy or a nuisance. These early decisions—some encouraging, some painful—can make impressions that last a lifetime.

It is also during the first five years or so that a child learns the basic concept of morality, of right and wrong, good and bad. Children are constantly watching the adults in their lives, parents and teachers, for clues about life, about what works and what doesn't, what is or is not acceptable. Young children can be taught gently and lovingly. They can often understand more than they communicate, but they also learn by watching and imitating the behavior of those around them. It helps to remember that they will accept as right the things you do, as well as what you say.

The Foundations of Emotional Development

It is during the first year of life that a child begins to learn the fundamental concept of trust, the first important stage of emotional development. If she cries, does someone come? If she's hungry or wet, will someone help? Do the routines and rituals of daily life happen predictably? It is by these simple experiences that she will learn to trust and rely on her parents. Without this basic trust, life becomes far more difficult. Children who have been shuttled in and out of foster homes during their early years, or who have been denied affection and consistent care, often refuse to make eye contact or to respond to even the most loving attempts later on. It can take a great deal of patience and determination to build in these children the willingness to trust that was stunted during their early years.

Most of us know people who have a hard time trusting themselves or others, and who seem to have little faith in their ability to influence what happens to them. Will your child go through life with an attitude of trust or mistrust, faith or doubt? It all depends on how he is treated in the first year of life (and the subconscious decisions he makes about his experiences), according to psychologist and human development expert Erik Erikson. This first critical year of life is also the first stage of emotional development.

The second stage of emotional development, which takes place during the second year of life, determines whether your child will go through life with faith in his autonomy (self-control and self-confidence) or will struggle with feelings of doubt and shame. The frustrations we all encounter in life often create thoughts of doubt and shame within us; however, Erikson believed that our experiences during the second year of life are especially crucial to developing a sense of autonomy that is stronger than the thoughts of doubt and shame.

The next stage of emotional development takes place during the preschool years, ages two to six. The experiences children encounter in their homes and/or preschools influence the development of initiative versus guilt—that feeling of having confidence in *my* plans and *my* ideas, as opposed to a lack of confidence (the "I can't do *any*thing" syndrome). Again, many times our interpretations of our life experiences leave us carrying a hefty sack of guilt on our shoulders, which makes us unwilling to take risks or to believe in ourselves and our own abilities. Hopefully, understanding the importance of this third stage of emotional development will motivate adults to learn the skills that will help children develop a sense of initiative that is stronger than their sense of guilt.

We will discuss each of these years and the experiences that help or hinder healthy emotional development. (Erikson's theory also covered later years. Those stages are beyond the scope of this book, but you may want to investigate them on your own.) In this chapter we will discuss the development of trust versus mistrust during the first year of life. In the next chapter we will discuss the second year of life and the development of autonomy versus doubt and shame. Following that we will devote a chapter to the preschool years and the development of initiative versus guilt.

The First Stage of Emotional Development: Trust Versus Mistrust

A sense of trust means that an infant "feels" or "senses" that she can rely on the affections and support of others. To develop a sense of trust during the first year of life, a baby needs to have his or her basic needs met consistently and lovingly. These needs include proper nutrition, a comfortable temperature, dry diapers, adequate sleep, and lots and lots and lots of touching, holding, and cuddling. Many parents feel confused about the difference between meeting their babies' needs and spoiling— and they're sure to hear many points of view (some welcome, some not).

Opinions range from "put your baby on a strict schedule (after all, he or she has come to live in your house and there is no reason to change your life too much)" to "forget about your life; hover around your baby and try to anticipate every need and whimper." Understanding the importance of your child developing trust instead of mistrust is a key factor in deciding what is right for you and your baby.

A neglected baby (one whose basic needs for food, comfort, and loving touch are not met) will develop a sense of mistrust in life. Perhaps surprisingly, an extremely pampered baby may also develop a sense of mistrust because he has never had to learn patience and self-reliance. Trying to figure out how to "walk" the middle line could cause considerable anxiety for parents, but as your understanding increases, so will your confidence. We need to use our heads and our hearts to be effective parents. The more information we have, the more we can trust our heads. The more we know how important it is to enjoy our children, the more we can trust our hearts. And when in doubt, always trust your heart.

What Is "Developmentally Appropriate"?

Part of understanding and managing young children's behavior involves knowing what is "developmentally appropriate." The more we know about the psychological, intellectual, and physical development of the child, the more we know what is "developmentally appropriate," and the better our ability to get into our child's world and shape his behavior will be. For example, it is developmentally appropriate to carry a baby in your arms. Being held, loved, and cuddled is helping him learn to trust. It is not developmentally appropriate to carry a two-year-old too often or he will not develop a strong sense of autonomy (as discussed in the next chapter). It is developmentally appropriate to discover and meet the needs of a crying infant by doing anything you can, but a crying toddler (or older child) will develop strong skills only if you help her help her*self* instead of doing too much for her. An understanding of developmental appropriateness helps us know that it is almost impossible to spoil an infant.

Spoiling, or "Help, I'm a Slave to My Baby!"

Don't worry about spoiling your baby during the first three months of life. It can happen, but it is very rare. Sylvia managed to spoil her infant because she hardly ever put him down. She held him as she puttered around the house; she held him as she fixed the meals; she even held him after he had gone to sleep. By the time her baby was two months old, he screamed every time Sylvia tried to put him down. There was no escape even when he slept; if she tried to lay him down, he would wake up and scream.

This example provides a good definition of spoiling—when the child becomes demanding and the parent feels like a slave to the child. Babies need to have their cries responded to—it teaches trust more effectively than anything else—but considering your baby's needs, your own needs, and the needs of other members of your family will help you introduce routines and begin to find a good balance.

If you feel at the mercy of your three-month-old baby's demands to be held, pick her up for just a few minutes, cuddle and coo, and then place her in a playpen with a musical mobile, or place her in a safe infant seat where she can watch what you are doing. The key is a balance that meets the needs of everyone concerned. A baby should not be left in a playpen or infant seat too long, and a mother should not feel like a slave to her child. The following story about nursing illustrates how good information can help a mother follow her head and her heart to meet the needs of her baby and herself.

Nursing: Making It Work

Jane, one of the authors (and mother of seven children), shares her nursing story and what it taught her about trusting her own instincts.

How I wish I'd had more information on nursing from the beginning; I wouldn't have created so much pain for myself and my children as I learned. My first child was born during the time (1956) when doctors were advocating a strict feeding schedule of every four hours. I didn't even question their reasoning. I just assumed they must know what they were talking about. Baby Terry would nurse and fall asleep. During the afternoon he would often wake up after an hour and start crying. I would think, "Oh no! Three more hours before he can nurse." I would walk the floor with him and try to comfort him, but he would just cry until he was screaming. I tried pacifiers and water. They might work for a few minutes, but soon he would be screaming again. (It is painful for me to even remember this.)

Finally, after two hours, I would "cheat" and nurse him before the four hours was up. He was so exhausted from crying that he would nurse for a minute or two then fall asleep. How could I have been so ignorant that I didn't know he couldn't get enough in two minutes? I was so intimidated by the doctor's advice that I didn't think. I just assumed that I had to wait another four hours. Terry would wake up hungry in about an hour and we went through another agonizing two hours before I would "cheat" again.

Because of my lack of information about nursing, I believed many myths. I believed that if my breasts weren't engorged, I didn't have any milk, that my milk must not be rich enough because it wasn't "milky white," and that Terry cried because I didn't have enough milk. The truth was that he cried because he wasn't nursing long enough to get enough nourishment and to build up my milk supply in the process. Another mistake was introducing him to cereal to fill him up. I didn't know that would only keep him from nursing long enough to build up my milk supply. I gave up in frustration after two weeks and put him on a bottle.

I tried nursing with my next three children—Jimmy, Kenny, and Brad—and even though I didn't wait four hours between each feeding, I still believed they needed cereal, apple juice, and baby food, and that I didn't have enough milk unless I was engorged. I gave up after a few weeks each time, thinking my milk just wasn't good enough.

When my fifth child, Lisa, was born, I tried nursing again. I was on my way to failure once more when my sister-in-law told me about La Leche League and their book, *The Womanly Art of Breastfeeding*. She told me there was no such thing as bad mother's milk, that engorgement wasn't a sign of "enough" milk, and that I should throw away all the formula bottles and supplemental foods and just nurse whenever my baby wanted to in order to build up my milk supply. I read the book, threw away the bottles and solid foods, and began a successful nursing experience.

I don't know when I have ever been happier! I loved nursing on demand. There were times when Lisa would sleep five or six hours. In the late afternoon and evening she would sometimes nurse as often as every hour—or sometimes every 15 minutes! But by the time she was three-and-a-half months old, she had regulated herself to a three-hour schedule during the day and would sleep through the night, even without cereal to "fill her up."

The *Womanly Art of Breastfeeding* answered so many questions that it became my "bible." I became confident that Lisa didn't need supplemental food until she was a year old. Every month my pediatrician would tell me I could introduce a new baby food, and I would just smile. Each month he would ask me if I had introduced the foods, and I would tell him I hadn't. He would tell me that maybe I should, just to make sure she didn't get anemic. (Iron is the only thing missing from mother's milk, but the baby is usually born with a year's supply of iron.) I would ask him if he would like to take a blood test to see if she was in danger of anemia. He would say, looking sheepish, "I can tell from looking at her that she isn't anemic." He really was a wonderful doctor whom I trusted for the health care of my baby; I just knew he didn't know as much as I did about nursing.

Introducing Solid Foods

Introducing solid foods was easy. When Lisa was seven months old, we occasionally offered her some mashed banana or mashed potato. I might blend other fruits or vegetables in a blender with some liquid. I say "might" because sometimes we did and sometimes we didn't. We didn't feel any pressure because we knew she was getting all she needed from breast milk during the first year. We saved a fortune (at least, it seemed like a fortune to us) on what we would have spent on formula and baby food. By the time she was a year old, she could eat many of the foods we cooked for our meals if we mashed, chopped, or blended.

Supplemental Bottles

Babies often thrive on breast milk only the first year. However, if you plan to be away from your baby (and an occasional night away is good for your own mental and emotional health, as well as your spouse's), it is easier if she is comfortable taking a bottle. I made the mistake of not introducing my last baby to a bottle until I needed to leave her with a baby-sitter when she was three months old. It took me three days of almost constantly pushing a bottle of apple juice in her mouth before she would finally take it.

La Leche League suggests expressing (that is, pumping) breast milk into a bottle and freezing it (it looks like milky dishwater) so it is available when you need to be away from your baby. This can allow Dad the opportunity to take turns with night feedings or other much needed "Mommy breaks." With time and practice, you will learn to gauge the needs of your baby. Some babies do well on a combination of nursing, formula, and foods; some babies never need anything but breast milk. Babies, like adults, are unique individuals. Patience and a bit of trial and error will help you learn to know your baby's requirements.

But I Don't Want to Nurse

In spite of the many nutritional and emotional benefits of nursing, it is not mandatory. Many emotionally and physically healthy babies have been raised on formula and baby food. The key is to have knowledge about what you are doing and to have confidence in your choice. Remember that a confident mother is better able to foster a sense of trust in her baby. Either choice, bottle or breast, can supply the nurture an infant needs; both must eventually come to an end.

Weaning

Lisa weaned herself by her first birthday; she simply refused to nurse any more. Many mothers believe weaning *can't* be that easy, but it can be if mothers are willing to watch for the signs of readiness in their babies. Somewhere between the tenth and twelfth month, most babies lose interest in nursing (or in taking a bottle). Many mothers ignore the signs and push the bottle or breast at the baby until they give in and start taking it again (unless they are as stubborn as Lisa). Mothers do this for one of two reasons: (1) They are not aware that a loss of interest during this window of time is a natural phenomenon that indicates a readiness for weaning, and (2) Mothers sometimes want their babies to keep taking the bottle because it is an easy way to calm them when they are fussy and/or to help them to go to sleep.

Keeping babies on the bottle or breast after they are ready to stop may squelch the first blossoming of their sense of autonomy, which we will discuss more thoroughly in the next chapter. It is important to realize that once the window of readiness to wean passes, nursing or taking a bottle becomes a *habit* instead of a need. The habit of nursing or taking a bottle can hinder the development of a child's sense of autonomy. Missing this opportunity for weaning isn't a traumatic, life-damaging experience. Many parents have been unaware of the signs of readiness for weaning and have allowed their children to develop the bottle or nursing habit. They have also learned (from hard experience) that weaning is more difficult when it has become a habit. We do survive, however, even if we miss this one factor that could increase autonomy a little bit and make weaning much easier.

As H. Stephen Glenn and Jane Nelsen point out in their book, *Raising Self-Reliant Children in a Self-Indulgent World,* "Weaning has never been easy for the weanor or the weenee, but it is necessary for the survival of both." Weaning (letting go) is an important parenting skill that is necessary to help children develop their full potential. Weaning is part of the larger, lifelong process of letting go and is vital to helping children develop their full potential. Weaning (and letting go) should not be confused with abandonment. Children need a lot of loving support during the weaning process. When parents wean and let go with love at developmentally appropriate times, children are encouraged to trust, to learn confidence, and to develop their full potential. Some parents, however, do choose to prolong the weaning process, as in extended nursing.

Extended Nursing

There are at least two sides to the story of extended nursing. We encourage you to become educated and aware before you decide what works for you and your baby. La Leche League and other groups encourage nursing for as long as four years or more. If you decide you want to nurse for an extended period of time, La Leche League offers classes and support. (The support can be very helpful since many people will be critical.) If you choose to extend nursing, you will have more confidence if your decision is based on education and awareness.

Uniqueness and Self-Trust

To say that people are different and unique isn't new or profound, but it doesn't hurt to be reminded. Because parents are unique, they will be comfortable with different methods of parenting. We must also remember that children don't all respond in the same ways.

What does all this have to do with the development of trust or mistrust? Erikson found that a key factor in the development of trust in children is the degree of the mother's trust in herself. Most mothers find they can trust themselves more when then have a basic understanding of child development and parenting skills—and faith in their own instincts. This is one reason it is important to be aware of the basic premises, such as the development of trust or mistrust in children, and then to use that awareness to choose what works best for you and your children.

An important part of awareness comes from education about effective parenting skills. All parenting skills taught in this book are based on the premise of treating children with dignity and respect—and of teaching them life skills. The first "skill"— it may just be a basic instinct that gets lost when we don't have the education and confidence we need for effective parenting— is simply to enjoy your children.

Enjoy Your Children

Does this really need to be said? We think so. We all have experienced getting confused and overwhelmed with the responsibility of parenting. Sharing your life with a child, especially during his first year of life, can be an overwhelming experience. Everything is new; the baby is demanding, and we all have moments when we worry if we're doing it "right."

Whenever you feel that way, just forget everything else and remember to enjoy. When you forget to enjoy, learning new skills and adjusting to life with a developing child can seem like a heavy burden. Your baby will sense your worry and doubt and his growing sense of trust may be hindered. When built on the foundation of enjoyment, awareness, and education, confidence will filter through your heart and you will know what to do. (Yes, you really will!)

Making Enjoyment a Priority

When you have small children you may as well forget about being a perfect housekeeper, running the PTA, or taking on anything that makes you feel stressed and robs you of time to enjoy your children. Discuss priorities with your spouse and make an agreement to put first things first—each other and your children. Agree to be satisfied with soup and sandwiches for a while instead of elaborate meals.

Why is this important? Isn't it possible to "do it all"? It may be; but keep in mind that infants can "feel" the energy of their parents. They often become fussy when their parents are upset. They also "sense" when you enjoy them—and know when you don't. How can infants develop a sense of trust if they don't "feel" the energy of enjoyment from their parents and know that they are loved, wanted, and appreciated? (We will explore communication and love further in Chapter 16.)

Ask yourself this question when circumstances get in the way of simply enjoying your children: "What difference will this make ten years from now?" Whether or not the house is clean, the lawn mowed, and the furniture waxed won't make any difference; on the other hand, time you spend with your spouse and your children will make all the difference in the world!

CHAPTER 4

*The Second Year of Life—
I Can Stand on My
Own Two Feet
(But Don't Abandon Me)*

What do toddlers want to do? Just about everything: explore, touch, examine, put their fingers in sockets, play with the television knobs, empty cupboards of every pot and pan, play in the toilet, unravel the toilet paper, eat lipstick, spill perfume, and investigate everything they can get their hands on.

What happens when parents don't allow toddlers to explore? What happens when parents slap their children's hands when they touch something they are not "supposed" to touch? Well-meaning parents who have not learned about this important developmental phase may not know that too much confinement and punishment can instill doubt and shame instead of a sense of autonomy. Notice we said "a sense of" autonomy—not autonomy itself.

In the first year of their lives, we work to help children develop a sense of trust rather than mistrust. Erikson believed that between the ages of one and two, children have the opportunity to begin their quest for a sense of autonomy that is stronger than feelings of doubt and shame. This search for a sense of autonomy continues throughout childhood, but the second year is when the foundation is established. A strong sense of trust developed in the first year and a strong sense of autonomy developed in the second year also build the foundation for healthy self-esteem.

What Is Autonomy?

Since a strong sense of autonomy is so important, we need to know what it is and how to help toddlers develop it. The dictionary defines "autonomy" as independence or freedom, having the will of one's actions. "What?" you might ask, "Give my toddler independence and freedom? My toddler is still a baby who needs to be dependent on me!" A toddler needs both autonomy and healthy dependence on you. He needs a balance between the security provided by parents and home, and the freedom to discover his own capabilities.

This is illustrated beautifully by the research of Harry F. Harlow using monkeys and their young. In this study, the mother monkeys took their babies into a room full of toys. The baby monkeys clung to their mothers while they surveyed the interesting toys in the room. Eventually, their need to explore took over, and they left their mothers to play with the toys. Periodically, however, they would return and jump into their mothers' arms for another dose of security before going back to their play. Children are not monkeys; but they, too, need a gentle blending of safety and freedom. Too much freedom, however, could be very dangerous and threatening for a toddler.

It is easy to misunderstand what autonomy means for a toddler. Possessing autonomy does not mean that children no longer need guidance and safe boundaries. They do. They also need a lot of freedom within those safe boundaries so they can begin that important journey toward independence—and, eventually, interdependence.

When children come into the world, they are totally dependent. Parents are most effective when they help their children learn the skills of independence (autonomy) and interdependence; but healthy independence is the foundation for healthy interdependence. The POSITIVE DISCIPLINE SERIES book *Clean and Sober Parenting* offers an excellent description of independence and interdependence:

> Many people have the mistaken idea that being an independent person means not needing anyone . . . This idea is unfounded. Independence means people know what they think, what they feel, and what they want. It means they have skills to express what they think and feel to others in a respectful manner. It means they have the skills to accomplish what they want most of the time, sometimes by themselves and sometimes with others. Only when members become independent and express their uniqueness can they break the co-dependent patterns and move toward interdependence. (57)

Aware parents can avoid the mistake of creating a codependent relationship with their children—in the name of love.

I Am Me, You Are You, and We Can Be Together

Interdependence is very different. *Clean and Sober Parenting* offers this explanation:

> Picture two people leaning on each other for support. If one moves, the other falls. This is co-dependence. Now picture those same two people near each other and available to help and connect, but with lives of their own and skills of their own. There is a lot of give and take through respect and support for individual differences. This is interdependence.

> Most people fantasize about interdependence when they think about building a relationship or a family. Then, without realizing it, they sabotage interdependence when their fears (or lack of information about effective parenting skills) keep them holding on and refusing to let go. (57–58)

This process begins at birth, as parents gradually "let go" when their children grow and begin to develop new skills and the confidence to use them. Growth toward independence and interdependence is a lifelong process that will be much easier for children who develop a strong sense of autonomy during their second year. Toddlers can only develop a sense of autonomy, not complete independence. Complete independence at this age is not only impossible, but allowing too much independence would be permissive parenting. And permissive parenting is rarely effective parenting.

Encouraging Autonomy Does Not Mean Being Permissive

Autonomy does not mean children should be allowed to do anything they want. One of the more persistent debates about parenting in early childhood concerns "childproofing" a home: removing poisons, plugging electrical sockets, latching kitchen cabinets, putting valuable or fragile items out of reach of young hands, and otherwise making the home environment safe for a child to explore. The importance of developing a child's autonomy is an excellent argument in favor of "childproofing" your home. Once the home is "childproofed," there will still be many things children should not be allowed to do, such as climb on sofas.

Some parents believe the best way to teach toddlers not to touch things or do what they shouldn't is to slap their hands. Think for just a moment. Toddlers would not be normal if they didn't want to explore and touch. They're doing their developmental "job," and it is an important ingredient in their sense of autonomy. Does it make sense to slap or spank them for doing something that is normal and important for healthy development? Slapping and spanking, especially for something that is a part of normal development, is far more likely to create a sense of doubt and shame than healthy autonomy.

Effective parenting can help children learn limits without creating doubt and shame. All require kindness and firmness at the same time. Non-punitive parenting methods are discussed later in this chapter and throughout this book.

A Need to Explore in a Safe Environment

An important part of the development of autonomy during the second year of life lies in the maturation of the muscle system. Providing a safe environment for exploration is one of the best ways to help toddlers develop healthy autonomy, as well as healthy muscles. As they explore, they exercise their muscles and enhance muscle maturation by experimenting with such activities as holding on and letting go (yes, dropping that spoon over and over is helping them develop their sense of autonomy). Children who are confined too much will not have the opportunity to develop a strong sense of autonomy. They need the opportunity to explore and test what they can and cannot do.

Jenny did not know about the importance of helping her toddler develop a strong sense of autonomy. She was an artist who loved to paint during the day when the light was good. Her daughter, Dani, seemed content to sit in a high chair eating crackers for long periods of time. When Dani would tire of the high chair, Jenny would move her to a playpen or wind-up swing. Dani was rarely let out to roam around the house.

Jenny was not a "bad" parent. She felt thrilled and lucky that Dani seemed so content with her confinement and that she could get so much painting done. Jenny didn't understand that she was hindering Dani's development of autonomy and muscle development by not giving her more opportunities to explore.

Positive Discipline methods help children develop a sense of autonomy, as well as the characteristics and the life skills they need when they can no longer depend on adults. Children, from birth through the preschool years, *always* need adults around. They also need opportunities to start developing the attitudes and skills they will need for the rest of their childhood and adult lives when parents are not around.

Punishment does not foster a healthy sense of autonomy and it does not teach life skills. Punishment (spanking and shaming children for doing things that are developmentally appropriate) fosters doubt and shame. Children will experience enough self-imposed doubt and shame as they encounter the "real" limits of their abilities. Hopefully, an understanding of this important developmental stage will help parents avoid adding to the frustration children experience as they progress in their desire for more independence.

Developmentally Appropriate Behavior

In the last chapter we introduced the concept of developmentally appropriate behavior by stating it is appropriate to carry an infant, but less appropriate to carry a toddler. This does not mean you never carry a two-year-old. It does mean you have an increased awareness about his need to develop autonomy.

Suppose you have a toddler who wants to be carried to the car. Instead of carrying him, you may stoop down, give him a hug, and tell him you are sure he can walk to the car by himself. If he still whines to be carried, you might say, "I'll hold your hand and walk slowly, but I know you can do it." You might even add, "I really need your help. Will you carry my purse?" (If it is a small one!) Yes, it would be easier to just pick him up and carry him to the car. Helping children develop the confidence and life skills they need is not always easy. But who said parenting would be easy? It need not be so difficult, either. Successful parenting is often a matter of knowing what is effective and what is not.

Distraction and Choices

Is it fair to punish children for doing things that are normal and "developmentally appropriate" for them to do? Children shouldn't be allowed to do whatever they want, but they shouldn't be punished for doing what comes naturally. It is normal and "developmentally appropriate" for toddlers to explore and want to touch, so providing them with many things and areas where they can safely do so is wise.

In the kitchen you might have a cupboard full of plastic containers, wooden spoons, pots and pans, and other items that can't hurt or be hurt by your child. In the living room you can provide a box of special toys. When your child wants to touch something that shouldn't be touched, such as a stereo, kindly and firmly pick her up and remove her from that item and place her by the toy box. Don't slap or say "no!" Instead say, "You can't play with the stereo, but you can play with your toys." This is called distraction, and you may have to do it over and over and over. (Too many parents don't realize that they spank over and over, or say "no" over and over. Distraction, much more peaceful for both parent and child, will be discussed in more detail in Chapter 13.)

Children may experience frustration by not being allowed to play with the stereo or to run into the street. This is what Erikson called the real "crisis" of this stage of development. However, adding punishment to the natural crisis is like pouring salt on a wound. The frustration is greatly eased when parents remember to be kind when they are being firm. Children "feel" the difference. It still feels like punishment to the child if distraction is accompanied by shaming words such as "bad girl."

Toddlers are interested in exploring so many things that it is not difficult to use distraction at this age. When a toddler wants to touch something that isn't appropriate, offer a substitute—or a choice of substitutes. "You can't jump on the couch.

Would you like to play with your truck or help me wash the dishes?" "It is time for bed. Which story do you want me to read when you've put on your pajamas?" (Yes, toddlers can learn to put on their pajamas, with or without your help, depending on their age.) "I need to talk on the phone now. You can play in the junk drawer (prepared in advance with age-appropriate items) or the pan cupboard while I'm on the phone." Be creative on the many possible ways to distract your child from unacceptable behavior to acceptable activities. One of the simplest discipline methods to use with toddlers is distracting and offering choices. By using this method, you also help your child develop a strong sense of autonomy.

Don't Slap Hands or Spank

To spank or not to spank is another major parenting debate. In the context of autonomy versus doubt and shame, it is obvious that spanking fosters more doubt and shame than the child experiences from natural limits. (We will discuss discipline in greater detail in Chapter 15.) A young child often does not understand the connection between what she did (reach for an electrical cord) and the response (a quick slap). Too many parents have had the unsettling experience of reaching for their child in love and having that child cringe away in fear, as if a slap is on the way—certainly not the sort of relationship that fosters trust and closeness, and certainly not what most parents would choose.

Take Time for Training

Some parents mistakenly believe that spanking is a good way to train children. Many parents say, "But I *have* to spank my children when it is a matter of life or death. I have to spank my child to teach her not to run into the street." But does spanking really teach your child what you intend? After you have spanked her, would you let her play near a busy street unsupervised?

Most parents are quick to realize that spanking is neither teaching nor training. Spanking and slapping are reactions, reactions often born out of fear, worry, and frustration. A parent might spank a child a hundred times, but even so, it would be unwise to allow that child to play unsupervised by a busy street. Children need to be supervised when they are near any kind of danger that requires mature judgment and skill for them to handle the situation on their own. It is much more effective to teach children judgment and skills about dangerous streets than it is to scare them by spanking.

How might you effectively deal with a child who has a fondness for the middle of the road? Take time for training every time you have occasion to cross a busy street by asking your child to look both ways and to tell you when no cars are coming. Ask your child to tell you when it is safe to cross the street. If you don't agree with his assessment, ask, "What about the big truck that's coming? What do you think will happen if that truck hits us?" Teach by asking questions, and encourage your toddler to ask questions, too. (The importance of asking "what" and "how" questions is discussed in more detail in the next chapter.) Skip the lectures. They invite avoidance or resistance, while questions invite thinking and participation. Education comes from the Latin root "educare," which means "to draw forth." Questions "draw forth." Lectures attempt to "stuff in"—a method that usually fails.

Toddlers can understand more than they can verbalize. Asking questions and allowing them to use whatever language they have to express themselves helps with their language development as well as their sense of autonomy.

Sometimes parents feel guilty when they discover new information, especially when it seems to point out ignorance or mistakes they may have made. You may be saying, "Oh my goodness! I didn't treat my children that way. Have I ruined them forever?" Absolutely not! As we say over and over, mistakes are wonderful opportunities to learn—for adults and for children.

Sometimes we need to tell our children about our mistakes and start over. "Honey, I thought the best way to show you how much I love you was to do everything for you. Now I know that's not the best thing for you. It may be hard for both of us when I stop being 'supermom' and help you learn how capable you are, but I have faith in both of us. We can do it!" And it's true. Don't waste any time on guilt. You will continue to make mistakes; so will your children. Isn't that exciting?

Understanding the importance of this developmental age can help parents learn the skills and provide the atmosphere (most of the time) that encourages children to learn important competency skills that will serve them all their lives. Parents can also interact with their children (most of the time) in ways that invite them to make healthy decisions about themselves, others, and the world. Notice we said "invite." We can never be sure how an individual will interpret his or her life experiences and what they will decide about them.

Unconscious Life Decisions

One thing children do not consciously understand and cannot verbalize is the unconscious decisions they are constantly making about themselves, about the world, about others, and about how they need to behave in the world to survive and thrive. They are making these decisions based on their interpretation of their life experiences. (This concept is covered thoroughly in Chapter 10: The Messages of Misbehavior.)

When you slap the hand of a one-year-old, she might understand that she shouldn't touch, but she is now faced with an existential crisis far beyond her understanding. She has been punished for doing something she needs to do in order to follow her ingrained developmental blueprint. What will she decide? That she is bad? That the world is bad? That *you* are bad?

On the other hand, when you distract her by removing her from what she can't touch and guide her to what she can touch, what will she decide? Distraction does not damage her self-esteem or self-confidence as spanking and shaming can. It does let her know that some things are acceptable to touch and some are unacceptable. This is an important life skill.

A child may still feel frustrated and upset about not being allowed to touch whatever she wants. She may even have a temper tantrum. However, when supervised with firmness and kindness, she will be left with a much different feeling than when she is controlled with force or punishment. A positive atmosphere is conducive to positive emotional and psychological development; a negative atmosphere promotes shame and doubt.

Children who are encouraged to develop a sense of autonomy will usually make healthier decisions later in life. Children who are not allowed to develop a sense of autonomy will make decisions based on doubt and shame. When parents realize this, they can work toward creating an environment in which children develop a stronger sense of autonomy.

Sleeping with Parents

Many parents wonder about letting their children sleep with them. There are many different opinions on this issue. Books have been written about the "family bed" and the benefits of allowing children to sleep with their parents. Other experts believe children become demanding and dependent when they sleep with their parents. We will discuss several possibilities for you to be aware of, so you can decide what fits your family.

Some people believe children have the opportunity to learn more cooperation, self-confidence, and autonomy when they sleep in their own beds. Other people believe children feel more loved and secure when they sleep in their parents' bed.

The first thing to consider is whether it works for you. Some parents find it very difficult to sleep when their children are in bed with them. Some couples find it greatly hampers their relationship (emotional and sexual). Many couples enjoy getting into bed to have a conversation, quietly read a book, and/or make love before going to sleep. (We purposely left out watching television, which can create a bigger wedge in a relationship than children in the bed.)

The second thing to consider is whether it works for your children. By "work" we mean does it help or hinder their development of autonomy, self-confidence, and self-reliance; or does it increase their sense of doubt and shame? We don't claim to have the answer. We do believe that educated parents will be more aware of what is happening in their child's world. Educated parents will be able to sense when their child becomes demanding or develops too much dependence (instead of healthy independence).

Alfred Adler, a pioneer in the field of families and children's behavior, believed that children should not sleep in their parents' bed because it hampers their striving for self-confidence and invites children to believe themselves incapable of the independence that eventually leads to cooperation and interdependence. He also believed there was a strong connection between daytime misbehavior and nighttime misbehavior—in other words, children who created difficulties during the day would also create difficulties at night.

Adler told the following story about a woman who came to him with a "problem" child. After hearing the woman's complaints about her problems with the child during the day, Adler asked, "How does the child behave during the night?" The woman replied, "I don't have any problems at night." This surprised Adler because of his theory that daytime and nighttime behavior are related. After a bit more discussion, Adler asked again, "Are you sure you don't have any problems during the night?" The woman assured him, "Oh no, I don't have any problems at night." Finally Adler guessed what might be happening at night. He asked, "Where does the child sleep?" The woman replied, "Why she sleeps with me, of course."

Adler explained to the woman that the sleeping arrangement was part of the problem. Of course the child was not creating any problems at night because her inappropriate demands were being met. During the day the child was only trying to get the same level of attention she received at night, and created problems when her mother did not cater to her as she did at night.

If your child is sleeping in your bed and is very demanding and dependent during the day, you might want to start the weaning process. (Remember, however, as we've mentioned before, "Weaning is never easy for the weanee or the weanor, but it is necessary for the ultimate good of both.")

Some parents don't allow their children to sleep with them during the night, but welcome them into their bed on weekend mornings for "morning snuggles." Other parents have a routine of lying down on their children's beds for story time. They make it clear to their children that they will leave when the story is over. They want to avoid the habit many children quickly adopt of insisting their parents stay in their bed until after they fall asleep.

Carmen allowed this habit to develop with her toddler, Juan. "Now," she complained, "I fall asleep before Juan does. That spoils the rest of my evening because I can't wake up soon enough to enjoy my older children, my husband, or the many things I was looking forward to accomplishing after the children were asleep."

Weaning—Again

"What if it is too late? I have already allowed these habits to develop and my child is now very demanding. She won't go to sleep unless I lie down with her or let her sleep with us. When I try to break her of the habit, she screams—and I can't stand it. I always give in. It has created all the problems you have discussed, but I can't stand to listen to her cry."

Knowing in advance that weaning is difficult helps—but only a little. Here are some tips to help you survive the weaning process.

1. Give up your "guilt button."   Children know when they can push that button; they also know when it is gone. (Don't ask us how they know—they just do!) Guilt is rarely a positive, helpful feeling. Knowing *why* you are doing something will help you do what is necessary for the ultimate good of your child.

2. Tell your child what you are going to do.   Even if your child is preverbal, he or she will understand the feeling tone behind the words. A little warning and time to prepare will help both of you avoid unpleasant surprises and misinterpretation.

3. Follow through.   If you say it, mean it; and if you mean it, follow through with action that is kind and firm.

4. Hang in there.   If you've followed the first three steps, it usually takes three days for your child to believe that you mean what you say. This means that he or she will try very hard to get you to maintain the old habit. He or she will probably cry (scream) for at least three nights. The crying time usually gets shorter each night, especially if you have followed the first tip. (Some mothers who can't stand to hear their child cry may choose to sleep at a friend's house for three nights!)

5. Take time during the day for lots of hugs and other special time with your child.   Make sure this isn't "guilt penance" time, but time for reassurance and enjoyment of your love for each other.

Love and Enjoyment

It always comes back to love and enjoyment. Nothing is more important to the emotional development of your child. Understanding how important it is for a child to develop autonomy can help parents know that overprotection is not the best way to show love. Instead they can have fun showing love by watching freedom and independence develop in their children, and by enjoying the promise of confidence and courage in years to come.

CHAPTER 5

"Me Do It"—
Initiative

"Me do it!" These words are the cry of the eager two-year-old who is trying to tell us, "I'm ready to start developing initiative." Do we listen? Or do we say "No, you're too little. You can't do it well enough. Wait until you're bigger. It is easier and faster for me to do it." Parents often do not realize they have just said the words that instill a sense of guilt instead of a sense of initiative. And years later, those same parents may find themselves wondering why their child "just won't do *any*thing!"

Again, we are talking about "a sense of" initiative—not actual ability. As in the first year children develop a sense of trust or a sense of mistrust, in the second year a sense of autonomy or a sense of doubt and shame, toddlers and preschoolers (ages two to six) begin to develop a sense of initiative—or a sense of guilt.

Preschoolers see the world as an exciting and fascinating place, especially as they develop more autonomy and a greater physical and intellectual capacity to explore. At the same time, however, they are often frustrated when adults get in their way. They experience frustration when they find they do not have the skills or abilities to get some of the things they want or accomplish what they want to do. And children may respond to these frustrations by withdrawing and adopting a sense of guilt about their inability to "conquer the world." Adults at home and school can help develop preschoolers' confidence and initiative by providing a range of opportunities, time for training, and encouragement for the many things they *can* do so children have the opportunity to gain a sense of initiative that is stronger than their sense of guilt.

Adults may need a slight attitude adjustment, too. Of *course* preschoolers are too little to do things perfectly. Which is more important—perfection or helping your children develop healthy self-esteem and strong life skills? Of course it is easier and faster for you to do things. Which is more important—ease and speed or helping children develop confidence and an ability to learn from mistakes? Who ever said parenting was easy and didn't take much time? Too many parents want confident, courageous, respectful, resourceful, responsible children, but they don't understand what children need in order to develop these characteristics.

Good day care centers and preschools are staffed by people who have studied early childhood education and are aware of the stages of development we have discussed. These centers and schools provide equipment, toys, and activities designed to enhance the development of trust, autonomy, initiative, social skills, intellectual skills, and life skills. For this reason, attending a good preschool or day care center can be an extremely beneficial experience for preschool children. (Please see Chapter 17 for more information on preschools and day care centers.)

One purpose of this book is to give parents the same kind of knowledge as early childhood educators in the areas of child development. Another purpose is to give both parents and teachers the kind of discipline skills that help children develop trust, autonomy, and initiative as well as crucial values and life skills. Since initiative does not equal ability, and skills take time to learn, training is essential for the child to develop a sense of initiative.

With training, two-year-olds can dress themselves, scramble eggs, and behave in the grocery store, at church, or in other public places. Learning these kinds of skills is an important part of developing initiative.

The Importance of Skills

One of the authors, a former elementary school counselor, was sometimes asked to counsel a child who was having difficulty in the classroom. She would ask the child: "Who dresses you in the morning?" Most five-, six-, and seven-year-olds having difficulty adjusting to the learning environment were still being dressed by a parent or an older sibling. Children who did not learn to dress themselves seemed to develop less autonomy and independence. Instead they learned to depend on others to "take care of them" and "do it for them." They used much of their intelligence to develop avoidance skills rather than self-reliance.

Such children often unconsciously expect their teachers to take care of them as their families do. Instead of learning "I can do it," they learn to manipulate others into their service—a skill that doesn't work well at school, the workplace, or in marriage. Sometimes these children believe they are not loved unless someone else is taking care of them. Again, well-meaning parents who did not understand the importance of helping their children develop autonomy and life skills thwarted them in the name of love.

Scrambling Eggs

Did you know that two-year-olds can learn to scramble eggs? Many parents are horrified by the notion and object that it would be too dangerous: "She might burn herself or make a huge mess!" Chances are good that your child will not burn herself if you take time to train *and* supervise. (Again, allowing children to develop a healthy sense of initiative does not mean they should not be supervised.) A two-year-old who scrambles eggs is developing the important belief: "I can do it." She is developing confidence, courage, and skills, the foundations of healthy self-esteem—and that just might be worth a messy kitchen!

Going Out in Public

With time for training, children can learn to behave in those famous child development observation laboratories: public places. Taking time for training can involve many strategies. Role playing and logical consequences, as well as other techniques that will be discussed in greater detail later on, can be used to help a child learn to behave when you're out in public—in a restaurant, for example.

Role Playing

Children love to play, so role playing can be a fun way to teach them skills and help them understand the difference between effective (respectful) and ineffective (disrespectful) behavior. Two-year-olds are not too young to understand role playing when you make it simple. (Remember, children understand much more than they are able to verbalize.)

One way to set up a role play is to say to your child, "You be the daddy, and I'll be the little boy. We are at the pancake house. How should I behave? Should I cry and run around and throw my food like this?" Then demonstrate crying and running around. "Or should I sit quietly in the seat and eat, or perhaps color quietly while I wait?" Then demonstrate by pretending you are sitting in the restaurant and have your child supervise your behavior. (Be aware that it is not developmentally appropriate to expect a small child to sit quietly in a restaurant, church, or anywhere else for unreasonably long periods of time.) Then reverse roles and let the child play herself being both disrespectful and respectful. Be sure to emphasize the benefits of respectful behavior!

Logical Consequences

Again, we want to stress that permissiveness is not the way to help children develop initiative. One alternative to permissiveness is logical consequences. (We discuss logical consequences, along with many other alternatives, in Chapter 14.)

Logical consequences must be related, respectful, and reasonable. If a child is misbehaving in a restaurant, a related consequence could be to take her out to wait in the car while the others in your group finish their meal. It is not respectful to scold or spank while removing her. Respect requires kindness and firmness at the same time. A parent can either say nothing, or say firmly (but kindly), "I'm sorry you didn't feel like behaving in the restaurant today. You can try again next time." Giving a child a chance to try again next time is reasonable and encouraging. It is not reasonable to say, "I'm never taking you out to eat again—or anywhere else, for that matter!" Besides being unreasonable, most parents do not follow through on such threats. This does not demonstrate kindness nor firmness, nor does it inspire trust.

Myrna and Lamar decided they would teach their son Mark to dress himself when he was two years old (excellent training for budding initiative). They purchased clothes that were easy for a small child to manage, such as pants with elastic bands, wide-neck T-shirts, and sneakers with Velcro fasteners. Mark was a willing student and pretty much mastered the art of dressing himself (even though he put his shoes on the wrong feet about half of the time).

Mark attended a preschool, and his job was to get himself dressed in the morning, help with breakfast, and be ready by 7:30 when his dad would drive him to school on the way to work. Myrna and Lamar had been warned about the possibility that Mark might use his initiative to "test" the routine. In preparation, they worked out a logical consequence with Mark in advance. Together they decided that any time Mark was not dressed in time to go, they would put Mark's clothes in a paper bag so he could dress in the car on his way to school. They weren't sure how much Mark really understood about their discussion of consequences, but they had faith that he would learn if they ever had to carry out their plan.

Sure enough, after several weeks of smooth mornings, the day arrived when Myrna noticed Mark wasn't following his routine. When it was time for Lamar to leave for work, Mark was totally naked. Myrna had prepared the sack of clothes, so Lamar kindly and firmly picked Mark up under one arm, took the sack of clothes in his other hand, and walked to the car through pouring rain—just as a neighbor was out picking up his newspaper.

Lamar sighed, and reminded himself, "Oh well, taking time for training with Mark is more important than what the neighbors think."

Mark cried and complained that he was cold while they were driving to school. His dad said, "You can get dressed if you want to."

Mark hadn't finished testing, so he continued to complain. When they arrived at the school, Lamar took Mark, still stark naked, into the preschool. Joyce, the preschool director, understood these moments well and smiled as the pair approached.

"Oh hi, Mark!" she said warmly. "I see you didn't get dressed this morning. That's okay. You can take your bag of clothes into my office and come out as soon as you are dressed."

Mark dressed in about five minutes. But a month later, he decided further research was in order and tested the routine again. This time he still had his pajamas on when his dad carried him to the car, and he got dressed on the way to school. He had learned that complaining didn't work.

Some people will object to this story, saying it was humiliating to Mark to be taken to school naked. We can assure you that this is not humiliating to a two-year-old. It *would* be humiliating to a six-year-old, and therefore not an appropriate method.

Piggy-Backing

Lamar could have made this experience humiliating to Mark by "piggy-backing," which means adding blame and shame to what would otherwise be a logical consequence. Lamar did not say, "It serves you right! Maybe next time you'll hurry up. You are making me late. All the kids will probably laugh at you for not getting dressed." That would have made the experience humiliating. Instead, Myrna, Lamar, and Joyce treated Mark kindly and firmly, which helped him learn the benefits of using his skills to help himself and cooperate with others.

"Oops, I Made a Mistake!"

By now you might be afraid that you have to be a perfect parent to raise a perfect child. There are no such things. Isn't that wonderful? An important definition of human beings—parents and children—is that they never quit making mistakes—NEVER! It doesn't matter how much we learn or how much we know. As humans beings we sometimes forget what we know and get "hooked" into emotional reactions—or we just plain goof up. Once we understand this, we might as well see mistakes as the important life processes that they are: interesting opportunities to learn. Instead of feeling discouraged when we make a mistake we can say, "Terrific! I've just been given another opportunity to learn!"

Wouldn't it be wonderful if we could instill this attitude in our children so they wouldn't be burdened with all the baggage we carry about mistakes? Many children (and adults) short-circuit the lifelong process of developing initiative because they are afraid to make mistakes. Mistakes aren't the same as failures, although we often behave as though they are. Asking "what" and "how" questions, instead of telling what and how, will help tremendously.

"What" and "How" Questions

Children do not develop a strong sense of initiative when parents and teachers spend too much time lecturing—telling children what happened, what caused it to happen, how they should feel about it, and what they should do about it. Telling may keep children from seeing mistakes as opportunities to learn. Telling instills guilt because it sends the message that children aren't living up to adult expectations. And last but not least, telling children what, how, and why teaches them what to think, not how to think. Parents are often disappointed when their children don't develop more initiative without realizing they are not using the kind of parenting skills that encourage initiative.

A powerful skill to help children develop thinking skills, judgment skills, problem-solving abilities, and initiative is to *ask* them, "What happened? What were you trying to do? Why do you think this happened? How do you feel about it? How could you fix it? What else could you do if you don't want this to happen again?"

When children are younger they need more clues as part of the "what" and "how" questions. For example, if a two-year-old gets stuck on her tricycle, she will be invited to think and use initiative if you ask, "What do you think would happen if you got off and backed up?" That is very different than telling her, "Get off and back up." Even though a question contains direct clues, it still invites thought and a decision. As children get older, they will benefit from questions with fewer clues.

Remember Joyce, the director of the preschool Mark attended? Joyce believes in the importance of giving children opportunities to develop autonomy and initiative using all of the concepts discussed in this chapter. Her staff looks for every opportunity to let children experience how capable they are by taking time for training and then letting the children do many things that are usually done for them by adults.

When Joyce goes shopping for groceries, she lets the children take turns going with her to help her put items in the grocery cart. When she returns to the day care center, she backs the station wagon into the play yard and calls the children to help take the groceries to the kitchen one item at a time. The cook helps the children remember where to put the items away.

During lunchtime the children dish up their own food. One little fellow named Matt consistently took too much food. After about a week, his teacher helped him explore what was happening by asking, "What happens when you take too much food?"

Matt responded, "I can't eat it all and I have to throw some away."

The teacher continued, "What would happen if you took smaller helpings of food?"

Matt looked like he had made a great discovery as he said, "I could eat it all."

The teacher said, "I'm sure you could." Then she asked, "If you took less food, ate it all, and were still hungry, what could you do then?"

Matt beamed as he said, "I could take some more?"

The teacher asked, "When will you start doing that?"

Matt looked like he could hardly wait as he crowed, "Tomorrow!"

After lunch the children each scrape their own food into a plastic dishpan, rinse their own plate in another dishpan, use a dish brush to scrub their dish in another dishpan filled with suds, rinse again in another dishpan, and then put the dish on a drying rack. This routine is definitely more time-consuming than having an adult clean up after lunch. But Joyce and her staff of teachers are more interested in helping children develop their full potential than in getting chores done quickly. They also love the children, enjoy them, and feel privileged to be part of their growth and development.

There it is again: love and joy. The more we know about what is developmentally appropriate, how we can enhance the environment in which children grow, learn the skills which will encourage them to reach their full potential, and forgive ourselves when we make mistakes, the more we can relax and just enjoy watching our children grow, knowing that they're learning to trust their own abilities, to believe in the support of the adults in their lives, and to experience the wonder of life all around them.

CHAPTER 6

Temperament:
What Makes Your
Child Unique?

Most parents and teachers cherish a fantasy about having "the perfect baby" or "the perfect child." The conventional description of this ideal baby is one who doesn't cry or fuss very often, who sleeps peacefully through the night, takes long naps, eats her food without spitting it out (or up), and who can happily entertain herself, gurgling and cooing angelically at her crib mobile. "Oh," we say when confronted with one of these enviable specimens, "what a good baby." Does this mean that all babies who don't fit this description are "bad"?

A "perfect child" is often pictured as the one who quietly obeys his parents, doesn't fight with his brothers or sisters, does his chores without complaining, saves his money, does homework without being reminded—and who gets good grades, is athletic, and very popular. Does this mean that a child who doesn't fit this description is "imperfect"?

The Myth of the Perfect Child

Of course, there is no such thing as a "bad" baby or child, even though most don't fit the fantasy description. Babies are born with different, unique personalities, as any parent with more than one child knows.

59

Frankly, we worry about a child who fits the fantasy description. Usually this is a child who doesn't feel secure enough to test power boundaries and find out who she is apart from her parents and teachers, who is afraid to make mistakes or risk disapproval. We say "usually" because a few babies do fit the fantasy description and still feel secure and aren't afraid to make mistakes. They are called "easy" children.

Drs. Stella Chess and Alexander Thomas investigated the miracle of personality in their longitudinal study of the nine major "temperaments" found in children. These "temperaments," the qualities and characteristics that contribute to individual personalities, serve to describe three types of children, the "easy child," the "difficult child," and the "slow-to-warm-up child." All are good; some are just more challenging than others! We will discuss these nine temperaments, but for more information we highly recommend *Know Your Child*[1] by Stella Chess and Alexander Thomas.

The Berkeley Studies

Scientific investigation of temperament theory began with the Berkeley Studies, a longitudinal study of two basic temperaments, active and passive. This study revealed that these two temperaments were lifelong characteristics; in other words, passive infants grew up to be passive adults, while active infants grew up to be active adults. Actually, activity levels can be measured in the womb.

Chess and Thomas expanded the temperament theory significantly, even though their nine temperaments all fit under the

---

1. Chess, Stella, M.D., and Alexander Thomas, M.D. *Know Your Child*, New York: Basic Books, A Division of Harper Collins Publishers, 1987.

general headings of active and passive. A major benefit of being aware of temperament differences is that parents and teachers can better understand their children and students, and learn to appreciate and accept them as they are. With understanding and acceptance, parents and teachers are equipped to encourage children to reach their full potential rather than trying to mold them into perfect fantasy children.

The Nine Temperaments

The nine temperaments are activity level, rhythmicity, initial response, adaptability, sensory threshold, quality of mood, intensity of reaction, distractability, and persistence and attention span. All children possess varying degrees of each characteristic. But what do they look like in real life? (You may want to think about children you know as we examine these aspects of temperament.)

Activity Level

Activity level refers to the level of motor activity and the proportion of active and inactive periods. For instance, an infant with high activity might kick and splash so much in his bath that the floor needs a good mopping afterward, while a low activity infant can turn over but doesn't often choose to do so. A high activity toddler or preschooler might delight in energetic running games, while a low activity child chooses something quiet, like drawing or looking at a book.

Activity level will influence a parent's interactions with a child. For instance, it is Sunday afternoon at the community swimming pool, and three-year-old twins Ned and Sally are keeping their mother company while their older sisters take swimming lessons. As the hour progresses, Ned plays happily with the bag of plastic animals that his mother has brought along. He takes them over to the drinking fountain and gets them wet, then pretends they are eating a "koosh ball" sea urchin. The entire hour passes with Ned happily absorbed in his play.

Sally is a different story. She begins coloring in the book her mother has brought along, but within ten minutes has marked up all of the pages and wants her mom to read to her. Halfway through the story, Sally decides she is thirsty so Mom takes her to the drinking fountain. Then Sally begins to climb on the bleachers. Before half an hour has passed, Sally has colored, heard a story, gotten a drink, and explored the bleachers. Sally's mother knows her daughter and is already expecting to take a walk to the swings—and she knows they'd better be ready to leave the minute lessons are over.

Ned obviously has a low activity level, while Sally's is high. This mother used to feel frustrated by the differences between her twins, especially since she thought she treated them the same way. Information about temperaments helped her understand them better. She decided she might as well relax and simply enjoy the uniqueness of each child.

Rhythmicity

Rhythmicity refers to the predictability (or unpredictability) of biological functions, such as hunger, sleeping, and bowel movements. An infant might have one bowel movement each day immediately after breakfast, while another's schedule seems different each day. One child might eat her biggest meal at lunch, while another prefers dinner—or a different meal each day!

Carla Jackson was so proud; she thought her little Jackie was toilet trained by the time he was two years old. She put him on his toilet chair several times a day, and he obligingly produced a bowel movement each morning and urinated on each succeeding visit. But Jackie wasn't toilet trained; his mom was trained. Jackie was so regular that when his mom remembered to put him on his chair, he performed. But whenever they were in a different setting and she forgot, Jackie would have an "accident." Jackie stopped having accidents when he was three—and really toilet trained.

Carla's other children were not so regular, and she reproached herself for having "failed" to train them. Learning about temperament helped her to realize that she hadn't succeeded or failed; her children simply had different temperaments of regularity, as well as other differences.

Approach or Withdrawal

This temperament describes the way a child reacts to a new situation or stimulus, such as a new food, toy, person, or place. Approach responses are often displayed by mood expression (smiling, speech, facial expression) or motor activity (swallowing a new food, reaching for a new toy). Withdrawal responses look more negative and are expressed by mood (crying, fussing, speech, facial expression) or motor activity (moving away, spitting food out, pushing a new toy away).

Some babies are open to just about any new experience— new foods, new people—while others are more reluctant. Older children might reveal this temperament in the way they cope with new experiences, either running to join a new group or hovering on the sidelines a while to check things out.

Monica, for instance, came to her new child care center when she was two and a half years old. Whenever the children gathered for a group activity, Monica would hang back and refuse to join in. Because her teacher was sensitive to her temperament, she did not insist that Monica join the group, although she made sure Monica knew she was welcome. For two weeks, Monica held back, watching what happened and gradually moving closer. By the third week she was happily playing with the others. Monica's initial response was withdrawal, and her teacher wisely honored this aspect of her temperament.

Adaptability

Adaptability describes how a child reacts to a new situation over time, her ability to adjust and change. Some children initially spit out a new food, but accept it after a few trial tastes. Others accept a new food, a new article of clothing, or a new preschool far more slowly, if at all.

When Mrs. Frank's baby arrived, his older sister and brother were already in grade school and involved in a whirl of sports, music lessons, and other activities. Because of their busy schedule, the baby was rarely at home for a regular nap time. But that posed no problem: this baby was a highly adaptable child, perfectly content to curl up and sleep wherever he happened to be at the time, whether at a basketball game or in the grocery cart.

Mrs. Evers also had an older son when her daughter was born, but she often found herself looking for rides for her son when activities fell during the baby's nap time. If they weren't home at the proper time, the baby fell apart, crying, whining, and fussing. The one thing she never did was fall asleep anywhere besides her own bed. She would stay awake well past midnight if her family happened to be away from home. This baby had low adaptability, and the entire family suffered when they didn't take her temperament into account.

Sensory Threshold

Some children wake up from a nap every time a door opens, no matter how softly, while others can sleep through a hurricane. Some children complain about tight clothes or rough sheets, while others scrape their knees and bump their heads without slowing down. The level of sensitivity to sensory input varies from one child to the next and affects how they behave and view the world.

Alice was celebrating her fourth birthday. She opened a present containing a beautiful flowered dress and smiled in delight. The smile changed to dismay, however, when she noticed that the puffy skirt was held in place by a layer of stiff nylon net. "Do I have to wear this part?" she asked in alarm. "It'll scratch my legs."

Such things didn't faze Andy, though. He loved to walk barefoot and took off his shoes at every opportunity. His parents would point with concern to the gravel playground or exclaim about the hot pavement, but textures and temperatures didn't bother Andy. His little feet padded along undaunted, while their owner enjoyed the feeling of each toe wiggling freely.

Quality of Mood

Have you ever noticed how some children (and adults) react to life with pleasure and acceptance, while others can find fault with everything and everybody? One baby might favor her family with smiles and coos, while another feels compelled to cry a bit, just "because." It can be discouraging for parents and teachers to deal with a child who always looks on the dark side, but there are ways to both accept this temperament and help a child to face life more positively.

Stephen Ellis came home from his parenting class with a new idea: he would ask his four-year-old son, Carl, about the happiest and saddest moments of his day. Stephen looked forward to making this a part of their bedtime routine and having a chance to get into his son's world. When Stephen asked Carl about his saddest moments, he often had a long list of troubles to relate, but when asked about his happy moments, he couldn't think of any. Stephen began to feel real dismay that Carl was so miserable.

In fact, Carl simply has a negative mood temperament and sees the world from that perspective. When Stephen learned about temperament, he was able to stop getting hooked by Carl's negative mood. He would listen to his son's list of troubles, then share some of his own sad moments. Then he would share his happy moments. As Stephen continued to show Carl that it was okay to see both negatives and positives, Carl started sharing happy times too. He still sees lots of negatives, but he is learning to see the positive things as well.

Intensity of Reactions

Children often respond to events around them in different ways. Some smile quietly or merely take a look, then go back to what they were doing; others react with action and emotion.

Mrs. Peters was getting ready for art time with her class. While the children played quietly, Mrs. Peters set out paper, markers, pastels, and scissors. She was carrying the box containing the trays of water colors and brushes when she tripped over a forgotten block, and the box of painting supplies crashed to the floor. The group of children reacted in a number of interesting ways. Some looked up, startled, then returned to playing. Little Steffi and Adam began to cry loudly. Mark got up to poke through the debris with his toe, while Angie ran around the room giggling. The children responded differently to the same situation because their intensity levels were different. Understanding that children react to stimuli with varying degrees of intensity can help both parents and teachers deal with behavior more calmly.

Distractibility

"If my daughter decides she wants to go out and play but it's lunchtime," one mom says, "she'll fuss and fuss, and won't get involved in anything else." "My little guy knows when he's hungry, and he follows me around the kitchen until I have his lunch ready," says another. "Well," shares another mom, "if someone walks by while my baby is nursing, she not only looks but stops sucking until the person is gone." They may not realize it, but these parents are actually talking about their children's distractibility, the way in which an outside stimulus interferes with a child's present behavior and his willingness (or unwillingness) to be diverted.

It is nap time at the child care center when Melissa makes the unfortunate discovery that her special teddy bear has been left at home. The teacher holds her, talks with her, and offers one of the center's toys as a substitute, but nothing helps. Melissa spends the entire nap time sitting on her mat whimpering for her teddy.

Melissa has low distractibility, which will be a real asset someday when she's hired to be an air traffic controller or the President's bodyguard. But for now, Melissa is not a child who should be brought to day care without her precious teddy. In fact, it might be wise to have two teddys, one for home and another for school, so this sort of crisis can be avoided.

Persistence and Attention Span

Persistence refers to a child's willingness to pursue an activity in the face of obstacles or difficulties; attention span describes the length of time he will pursue an activity without interruption. The two characteristics are usually related.

A child who is threading beads on a string might give up if a bead doesn't go on immediately; another will try again and again until she succeeds. These children are demonstrating different levels of persistence. A child who is content to tear up an old magazine for half an hour at a time has a fairly long attention span, while another who plays with ten different toys in ten minutes has a short one. Again, no combination is necessarily better than another; they're simply different, and present different challenges in parenting and teaching.

Mitchell has been tracing a map from his atlas every morning for a week. He has carefully continued his work, adding details and humming contentedly to himself as he draws. When Mitchell's best friend, Erica, came over to play, she sat down to help him—for a while. But within half an hour Erica had three hastily completed drawings, and had turned her attention to Mitchell's new Play-Doh. Someday Erica may be discovering new strains of bacteria and new medications with her ability to detect and investigate new things, while most of us would be very comfortable with the future Dr. Mitchell performing our six-hour open-heart surgery!

Temperament: Challenge or Opportunity?

If asked, most parents and teachers would probably prefer children with a long attention span and high persistence; they're much easier to teach and entertain. However, few children fit this ideal description. In fact, most families include children of different temperaments, while teachers can find themselves working with quite an assortment!

Parents who understand their child's temperament can be knowledgeable consultants to teachers and other people who may be working with that child. For example, if your child is slow to adapt, ask for a conference and explain to the teacher that your child adapts slowly but responds to patience and kind firmness. If your child has a short attention span, find a teacher who appreciates creativity and provides a variety of experiences during the day. Avoid authoritarian teachers who require children to spend a great deal of time sitting still, and who punish children who do not conform to expectations. Be sure that it is your child's temperament and not your own that motivates you. You should always be your child's best advocate and supporter.

Teachers may need to provide information about temperament to parents, too. An understanding of temperament can help both parents and teachers encourage acceptance instead of unrealistic expectations.

Evan's parents were very artistic people. They designed beautiful wall hangings and non-traditional clothing, and they became concerned that Evan wasn't being given ample opportunity for artistic expression at his preschool. Evan never came home with paint on his clothes or clay under his fingernails.

But in fact, Evan had many opportunities to explore the world of art. He just wasn't interested. Evan was a precise, orderly youngster who preferred to work quietly putting together puzzles or exploring counting materials. He didn't like the slippery feel of paint on his hands, or the gooey mess of clay. Evan's parents were viewing their son in light of their own temperaments, not his. When Evan's teacher explained the facets of his temperament, they were very grateful. Now they could begin to accept Evan for the unique person he was and encourage him to follow his own dreams, not theirs.

Goodness of Fit

Chess and Thomas emphasize the importance of "goodness of fit," the depth of understanding parents and teachers have of a child's temperament and their willingness to work with that child to encourage healthy development. Children experience enough stress in life as they struggle for competency and belonging. It does not help to compound that stress by expecting a child to be someone he is not.

Understanding a child's temperament doesn't mean shrugging your shoulders and saying, "Oh well, that's just the way this child is." It is an invitation to help a child develop acceptable behavior and skills. For instance, a child with a short attention span will still need to learn to accept some structure. Offering limited choices is one way to be respectful of the child's needs and of the "needs of the situation," behavior appropriate for the present environment. In school, for example, the needs of the situation are that learning must take place, and children should respect themselves and one another. Giving a child a limited choice of more than one way to learn or do an activity would fit the needs of the situation, take the child's temperament into account, and still be respectful to everyone concerned. A child with a long attention span may need encouragement to expand her horizons to include a variety of interests and activities.

Needs of the Situation

An awareness of temperament in children helps us understand why different methods are more effective with some children than with others. There are some universal principles, such as everyone's right to dignity and respect, but this doesn't necessarily mean that we can just demand our children treat us with dignity and respect—or that children will automatically know how to do so.

Each individual must learn to take personal responsibility for his own dignity and respect. You may not be able to demand that your child treat you with respect, but you can treat yourself with respect. If your child is behaving disrespectfully, you can choose to leave the room, or find another positive discipline method to deal with the behavior. You should not withdraw love or acceptance from a child because her behavior needs work.

Three-year-old Tammi had learned some pretty exciting profanity at her preschool. The first time Tammi tried the "F" word on her mother, Barbara overreacted.

"Tammi!" Barbara said strongly, "don't you EVER let me hear you talk like that again!"

Tammi was delighted that she could create such excitement. The next day she tried out some new words for her mother to hear, but this time Barbara was prepared.

She said, "I don't appreciate listening to that kind of language. It's very disrespectful. So I'm going to my room to read for a while. Let me know when you're ready to speak respectfully."

Tammi wasn't quite as delighted to find herself without an audience. Soon she was knocking on her mother's door saying, "I'm ready to talk good now, Mommy."

Later that evening, as she tucked her daughter into bed, Barbara took a moment to explain things to Tammi.

"Honey," she said, "most people don't like hearing those words. If you choose to use them you can either go to your room where others can't hear you, or I will go to my room for a while. It's up to you."

Tammi snuggled closer to her mom, and Barbara asked her, "What could you do or say when you hear other people using disrespectful language?"

Tammi, inspired by her mother's example, decided that she could leave just like her mother did.

"Could you give them a chance to change their behavior, like I did with you?" asked Barbara.

Tammi said, "I could play with them again when they stop."

A few days later, Tammi heard one of her friends at preschool using one of the "bad" words. She said, "That isn't respectful. I'm going to play with someone else until you're ready to stop saying those words."

We can teach children so much through example, and by exploring with "what" and "how" questions. Barbara also demonstrated that adults, too, can learn from mistakes and improve their behavior later. Parents and teachers can ask themselves several questions when responding to a situation. First, is it respectful to child, adult, and the needs of the situation? Second, does it allow for differences in temperament? Third, is it encouraging children to gain confidence and healthy self-esteem? And fourth, does it teach life skills for now and for the future? When you can answer "yes" to these questions, you'll know you're using positive discipline skills and effectively shaping your actions to your child's unique self.

Positive Discipline Skills for Parents and Teachers

Many of the skills we suggest are appropriate for children of all temperaments because they invite children to learn cooperation, responsibility, and life skills. However, an understanding of temperament helps us understand why different methods may be more effective, depending on the temperament and needs of an individual child.

For example, time out, when properly used, can be an encouraging way to help children who need time to calm down and cool off (see Chapter 15 on discipline). Family meetings and class meetings are essential to help all children learn problem-solving skills and cooperation. Positive discipline parenting skills help children who are misbehaving redirect their energy in useful ways. Asking "what" and "how" questions encourages children to focus on personal accountability as they explore what happened, what caused it to happen, how they feel about it, and what they might choose to do differently next time. Parents and teachers can help children develop into the best people they can be when they understand and respect differences, individuality, and the creativity of each child.

Individuality and Creativity

Parents and teachers may not be aware of how they squelch individuality and creativity when they buy in (often subconsciously) to the "myth of the perfect child." It is tempting for adults to prefer the "easy" child, or to want children to conform to the norms of society. Egos often get involved; we worry about what others think and fear that our competency may be questioned if our children aren't "good" in the eyes of others.

The following song, "Flowers Are Red" by Harry Chapin, is used by the kind permission of Elektra/Asylum Records. It beautifully (and sadly) illustrates how we can kill the individuality that makes our children special in our desire to make them "fit in." The music to this song is delightful, and we hope you will make the effort to find the "Living Room Suite" by Harry Chapin.

Flowers Are Red

The little boy went first day in school; he got some
   crayons and he started to draw. He put colors all over
   the paper, for colors was what he saw.
And the teacher said, "What're you doing, young man?"
   "I'm painting flowers," he said. She said, "It's not the
   time for art, young man; and anyway, flowers are green
   and red. There's a time for everything, young man, and
   the way it should be done. You've got to show concern
   for everyone else for you're not the only one."

And she said, "Flowers are red, young man, and green
   leaves are green. There's no need to see flowers any
   other way than the way they always have been seen."

But the little boy said, "There are so many colors in the
   rainbow, so many colors in the morning sun, so many
   colors in a flower, and I see every one."
The teacher said, "You're sassy. There's ways that things
   should be. And you'll paint flowers the way they are; so
   repeat after me."

And she said, "Flowers are red, young man, and green
   leaves are green. There's no need to see flowers any
   other way than the way they always have been seen."

But the little boy said, "There are so many colors in the
rainbow, so many colors in the morning sun, so many
colors in a flower and I see every one."
The teacher put him in a corner. She said, "It's for your
own good. And you won't come out till you get it right
and are responding like you should."
Well, finally he got lonely. Frightened thoughts filled his
head. And he went up to the teacher, and this is what
he said:

And he said, "Flowers are red, and green leaves are green.
There's no need to see flowers any other way than the
way they always have been seen."

Time went by, like it always does, and they moved to another town. And the little boy went to another school,
and this is what he found. The teacher there was smiling. She said, "Painting should be fun. And there are so
many colors in a flower, so let's use every one."
But the little boy painted flowers, and he drew them green
and red. And when the teacher asked him why, this is
what he said:

And he said, "Flowers are red, and green leaves are green.
There's no need to see flowers any other way than the
way they always have been seen."

It is easy for us to say, "Oh, I could never be that
mean!" But are we? We don't believe parents and teachers
discourage individuality or creativity intentionally. Even the
teacher in the song truly believed "it was for his own good."
Hopefully, an awareness of temperament will help us avoid
the "meanness" that comes from a lack of information and
understanding.

One of the primary motivators for Chess and Thomas was
the desire to stop society's tendency to blame mothers for the

characteristics of their children. Chess and Thomas stated, "A child's temperament can actively influence the attitudes and behavior of her parents, other family members, playmates, and teachers, and in turn help to shape their effect on her behavioral development" (p. 36). In this way the relationship between child and parents is a two-way street; each continuously influences the other.

What if the mother whose twins behaved so differently at the swimming pool had been two different mothers? It would have been easy to decide that quiet, busy Ned's mother was very effective, while active, bouncy Sally's mother "just couldn't control that child!" It may be wise to ask yourself occasionally, "Are you looking for blame, or are you looking for solutions?" The more we know about temperament and effective parenting skills, the better we will be at finding solutions that help our children develop into capable individuals, despite their differences and uniqueness.

Work for Improvement, Not Perfection

Even with understanding and the best intentions, most of us will struggle occasionally with our children's temperaments and behavior when we get caught up in a lack of patience or our own ego, or simply get "hooked" into reacting to behavior instead of acting thoughtfully. Awareness and understanding do not mean we become perfect; mistakes are inevitable. However, once we have had time to "cool off" after we make a mistake, we need to resolve it with our children. They're usually more than willing to hug and offer forgiveness, especially when they know you'll do the same for them. It is important to help our children work for improvement, not perfection; we can give this gift to ourselves as parents and teachers as well.

Kindness and Firmness

Rudolf Dreikurs continually made a plea for parents and teachers to use kindness and firmness with children. An understanding of temperament shows just how important this is. Kindness shows respect for the child and his uniqueness; firmness shows respect for the needs of the situation. By understanding and respecting your child's temperament, you will be able to help him reach his full potential as a capable, confident, contented person.

CHAPTER 7

Understanding Developmental Appropriateness

Each human being is a work of art. Look at the variety we see in appearance alone: skin color, hair color and texture, shape of the nose, color of the eyes, height, weight, shape—each one of us is unique. And physical characteristics are only the beginning of our uniqueness. Temperament, as we have discovered, is as individual as a fingerprint. So is the rate at which we develop and grow. Understanding "developmental appropriateness"— the sorts of things children do, think, and are capable of at different stages—can help parents and teachers work effectively with children just as they are at the moment.

Windows of Opportunity

Children are, in many ways, similar. Johnny and Mary, for instance, will both be learning to walk in the first year and a half of life. But children are different, too. Mary doggedly pulled herself along the furniture and took her first steps at ten months of age, while Johnny was contentedly crawling at eleven months. By thirteen months of age, both children were walking, exploring their world on their own two feet. Similar, yet unique!

Picture a window in your mind. Although the window is "framed" on all sides, there is a great deal of space in the middle. In the same way, many behaviors and early experiences in our children's lives take place in just such a "window." The window for getting a first tooth can be anywhere from six to ten months of age. There are similar windows for physical, intellectual, and emotional development, and each child has his or her own individual schedule, neither exactly like nor completely unlike anyone else's.

Very few things in the world of parenting come in only black or white. This book is all about choices, windows, and possibilities. Understanding your child's individual progress—her development of trust, autonomy, and initiative, her temperament, her physical development—will help you make the best choices for her, and for you. Let's take a look at some of the ways developmental stages influence your child's perceptions and behavior.

Process Versus Product

It's a busy Friday evening, and you're off on a quick trip to the grocery store with your toddler. You have a definite goal in mind, namely to grab the necessary ingredients for dinner in time to get home, prepare and eat it, and still be on time for your older son's soccer game. For you, going to the store means obtaining the desired "product."

For your toddler, however, the product just isn't the point. Children are firmly rooted in the here and now; they think and experience life differently than adults do. A trip to the store is all about the "process"—the smells, the colors, the feelings, the experience. Being sandwiched into a busy schedule just doesn't allow time to enjoy the process!

Children do not share our goal-oriented expectations. It isn't always possible to go along with a child's relaxed approach, either. Sometimes we really *do* need to run in, grab the chicken, and run home again. But being aware of your child's tendency to focus on process rather than product can help you provide a balance. There may be times when you can take a leisurely browse through the store, enjoying the flowers in the floral department and the magazines in the rack. Children are miniature Zen masters, able to focus on the moment and enjoy it—an ability many adults would do well to learn.

When you must hurry, take time to explain to your child why you must shop quickly this time. You can explain that you want him to hold your hand, and that you will have to walk past the toys and other interesting things. You can offer to let him help you find the chicken and carry it to the checkstand. Then you will walk back to the car and drive home. Helping a child understand clearly what is expected and what will happen makes it more likely he will cooperate with you.

When we understand this characteristic trait of young children, we can find many ways to use our knowledge. Patsy Green arrived at the child care center one afternoon just in time to see Laura Anderson and her son carrying a huge, colorful painting out to the car. Patsy looked around eagerly to see what her son, Paul, had painted, but none of the pictures had his name on them.

Baffled, Patsy cornered the teacher and asked why Paul hadn't had a chance to paint that day.

"Well," the teacher said, "Paul was very interested in the paint—but not in putting it on the paper. He stirred the colors and experimented with the feeling of the paint on his fingers, then decided he'd really rather build with blocks." She smiled, for she understood that Paul was interested in the *process,* in texture and balance and fit, not in producing a *product.* When Paul's mom can understand this as well, she'll be better able to help Paul benefit from the different experiences in his life.

Sex Identity

Alice Billings walks into the preschool shaking her head. She prides herself on being a "no frills" sort of person; she wears no makeup, pulls her hair back simply, and usually dresses in jeans and T-shirts. Right behind mom is her daughter, Sally—and Sally is a sight to behold. She is wearing a lacy pink dress, ribbons in her hair, her best shiny shoes, and a jangly assortment of bracelets on her arms.

Alice looks at the teacher in despair. "Where does Sally get this 'Barbie doll' taste in clothes?" she laments. Sally's teacher laughs as she welcomes them for the day.

As it happens, Sally is four years old and is making a very big discovery. Sally, it seems, is a *girl*. Not only was she born a girl, but she will remain one for the rest of her life, despite her earlier declaration that she would become a boy after her next birthday. Sally may not always insist on ruffles and bracelets. She is simply exploring *all* the aspects of what it means to be a girl from her perspective as a four-year-old.

Sex role identification takes place even when parents are careful to minimize gender stereotypes. On playgrounds everywhere games emerge during the preschool years that focus on gender. "No boys allowed," say the girls. "Girls, *ick*," reply the boys with equal fervor.

Although we understand this natural phase, we can still teach young children to respect *all* people. Children naturally learn that they are either male or female, but this learning process needn't involve the learning of prejudice or gender-based limitations. Girls can play army and boys can play with dolls with no particular implications for the future; both can learn to develop their own special abilities, regardless of sex.

Children will also begin to notice physical differences between boys and girls, and often will ask what they mean. In these days of explicit television and advertising, questions may come earlier than ever before (an excellent reason for staying tuned in to what your child is watching on the tube). A little boy may want to touch dad in the shower. Watching mom nurse a baby brother or sister may lead to all sorts of interesting questions. As much as possible, try to remain calm, relaxed, and "askable." Children don't need a great deal of detailed information about sexuality (in fact, their eyes will probably glaze over if you try), but most experts agree that it is wise to answer questions or offer explanations in simple, accurate terms. There are a number of wonderful, illustrated books available for young children. Being open helps establish an atmosphere of comfort and trust, and will enable your children to seek further information later on, when they really need it.

Children who are raised in homes where mutual respect flourishes will feel good about being who they are. Their tastes in clothing will change, as will their desire to have same- or opposite-sex friends. Gender roles are a topic of much debate and controversy in our society, and what to teach your children requires careful consideration. Be sure you let your children know that being a boy or a girl need not place restrictions on the opportunities life offers.

Racial Identification

Children naturally notice differences between themselves and others. But the conclusions they draw about those differences can vary, depending on what they're taught.

Randy was the child of biracial parents. When he was three, the black couple next door announced that they were expecting their first child. With the innocence of childhood, three-year-old Randy wondered aloud whether the baby would be black or white. To him, anything was possible. By the time Randy was four-and-a-half, he had noticed that his skin looked different than that of his playmates. What decisions will Randy make about who he is?

Wouldn't life be boring if we all looked the same? Parents and teachers have the opportunity to teach children to value differences, not condemn them, and to enhance development with experiences and information that celebrate the variety and worth of all humanity. Prejudice, whether it concerns race, religion, or nationality, is learned. Even young children can learn to respect differences in race, age, gender, and physical ability. And because children of this age are learning so much about themselves, it is vital that they learn about others in ways that are respectful and positive.

Lying and Stealing

As we've already discovered, children don't have the same grasp on fantasy and reality that adults do, nor do they automatically understand the difference between acceptable and unacceptable behavior. Lying is often a problem for parents with children around the ages of four or five, and developmentally it makes some sense. After all, a child is only vaguely beginning to understand the difference between things that are real and those that are unreal. Lying needn't provoke horror and punishment; parents and teachers can help children tell the truth by making it safe for them to do so and by understanding why they sometimes do not.

Dad was not thrilled to find the broken egg on the kitchen floor. "Hey," he called, with exasperation in his voice, "who broke this egg?"

Four-year-old Sammy replied calmly, "An alligator did it."

Now, Dad knows there probably aren't any alligators here in Kansas. Can he find a way to handle the situation that both solves the egg problem and teaches Sammy the importance of telling the truth? Let's look at a couple of possibilities.

Dad could join in the pretending with his son. "An alligator!" he exclaims. "Was it orange? I think I just saw it in the driveway." Sam smiles and agrees that it was an orange alligator.

Dad smiles too, then says, "You know, I'm just pretending that there was alligator. I know we don't have alligators around here. Isn't that right, Sam?"

Sam happily admits that there are no alligators. Dad suggests that they clean up the broken egg together, knowing there will be opportunities to talk as they work.

"Sam, were you afraid I would yell at you about the egg?"

Now Sam drops his eyes and nods slowly.

Dad makes his voice warm and gentle as he says, "I know it's tempting to blame things on an alligator, or to make up something that didn't really happen. But it's important for you to know that you can tell me the truth, even when you feel scared. Do you know why it's important to tell the truth?"

Sam shakes his head.

Dad continues, ruffling his son's hair as he speaks. "I want to be able to trust what you tell me, kiddo. I love you very much, and I want to know that when you tell me something, it's what really happened."

Sam looks up now and says slowly, "I love you, too, Daddy. I was just pretending."

Dad says, "Yes, I know we were pretending. And it's fun to pretend sometimes. It's important to trust that we can tell the truth, though. We're pretending when we make up a story together. We're lying when we use a story to avoid admitting we've made a mistake."

Sam will probably have to learn this lesson more than once. His Dad could also simply have asked Sam if he felt scared. Or he could have asked the original question in a less threatening way, saying "Sam, this broken egg made a mess. How can we solve this problem? Can you clean it up by yourself, or would you like me to help?"

Removing the sense of fear and getting the message of love through to our children (or even participating in a bit of nonsense with them) can help them learn to tell the truth. It is probably wise to remember, too, that few adults can claim to be completely truthful all of the time. Realistic expectations and acceptance will help your child learn trust and truthfulness.

Young children don't make the same assumptions about property rights that adults do. And because children learn by watching adults, they sometimes make surprising decisions about what they've seen.

For instance, Jason goes into the supermarket with his mom. He watches Mom pick up a copy of the free local paper and place it in her purse. Further down the aisle a woman is offering samples of cookies. Mom takes one for herself and offers one to Jason, who munches on it happily as they complete their shopping.

When they arrive at the car, Mom lifts Jason into his car seat and discovers a bulge in her son's pocket. Further examination reveals a candy bar.

"You stole this," Mom exclaims, shocked.

"What on earth is 'stealing'?" Jason wonders.

It's not really surprising that Jason is confused; what difference is there between the paper, the cookies, and the candy bar? These are the moments of truth parents face each day, and they can be either occasions for disappointment or opportunities for teaching.

If Mom is paying attention, she may realize that the problem is not one of dishonesty but differing perceptions. She may remember picking up the newspaper and the cookies. And she may choose to help her little boy understand why we can take some things out of the supermarket but not others.

If Mom lectures Jason, shames him, and makes him feel guilty and afraid, he may be more likely to believe that right and wrong are a matter of getting caught. He may also be less able to apply what he has learned to a future situation.

Understanding the developmental limitations in your child's thinking will help you focus on their underlying beliefs and invite real thinking and learning to take place.

The "No" Word

Toddlers and preschoolers are experiencing individuation, learning to see themselves as separate, independent beings. It's a natural and healthy process, but one that is frequently trying for parents and teachers. It doesn't take long for a young child to learn the power of the word "no," or that by using it he can provoke all sorts of interesting reactions. Adults can't always avoid these confrontations, but changing your own behavior and expectations can lessen their impact. There are actually three types of "no": the ones you can avoid saying, the ones you can avoid hearing, and the ones that you just learn to live with.

How Not to Say "No"

"Sometimes I listen to myself talking to my two-year-old," one mom confided to a group of friends, "and all I hear myself saying is 'no' and 'don't.' I sound so negative, but I don't know what else to do." There are actually a number of ways adults can avoid saying the "no" word themselves.

1. Say what you *do* want.   Elizabeth, who is three years old, is delightedly throwing blocks across the room. Her teacher walks in and immediately says, "No throwing blocks!" Now Elizabeth knows what *not* to do, but she may have a hard time figuring out what she *can* do. It might be more effective if her teacher says, "Blocks are for using on the floor" or "You look like you want to do some throwing. Would you like me to help you find a toy you can throw?" The next time you start to tell your child "no," ask yourself what you want to have happen. Then tell your child what you want.

2. Say "yes" instead.   It's really very easy to say "yes" instead of "no." Imagine that your five-year-old has just asked you if she can watch television. Your response might be, "No, you haven't cleaned your room." You might be surprised to learn that you can say "yes" and still communicate the same message. "Yes," you tell your daughter, "you can watch TV just as soon as your room is clean." If your daughter responds "But I want to watch TV right now!" you can simply say, "You can watch when your room is clean." Eventually your daughter will figure out that she can choose to either clean her room, or not watch television.

Many parents are programmed to respond with an automatic "no." When you are about to say "no," try asking yourself "why not?" Take a look at eighteen-month-old Cindy. She is playing in the kitchen sink, splashing water everywhere, and having a wonderful time. When Mom enters the room, her first response is to grab Cindy and say, "Stop that!"

But why? Cindy's eyes are sparkling; she is absorbed in the feel of the water and the magic of the droplets flying around. Her clothes can be changed, and she'll probably think it's a terrific game to help Mom mop the floor afterward. In other words, there may be no reason to say "no" this time. Mom *and* Cindy may be better off if they forget the "no" and simply enjoy themselves.

3. Use questions or statements.

It's art time at the child care center, but two of the boys have a better idea than making collages. Chris and Peter are having a marvelous time throwing the pieces of colored paper around the room. When the teacher comes over, she can say "Stop throwing the paper around!" Or she can say, "Who can show me what to do with these colored papers?" Or even, "There is collage paper on the floor." These responses give the boys an opportunity to demonstrate their knowledge of appropriate behavior and clean up the mess. They can do this without experiencing shame or humiliation—and without receiving undue attention (more about that later).

4. Agree to discuss the subject.   Family or class meetings are an excellent place to explore situations that provoke a lot of "no's" (see Chapter 18 for more information). If you find yourself saying "no" frequently when in the vicinity of the candy rack at the store, you may want to place "candy buying" on the agenda for your next family meeting. A child three years old or older can usually help make an agreement about when you will or will not buy candy. Once that agreement is understood, you can follow through with kind and firm action.

5. Draw a picture.   Simple pictures can help a child understand what is expected of him, especially if that child hasn't yet mastered language. Some children respond better to visual clues than auditory clues.

Andy had brought his favorite toy fire engine to the child care center and was busily creating havoc with it. Max, his teacher, told Andy that he needed to put the engine on the shelf until it was time to go home. Andy reluctantly complied, but a few minutes later Max noticed that Andy had taken it down and was running through the playroom with his "siren" on.

Max approached Andy again, and was met with a scowl as the boy clutched his toy tightly. Max paused for a moment, then picked up a pencil and a piece of paper. He drew a simple picture of the fire engine sitting on a shelf and said, "This is the shelf with your fire engine on it." Andy was fascinated. Then Max drew the figure of a little boy running. "This is Andy," he said, "playing outside without a fire engine."

Andy looked at the pictures for a moment, then calmly went to the shelf to put away his fire engine and headed out the door to play. Max was astonished, but Andy had simply needed the additional visual clues and encouragement the picture gave him to choose the right behavior. (There's also something to be said for doing the unexpected!)

Another teacher decided to try the picture approach with Jenna, a three-year-old who refused to stay on her cot during nap time. The teacher drew a simple stick figure of a little girl lying in the center of a rectangle. She showed the picture to Jenna and said, "This is Jenna lying on her cot." Amazingly, Jenna went over to her cot and lay down. Drawing a picture may not work for every child every time, but can be very helpful for children who are helped by receiving visual clues.

How to Avoid Hearing the "No" Word

Would you prefer that the youngsters in your life say "no" a bit less often? Try asking fewer questions that allow for a "yes" or "no" answer. Asking "are you ready to eat?" invites a "yes" or "no" answer. Giving limited choices such as "would you like milk or apple juice with your dinner?" can avoid the entire problem.

Instead of asking "Did you have fun today?" ask "What was the happiest time of your day?" You're inviting thoughtful answers, instead of single-syllable ones.

Another good way to avoid hearing "no" is to look for cooperation instead of giving orders and commands. If your boss stomps in and tells you, "Get over there and finish that job!" most adults would be tempted to respond with something stronger than a simple "no." Children are no different. Most of the time, if you invite their help and cooperation in a friendly way, they will respond. Try it and see!

When You Must Say "No"

There are times, of course, when we must say "no." Children need safe, secure boundaries as they develop and grow, and they will respect adults who can gently and respectfully draw those boundaries (even if a temper tantrum comes first). Children, too, will say "no" from time to time. In fact, the ability to say "no" and mean it can prove important, especially as a child grows up and faces peer pressure about drugs, sex, and other serious issues. (Many adults wish they could learn to say "no" comfortably, especially when asked to serve on yet another committee or help with yet another fund-raiser!)

Give your children an opportunity to practice saying "no" in acceptable ways. Ask your child, "Do you want more milk?" "No," especially with a "thank you" attached, is a fine answer. When children are between the ages of eighteen and twenty-four months, they enjoy saying "no" just to say "no"! Ignoring the "no" and redirecting your child's attention to something else will probably solve the problem.

"All the World's a Stage"

Parents constantly hear the words, "It's just a phase." And there's a great deal of truth in the concept—children usually are in one stage or another. Understanding your child's development will enable you to deal effectively with behavior and shape your child's world into a place where he can love, be loved, and learn.

CHAPTER 8

"You Can't Make 'Em Do It": Sleeping, Eating, and Toileting

There is a familiar children's fable about a wager between the North Wind and the Sun. A man was walking along the beach one day wearing a heavy woolen overcoat. The North Wind boasted to the Sun that he could make the man remove his overcoat. The Sun agreed to the bet, and the North Wind began to blow. He blew steadily along the beach and the man buttoned up his coat. The North Wind blew harder and turned icy cold, but the man only held his coat about him more tightly. After a great deal of blustering and wild blowing, the North Wind surrendered.

Now the Sun took her turn. She shone brightly on the man, letting her warm rays caress him. Soon the man undid his coat. The Sun shone harder and the warmth increased. The man eventually removed his coat and the Sun won the wager.

This story is a lovely example of the power of gentle persuasion, and it is a great deal like parenting young children. When we offer gentleness and understanding, warmth and trust, firmness and kindness, our children open up to us. The more severe and punishing we are, the more our children "button up" and resist us. Yet many parents insist on blowing like the North Wind, especially in the three areas of their children's lives where they actually have little or no control. Can you guess what these battlegrounds are?

91

S*E*T

Meet the terrible trio: sleeping, eating, and toileting (think "S*E*T"). There are very few parents who don't have war stories to share!

For instance, Joey's mother storms into his child care center and demands that the teacher make sure he eats *all* of his lunch today. Or Grandma purses her lips and tells her son that it's a disgrace her granddaughter is still wearing diapers. Or a bleary-eyed young couple ask their parenting class if *anyone* knows how to get their daughter to go to bed. These are battlegrounds where no amount of force, threats, or manipulation will succeed, for these areas are the child's ultimate responsibility and are within his control.

Of course, that doesn't mean you should just give up or let children do as they please. Parents and caregivers need to learn the methods of steady, gentle persuasion available to them in these challenging areas.

Routines

Children in the preschool years thrive on routines. They like their lives to be clear and predictable, and they enjoy the security of comfortable repetition. A familiar routine in the morning, at mealtimes, and at bedtime can eliminate the need young children often feel to test their boundaries. Clear expectations and predictable activities can smooth the rough spots out of a youngster's day (and that of his parents and teachers).

As children grow older, using routines can eliminate many of the hassles surrounding chores or homework, especially when the child is old enough to help create the routine during a family or class meeting (usually around the age of three). The routine can then become the "boss." A teacher or parent has only to ask, "what is our routine?" and everyone knows what should happen next. Routines will vary from family to family, from preschool to preschool, but they are useful ways to take the struggle out of the "terrible trio" of sleeping, eating, and toileting.

Sleeping, or *"Doesn't She Ever Get Tired?"*

It is nap time at the preschool and all of the children are asleep—except Margaret. The teacher has read a story and offered back rubs, but Margaret is still squirming. The teacher has even stroked Margaret's eyelids gently but in spite of her best efforts, Margaret is still awake.

Mary is a different story. Mary's mother worries that Mary sleeps too long at nap time, which makes it difficult to get her to bed at night. The teacher promises to keep Mary awake longer or to wake her up earlier, but despite her best efforts, Mary is usually the first to fall asleep and the last to wake up.

The bottom line is that you can't "make" a child sleep, and it is sometimes hard to control when they will wake up. Sometimes we feel so in need of time to ourselves that we try to establish a bedtime or nap time that just doesn't coincide with our child's needs. Most parents have experienced the frustration of a child who is happily wide awake long past bedtime, tumbles out of bed at awkward moments, or refuses to wake even when mom and dad have urgent business to attend to. Is there anything parents can do to help children settle into a sleep cycle that works for everyone?

The Importance of Comfort

In addition to adjusting our expectations, parents can set guidelines and develop routines to give a child the best opportunity to fall asleep; the rest is up to her.

Parents can keep a number of things in mind. We can make sure children are comfortable in pajamas that fit, in beds or cribs that are secure, and with the appropriate number of blankets.

Remember your child's temperament. Is the sleeping area warm or cool enough? Does your child need absolute quiet or a steady hum of activity?

If your child spends time in more than one household, special smells and textures can make bedtime much less stressful. A pillow or "blankie" that travels with your child from home to home or a special cuddly toy at the child care center are very important. Children have been known to curl up with their jackets tucked under their heads, drawing comfort from the familiar feel and smell.

An evening snack containing calcium, such as milk or yogurt, may help your child relax enough to sleep. Some people believe that sugar stimulates children. Although research is inconclusive, avoiding sugary food late in the evening may prove helpful. (Be sure to read labels; you may be surprised at the sugar content of some "healthy" foods!) Use trial and error to discover what works best for your child.

How many times have you heard that plaintive cry, "Mommy, I'm thirsty"? It may be helpful to agree with your child on how many drinks of water she will get. When children are allowed to negotiate the number of requests they can make, they seldom use their full quota. Whatever your agreement, follow through with kind and firm action.

Like adults, children have different needs regarding light and dark, noise and quiet. Some children enjoy solitude, while others need people close by; some children prefer total darkness, while the steady glow of a night-light comforts others. There is no "right" or "wrong"; finding out what works best for your child will take patience and a bit of trial and error.

Building a Bedtime Routine

Having a predictable, familiar routine can take a great deal of the struggle out of bedtime. But how do you find a bedtime routine that works? The following ideas may help you build a routine for your child that helps him (and you) have sweet dreams:

Playtime. A family playtime may be a good way to begin your nighttime routine. One family enjoys playing table games, while another likes a rousing game of tag or a pillow fight. It may be best to place more active games toward the beginning of your routine. The idea is to move steadily toward quiet, calming activities.

Bath time. A soak in the tub can be wonderfully soothing—and a time for closeness and play, too. There are many wonderful bath toys available (although your kitchen measuring cups and spoons will probably do quite nicely), and the sound and feel of warm water helps relax most children. An evening bath time should probably follow your active games and begin the "settling down" part of your routine.

Brushing your teeth. Did you know that toothbrushing can be fun? Some families put toothpaste on each other's brushes and all scrub happily away together, not only teaching good oral hygiene but having some good, clean fun as well!

Story time. Telling or reading stories is a familiar part of bedtime, for good reason. Young children love to hear stories; in fact, some never tire of hearing the same story over and over—and woe to the lazy parent who tries to leave a paragraph out! (How many parents have scurried to hide a particularly familiar book before their little one can request it yet again?) A child's earliest "reading" experience may consist of reciting a book to you, even turning the pages at the right spot. Children's poetry and simple rhymes are wonderful, too. As your child grows older (or if she often has difficulty falling asleep), you may want to let her look through books as she lies quietly in bed.

A variation on this theme is to play a story tape and let your child follow along in the accompanying book. Or you might tape yourself reading or telling a favorite story; then, if your child has more than one home or if you must be away for a while, he can hear your reassuring voice even when you can't be with him.

Special activities.   Since children often feel cozy and willing to talk just before they fall asleep, bedtime can be one of the best parts of your day together—if you let it be. You may want to pray together or sing a special song. One dad carries his small son around his room to say "good night" to each stuffed animal and picture. A tape of soothing lullabies or soft music can create a relaxing atmosphere.

Some parents enjoy asking their children to share the happiest and saddest moments of their day, and then letting their children ask them the same questions. (Because children's grasp of time is a little fuzzy, you may hear about things that happened this afternoon, last week, or even last month!) You may be amazed at how much you and your children learn about each other. Such moments go far beyond helping a child sleep; they are filled with shared love, trust, and closeness.

Hugs and kisses.   There are families where hugging, kissing, and saying "I love you" happens daily. In other families, these things rarely happen. Not surprisingly, researchers have discovered that a daily ration of hugs encourages emotional health, and if you haven't been dispensing regular hugs and kisses, you might consider giving it a try.

Bedtime is the perfect time for hugs, kisses, and gentle reassurances of love. Rick and Tracy McIntyre love to sit on the edge of three-year-old Cissy's bed and say, "If we were to line up all of the three-year-old girls in the world, guess which one we'd pick? We would say, 'We want *that* one!'" Rick and Tracy would both point at Cissy, who would giggle happily and launch herself into her parents' arms for a hug. The glow from your child's face during moments like these can illuminate the entire room!

Remember, it isn't necessary (or even wise) to do everything on the list as part of your bedtime routine—you might all be up until midnight! Nor will a bedtime routine guarantee that your child will never have difficulty falling asleep. If a child says he "can't sleep," tell him it's okay. He just needs to lie quietly in bed and look through a book or think quiet thoughts. Keep in mind that falling asleep is your child's job; you can only provide him with the opportunity. The hardest part of your job may be to ignore (with kindness and firmness) demands for more drinks and stories after you have completed a loving bedtime routine.

A bedtime routine may make it possible for you and your young child to enjoy sharing a special part of the day together, rather than rehearsing for World War III. The possibilities are endless. Pick out some ideas that appeal to you—or use your own creativity to find a routine that works for you and your child. Whatever you decide on, practice it often enough that it becomes a familiar, predictable part of your day—and a peaceful way to help and encourage your child to fall asleep.

Eating

Imagine for a moment that instead of your family, you're sitting down to dinner with some friends. Suppose you've invited Mary, her husband James, and your neighbor Sam over for a meal. As you pass around your favorite lasagna and a bowl of broccoli, the conversation goes something like this:

You: "I'm so glad you're all here for dinner. I'll pass around the lasagna."

James: "Just a small serving for me, please. I'm not very hungry tonight."

You: "Oh, nonsense! A big man like you needs lots to eat. Here—I'll give you a proper serving. Sam, have some broccoli."

Sam: "No, thanks. I'm not much of a broccoli eater."

You: "Sam, broccoli is good for you. You have to try a little bit or there will be no dessert for you! Now, Mary, I expect to see your plate all clean; there are still some yummy veggies there."

How do you think James, Mary, and Sam would feel? Would this be a successful dinner party? Does this sound a *little* bit like the conversation around your own dinner table?

All too often, the dinner table becomes a battleground for parents of young children. Parents worry about what their children eat—or refuse to eat. Have they had enough? Did they get enough vitamin C? Too much sugar? Enough calcium and protein?

But eating under surveillance is not relaxing, and children don't enjoy it any more than adults do. Listen to your own mealtime comments and ask yourself, "Would I say this to an adult guest?" Children treated with respect learn to treat others the same way. Just because they are small people doesn't mean they aren't entitled to opinions about food. It may help to remember, though, that those opinions often change as they grow and mature.

Mrs. Chong fretted constantly about what a picky eater her son Jimmy was. Jimmy rejected most foods and seemed to like only the things that Mrs. Chong considered "junk food." She worried about his health, charting the nutrients and vitamins he received each day. But no matter how much she fussed, Jimmy ate what he pleased. Oddly enough, he seemed healthy.

When he reached his teen years, Jimmy suddenly developed an appetite and began to eat everything his startled mother put in front of him. Although Mrs. Chong's years of fussing had very little effect, Jimmy eventually developed his own healthy eating habits.

Studies have shown that young children will usually eat a balanced diet *over time;* that is, they may not eat what their parents think healthy in any one day or even in a week, but over the course of time their bodies tell them what is needed. Arguing over the vegetables accomplishes little except raising everybody's blood pressure and making mealtime an unpleasant ordeal.

Martha Black was convinced that her son needed a warm bowl of oatmeal to start his day off properly. When three-year-old Ben refused to eat his oatmeal one morning, his mother decided she'd better teach him how important it was to eat the right foods. Martha got out some plastic wrap and covered the bowl of oatmeal. When Ben came in for lunch, Mrs. Black microwaved the oatmeal. After half an hour it had turned as cold (and as hard) as stone. Ben glared at it but refused to taste it, so Martha resolutely covered it up again. Can you imagine how appetizing that oatmeal looked at dinner after another trip to the microwave? Ben would willingly have starved before letting a spoonful pass his lips. What, do you suppose, has Ben learned about oatmeal? And what has his mother learned about Ben?

There is an important truth about food, eating, and young children. You provide the food; the children do the eating—or not, as the case may be. It is interesting to note that parents who raised children during the depression didn't experience eating problems. Since food was scarce, members of the family were delighted if someone didn't want their share. Coaxing someone to eat was not considered. In this atmosphere children were allowed to follow their own instincts about eating or not eating—and usually chose to eat as much as they could.

It *is* important to offer children a wide selection of nutritious food. (Special menus only reinforce finicky eating.) Be sure that at least *one* food on the table is considered edible by your child, then serve whatever else you wish. Even toddlers can learn to dish up their own food (with training) and often get so caught up in the activity that they forget to say "No." An important part of training is to teach them to take small helpings because they can always take more if they want it. It is not helpful to make them eat everything on their plate when they make a mistake and take too much. It is helpful to help them explore, through "what" and "how" questions, what happens when they take too much and how they can solve the problem.

There are a number of things parents can keep in mind to encourage healthy eating habits in their children and to make mealtimes together pleasant for the entire family.

1. Timing.   Young children see no reason to get hungry on anyone's schedule but their own. Infants nurse on demand; toddlers want food when they're hungry; and preschoolers often just can't make it from one meal to the next without something in between. These are normal variations; the key is to be certain that the choices available to your children are healthy ones. If your children aren't eating full meals, their snacks should provide them with the nutrients they need. A pile of carrot sticks or even a baked potato, for instance, is much better than french fries and a soda—especially when followed by a dinner skirmish over the peas.

A child who doesn't eat his entire lunch at the child care center can snack out of his lunch box on the way home. After all, *when* children eat is not as important as *what* they eat. Lunch food is just as nutritious eaten at 5:00 as it would have been at noon.

2. Simplicity.   Your church group may have raved about your prawns in Cajun sauce, but your preschooler may be totally unimpressed. Children are often suspicious of unfamiliar foods or unusual mixtures. A cheese sandwich with lettuce and tomato may be spurned, while a piece of cheese, some tomato slices, and a few crackers will be consumed quite happily. If your little one looks askance at the pasta and vegetable salad, try serving the ingredients to him separately. You certainly don't need to provide a separate menu—nor should you—but being aware of your child's natural preferences will help you find ways to encourage cooperation and experimentation.

3. Choices. Allowing children to develop their own eating habits requires mutual trust. Children will eat foods their bodies need, and if you provide a *variety* of healthy and appetizing foods, they will be more likely to choose foods that are nourishing. Remember, though, that even adults need a splurge now and then; thousands of children have been raised on occasional doses of fast food, pizza, and hot dogs without suffering permanent damage. The key, as always, is *balance*. Providing a regular diet of nutritious foods will help you feel better about the Easter jelly beans, chocolate Santas, and Halloween tummyaches that seem to be an inevitable part of childhood. However, if you have jelly beans, potato chips, cookies, cupcakes, and soft drinks around the house all the time, you are inviting poor eating habits and food battles.

4. Choose your battles. It may be absolutely imperative to you that your four-year-old eat her lima beans. Or you may feel comfortable watching your child eat a steady diet of salami slices, raisins, and crackers. But be aware that if you *in*sist, your child may feel compelled to *re*sist—and it's doubtful that staring at a plate of cold peas after everyone else has left the table ever persuaded a child to love veggies.

Some parents gloat about making their children sit at the table until they finish their dinner—and claim it works. If you talk to the children, you get a different story. They either figured out how to feed most of the food to the dog, or hide it in their napkin (weren't the parents suspicious when their children offered to clean up the table?). Or they developed eating problems as adults: Some got fat because they felt they "had to clean their plate"; others became bulimic to prove no one else could control what they ate. Someone will always lose in battles over food—short-range or long-range.

Mealtime Routines

Yes, routines work for eating, too. Mealtimes in our busy families often become hectic, stressful occasions that no one truly enjoys. Parents arrive home tired after a long day's work; children are often both hungry and cranky. Comfortable routines can make mealtimes proceed far more smoothly. The elements are simple; here are some suggestions, which may help you create routines for your own family.

1. Take time to relax.   If dinnertime is often rushed in your home, try beginning the process differently. For instance, Tom Shelton always packs an extra-large lunch for his four-year-old daughter, Katie. During the drive home after work and preschool, Katie opens her lunch box and enjoys whatever is left over from lunch. When they arrive home, Katie is not urgently hungry and her dad doesn't feel pressured to serve dinner immediately.

Taking time to wind down at the end of the day is almost always worth the investment. You may want to spend a few minutes curled up on the sofa with your child, reading or sharing moments from your day. A warm bath or shower might refresh you for the evening ahead, or you may want to take time for a walk or a quick game together. Slices of fruit or a bag of crackers may satisfy the hunger pangs long enough for the entire family to catch its breath. "But I don't have time," you may be saying, "I simply have too much to do!" Regardless of how busy your lives may be, taking time to relax and reenter your family's world will eliminate the hassles that often consume even *more* time.

2. Prepare the meal together.   Nothing encourages a finicky eater better than helping plan and prepare the meal. And most parents fail to recognize the wonderful little helpers they have right there beside them. Even an eighteen-month-old can find something useful to do in the kitchen. Get a big apron, pull up a stool to the sink, and invite your child to slosh and tear the lettuce for tonight's salad. A two-year-old can use a brush to scrub vegetables, and at three, your child can place silverware and napkins on the table.

Giving your children a way to contribute encourages the growth of their sense of initiative and helps teach life skills. It also invites children to see themselves as contributing members of the family, building their sense of belonging in the process.

3. Create moments that draw you together.   Lunch at the Roundtree Childcare Center is a special time. The children join hands around the table, and each day one child is invited to share something she feels grateful for. After the other children have listened respectfully, they take turns squeezing the hand of the person on their right. When the "squeeze" has gone all around the circle, the children begin their meal.

Mr. Linski is from a traditional Jewish family. Before each meal in the Linski household he recites special Hebrew prayers. In the Jones family, each person stands at his place at the table, and when all have gathered, they sing a grace together.

There are innumerable ways that families can add special beginning rituals to their meals, moments that create a sense of family identity and closeness, warmth and love. Some of these rituals are religious; some are not. In our busy families, meals are often eaten on the run—everyone has somewhere to go, and the moments of communication and togetherness can be lost if we're not careful. Rituals can be wonderful ways to preserve the sense of family and teach our children to value it.

4. Set some guidelines for finishing up.   Should children be expected to sit quietly until everyone has finished eating? Or should they be allowed to leave the table to play quietly? There is no "right" answer, but it may be wise to decide the matter beforehand, rather than arguing over the cold mashed potatoes.

Even young children can be involved in some aspect of cleaning up after a meal. If your child can walk well on his own, he probably can clear away his plate, scrape away uneaten food, or load his utensils into the dishwasher.

Remember that allowing children to be involved, encouraging mutual trust and respect, and having realistic expectations will take much of the struggle out of eating, and may make mealtimes together an event the entire family looks forward to.

Toileting

No other topic in the world of raising young children arouses such strong emotions, it seems, as "potty training." The Petersons took a great deal of pride in the fact that their first child was using the toilet at the age of eighteen months. They were *so* pleased, in fact, that Paula Peterson thought about writing a book about toilet training to help other, less fortunate families. Before she could get around to it, however, her second child was born. Much to the Petersons' surprise, this child wanted nothing to do with his parents' prize-winning toilet training techniques. In fact, despite being placed on the potty for long periods of time, this child was almost three before the training worked.

So much for genius. The reality is that children will use the toilet when they are ready to do so. Parents can cheer, beg, and threaten, but hang on to your diapers. Each child has his or her own unique schedule—and absolute control. What *can* parents do to set the stage for this important developmental milestone?

Readiness

Physical factors can influence a child's ability to use the toilet. He must have a bladder large enough to allow him to wait for increasingly long periods of time before urinating, especially to wait overnight. As a general rule, bladder control will come before bowel control, and daytime control will precede nighttime control.

A child may also need to communicate well enough to ask for help. And she must be interested enough in the whole process to start paying attention to her body's signals and to interrupt her play when necessary.

Perhaps the best advice is simply this: *relax.* Using the toilet on his own is a very significant thing for your child to do. When he's ready, he'll do it—and probably not a moment sooner. There *are* ways, though, that parents can gently encourage children to move toward toilet training.

Setting the Stage for Success

Imagine for a moment that you are a very small child. You know that mom and dad are eager for you to learn to use the potty, to be a "big boy" and wear "big boy pants." And suddenly you feel that strange tingly feeling that is beginning to mean you have to "go." So you head toward the bathroom, becoming aware as you trot down the hall that there may not be a lot of time.

Somehow you know you have to get your pants down, but the buckles on your overalls are stiff and your fingers are so small. Then you glance at the toilet, which looks *huge* from your point of view. Maybe, you think, a little assistance is called for. But by the time you alert mom and dad, it's too late. No wonder children often decide that it's easier just to stay in diapers!

Not surprisingly, "potty training" is just that: *training.* And there are many things parents can do to make it easier. The first involves your attitude. Knowing your child's temperament and abilities will help you keep your expectations reasonable. And if you are relaxed and comfortable, your child is likely to feel the same way. Pressure to "succeed" will only frustrate both of you. If accidents happen—and they will—be patient. If your child is wet, change her. If she is old enough, she can change herself (which often encourages a child to be more aware of her body's signals). Be sure, however, that you *never* humiliate or shame a child about toileting setbacks. Dry pants aren't worth damaged self-esteem.

It can help to train your child in the steps he must master along the road to successful use of the toilet. It's a good idea to provide clothing that is easily pulled down (and up); elastic waistbands are perfect. If the weather is warm, wearing under-pants alone (or nothing at all) may simplify the process.

A child will need comfortable access to the toilet, either in the form of a "potty chair" or a seat with steps that helps her up to the big toilet. A child may need to be reassured that she will not be flushed away (don't assume the child knows this al-ready—it can be a very real fear). It may be necessary to show her that her body will not fit down the toilet. And although you may be really pleased with what she has produced, let her know it's okay not to save it. If this is a big issue, simply flush later.

Be sure to teach your child the importance of washing his hands. Have a stool available so he can reach the sink, with soap and a towel for drying within easy reach. One preschool teaches children to sing this song while they wash their hands (the song lasts about 11 seconds, just the time it takes to kill e. coli bacteria).

> "Wash, wash, wash your hands,
> Wash your hands together.
> Scrub, scrub, scrub your hands,
> 'Til they're clean and sparkly."
> (to the tune of "Skip to M'Lou")

Having regular toilet times may encourage youngsters to develop the habit of using the bathroom regularly. And when leaving for an outing (even a short one), it is wise to invite a young child to use the toilet beforehand. (Most parents quickly learn where the restrooms at the neighborhood grocery store are located!)

One preschool teacher decided to take her class on a "field trip" to pick blueberries. They blithely sailed out of the preschool together and into a nearby field. Trouble soon arose, however; the teacher had forgotten to remind the children to use the toilet before leaving and now the only option was a well-used outhouse. This teacher spent most of her field trip holding one child after another over the outhouse, and she never forgot pre-outing reminders again!

When readiness and training have been taken into account, it is time to relax and trust that successful toileting will result. It's helpful to know that a number of things can cause a temporary setback, though.

Setbacks, or "Whoops!"

When a child is experiencing new things—a new preschool, a new house, or a new sibling—it's common for potty training to suffer a setback. A new environment or an especially exciting activity can cause a child not to pay attention to his body's signals; and other major life events, such as death, divorce, illness, or travel, can interfere with toileting. All of these events represent major adjustments in a child's life, and toilet issues often take second place to coping with change.

Your attitude as a parent or caregiver will make all the difference in how your child handles "accidents." Imagine how confused a child might feel when she not only loses control of her body, but faces a parent's anger and disappointment as well.

Ann was four years old when she was asked to be flower girl in her aunt's wedding. She wore a lovely, long white gown made especially for her with a lacy veil and tiny pearl necklace. People smiled and nodded at her as she walked down the aisle scattering rose petals, and Ann glowed with the attention and excitement.

The reception was beautiful and Ann was thrilled by the festivity around her. She had crawled under a table and was listening to the adults talking when she became aware of something she'd been ignoring all afternoon. Before she could get up, it happened: she had a bowel movement, soiling her lovely white dress.

When Ann's mother discovered her, she was horrified.

"I can't imagine what got into Ann," she told the assembled aunts and grandmothers. "She never does this anymore."

Turning to her crying daughter, she said coldly, "You should be ashamed of yourself." Ann was changed into her old play clothes and spent the rest of the day feeling disgraced. And for months, just the word "wedding" was enough to make Ann hang her head in shame.

When children have toileting accidents, the last thing they need is a disapproving audience. Ann's mother could have taken her quietly aside, helped her to change, and explained to her daughter that excitement can sometimes make us forget to do the things we should.

It may be wisdom to keep a change of clothing nearby when your child is learning to use the toilet. It is also immeasurably helpful to be patient, and to offer your child unconditional love and acceptance. Once you have taken into account your child's personal time clock, provided him with appropriate clothing and accessible facilities, and taken time to train him in the skills he needs, it is time to relax, celebrate his successes, and sympathize with his disappointments.

"All S*E*T"

There are many ways to get the message of love through to children. One of the most important is to offer your trust. Sleeping, eating, and toileting can be battlegrounds where parents and children oppose each other, or they can be opportunities for sharing respect, kindness, and encouragement. Healthy sleeping, eating, and toileting habits are gifts that will serve your children well. And although "you can't make 'em do it," there is much you *can* do to set the stage for success.

CHAPTER 9

"You Can't Come to My Birthday Party": *Learning About Social Skills*

Did you know that a crying baby is practicing social skills? In the first months of a baby's life, crying brings adults, who provide food, comfort, and entertainment. By four months of age or so, the baby's social repertoire expands—he smiles at the adults who surround him. And by five to eight months of age, the baby is giggling, cooing, and otherwise enchanting his grown-up companions.

Still, children don't truly discover that the world holds other people than themselves until they are between fourteen and twenty-four months of age. When a baby looks into a mirror, she sees an unknown being. It is well into the first year of life before a baby even recognizes the person in the mirror as herself! Knowing this can help adults comprehend how primitive her social interactions will be for a while. And when adults understand that social skills don't develop naturally but must be taught, they may be less dismayed that children often hit, bite, push, and fight as they discover how to get along with others.

Social skills like sharing and playing develop through training, practice, and mistakes—especially mistakes. The road is not smooth; emotional bumps and scrapes mark the landscape of

111

early social experience, with an occasional real bite and scratch thrown in along the way. A knowledge of how social skills develop in young children will help parents and teachers provide both training and understanding as children learn to interact with their equally inexperienced peers.

Sharing

Sharing is a big issue in the world of young children. We expect little people to take turns, to be happy with equal portions, to give up playing with a favorite toy. But children under the age of two are egocentric; that is, they are the center of their own world and everything else exists only as it relates to the center. Which is, to be exact, "me." This is not selfishness—it's natural human development.

When toddlers play together, most of their play is "parallel play." They play *near* other children rather than *with* them. Jeffrey, for instance, is sixteen months old. When he takes his bath, it is Dad who splashes and floats the rubber duckie to him. It is Grandma who rocks him to sleep. And at the child care center, the teachers feed him, carry him, comfort him, and change him. There are other children present, but they are more like mysterious new toys than other people. Jeffrey has begun to be curious about them and to explore them; he knows they cry when he pokes them, and when he tried to put one's hair in his mouth it created quite a commotion. For now, Jeffrey is content to do his own thing while other children do theirs—at least, most of the time.

Sharing requires two participants. When one (or both) of those participants is the center of the universe, trouble is bound to result. Parents and teachers can help toddlers learn to share by taking time for training. They can demonstrate sharing and give it a name. They can encourage any moves in the direction of sharing. And they can understand that the process takes time so they must have patience and allow for mistakes along the way.

It helps to remember that training at this stage is mostly preparatory; toddlers aren't quite developmentally ready to share. Simply redirecting a toddler's attention can effectively defuse a combustible situation.

When Susie is twenty months old and grabs another child's toy, an adult can step in, remove the toy gently from Susie and return it to the other child, and carry Susie away to find some other interesting object to play with. Saying, "Tommy is playing with that toy right now" or "Let's find a toy that Susie enjoys" is all that is needed.

When Susie is two-and-a-half and begins to attend a preschool, things change a bit. Susie is moving from a world where everything is "mine" to recognizing that the world contains other people. She no longer merely plays next to her companions, but enjoys running and chasing around the playground with them.

When Susie grabs a toy now, adults can respond differently than they did earlier. Susie is ready to learn and practice the social skill of sharing. A more appropriate response now is to take the toy and explore ways of learning to share with another child.

Susie and Tommy are playing in the block area when Susie grabs the toy car that Tommy has just picked up. Both children begin to yell, "It's mine! Give it to me!"

Naturally, the uproar draws the attention of Mrs. McGee, the children's teacher. She walks over and gently takes the car.

"Susie," she asks, "do you want to play with this car?"

"I want it," Susie agrees firmly.

Now Mrs. McGee turns to Tommy. "Are you playing with the car, Tommy?"

Tommy's lower lip juts out a bit as he says, "It's mine."

Mrs. McGee places the car in Tommy's hands, and turns to Susie. "Susie, what do you think you could say to Tommy if you want to play with the car?"

"I want to play with it?" Susie offers (with only a little sulk in her voice).

Mrs. McGee agrees that that's one way to ask. She suggests that Susie could also try saying, "May I play with the car?"

Tommy has been watching this exchange with interest. When his teacher asks him what he might say to Susie when she asks for the car, he responds right away.

"Here, you can have it," he replies, handing the car to Susie.

Mrs. McGee smiles. "It's nice of you to share, Tommy. What might you say if you weren't finished with the car?"

This is a new thought for Tommy. The teacher has made it clear that just asking may not be enough. She is helping Tommy learn that he has some options and can assert his own needs, but Tommy is momentarily baffled.

Mrs. McGee turns to Susie. "Can you think of something Tommy can say, Susie?"

Susie has just the answer. "He could say 'in a minute.' "

Mrs. McGee nods. "That's a good idea. Perhaps he could say that he will give it to you in ten minutes. Would that work, Tommy?"

Tommy nods, and Mrs. McGee encourages him to practice saying "I'm not done yet" to Susie.

Throughout this conversation, both children were invited to explore the possibilities available to them. Sharing is a skill that must be taught and practiced (even by adults). How will a child know what to do if no demonstrations are given? Remember, this is a period of intense language development. Providing the necessary words and ways to use them is part of the training process. Teaching and encouraging young children to "use their words" is a wonderful way to nurture social skills.

Playing "let's pretend" with dolls or puppets is another way sharing can be modeled and practiced. Adults can act out a conflict between two children, showing what happened as well as other, more appropriate responses. Then children can practice, holding the puppets and exploring both the inappropriate and appropriate behavior. This invites children to recognize inappropriate behavior in others and eventually, to notice and take responsibility for their own.

There are many other ways to take time for training in sharing. Model sharing yourself by saying, "I want to share my cake with you" or "Let's take turns bouncing the ball. I'll count to ten while you bounce it, then you count to ten while I bounce it." Give opportunities for sharing by saying, "I know that's your favorite toy. Which of your toys would you be willing to share with Michael for a while?" When children have difficulty sharing, acknowledge their feelings by saying, "I know it can be difficult to share. Sometimes I don't like to, either. You don't have to share all the time. I have faith that you will share when you are ready." Shaming a child, labeling her "naughty," or forcing a reluctant apology are unlikely to encourage sharing.

When children between the ages of three-and-a-half to five years of age quarrel, it may be helpful to ask them to sit quietly for a few minutes. You can ask them to explore and name their feelings, and invite them to explore ways they could handle a situation next time. Teaching social skills with the same attention we give to other types of skill development will produce children who can play together peacefully. When children experience continuous modeling and training, they can learn to get along quite well with other members of the world around them.

Hitting and Aggression

Toddlers are short on both language and social skills, and when they play together they can easily become frustrated. When they lack the ability to express what's wrong in words, hitting and other types of aggression sometimes result.

When you set one toddler down to play with another, neither is particularly sure of what the other is all about. Watch them eyeing one another and you can guess at what they might be thinking. "What is this creature? Does it break? Can I taste it? What happens when I pull its hair or examine its eyelashes?" Walking up and hitting another child may be just a primitive form of saying "hello!"

Still, children under the age of two need to learn that pulling hair, poking eyes, and hitting hurt people and cannot be allowed. Firmness, coupled with removing the child temporarily and redirecting his attention to something else, works best.

For preschoolers, a big part of learning social skills involves learning about feelings. We will explore this subject in detail later on, but it helps to know that children often hit because they are acting upon their feelings of frustration and anger. This can be a good opportunity to teach that there is a difference between a feeling and an action, and to help a child learn to identify and cope with his feelings.

Three-year-old Jack was on a rampage. He had been hitting the other children at the preschool, knocking over their towers of blocks, and kicking gravel on the playground. One afternoon Jack got angry when another child ran in front of him. He pushed her down, causing her to scrape her knee.

Miss Terry, Jack's teacher, gently led the raging Jack away from the other children and toward the book corner. As Jack calmed down, he looked over and noticed that one of the books had a picture of a sad-looking boy on the cover.

"Why does he look like that?" Jack asked Miss Terry.

"Well," his teacher replied, bending over to look at the picture, "he looks sad to me. Why do you think he might be sad?"

Jack began to explain that the boy in the picture was sad because his favorite baby-sitter had gone away and he wasn't going to see her anymore.

Miss Terry set Jack gently on her lap. "That little boy must feel very lonely and sad," she said. Jack began to cry in his teacher's arms.

When Jack's sobs had slowed to sniffles, Miss Terry asked if he could think of a way to help the child he had pushed feel better again.

"I bet she's sad, too," Jack said. "Maybe I could play a special game with her and help her put away her lunch stuff."

Miss Terry wrote a note to Jack's parents explaining what had happened and mentioning Jack's sadness over the loss of his baby-sitter. Jack helped by making a mark at the bottom to serve as his signature.

Jack had an opportunity to explore his feelings in safety. He also learned that he was responsible for his behavior toward other children. Identifying and accepting feelings can help children learn effective social skills.

Older children who are hitting or pulling hair should be firmly separated. A parent or teacher can say, "I can't allow you to hurt others" and can help the combatants explore other ways of acting when they feel angry or frustrated. It is important to understand that behavior often contains a coded message about how a child is feeling. As we will learn in the next chapter, interpreting the beliefs a child has about himself will provide clues about how parents and teachers might respond.

It will take more than one such occasion to teach children to play cooperatively together. Patient repetition and guidance will help children learn more quickly the pleasures of getting along; it *won't* turn them into angels! Remember that social skills "mistakes" can always be turned into opportunities to learn.

Friendship

"Will you be my friend?" Every preschool teacher has heard that plea. The first years of life are filled with so much growth, and that growth can be traced in the development of friendships.

Just what does friendship mean to a young child? When a child is younger than two years old, his friends are most likely to be the children of his parents' acquaintances or neighbors, with whom he is plopped down to "play" while the adults socialize. Between the ages of two and three, children begin to interact more with their peers. There is no greater statement of friendship from a preschooler than "you can come to my birthday party." They are saying "I like you enough to share the most important day in my world: the celebration of 'me'!"

Jenna is three-and-a-half years old. It is June and her birthday is not until December. Even so, hardly a day goes by that Jenna does not invite—or uninvite—someone at her preschool to her birthday party. When a parent wandered in to discuss enrolling her daughter, Jenna immediately went up to her and said, "I'm going to be four. You can come to my party." Jenna is a generous soul and includes everyone she meets in this grand event.

A short while later, however, when Jenna's friend Ilsa won't share the dress-up clothes, Jenna sticks out her lip and announces in a voice of doom, "You can't come to my birthday!" Ilsa trembles at such a threat and quickly hands over one of the dress-up scarves.

For young children, birthday invitations (or the threat of their withdrawal) are an early social tool. They represent an offer of mutual companionship and acceptance—or momentary rejection. As children mature and develop a less self-centered view of the world, they learn to interact in different ways.

A Word About Siblings

Are brothers and sisters a blessing or a curse? Most children occasionally wonder. We do know that brothers and sisters are forever; most of them will outlive their parents, and children usually learn their first lessons about friendship through their relationships with their siblings.

It is heartwarming to see eighteen-month-old Timmy go up to his four-year-old sister and say "Wuv you, Bef." It isn't so heartwarming to watch Timmy pull Beth's hair when she tries to rescue her favorite book from his clutches. When children are two or three years old, sibling fighting is the result of their immature social skills and the actions of the adults involved. Social skills training is important for siblings, especially because of the unique aspect that sharing (and vying for) a parent's love and attention brings to their conflicts. (Keep in mind that sibling fighting is *not* the same as sibling rivalry. Sibling rivalry is about the decisions each child in the family makes based on their birth order and role in family life—and can be a hidden basis for sibling fights. For an excellent discussion of sibling rivalry, see Chapter 3 on birth order in *Positive Discipline* by Jane Nelsen, Ballantine.)

It is helpful when parents learn to see sibling fighting for what it usually is. Just as puppies roll around, nip at each other, and roughhouse together, so young children sometimes tussle as they investigate their relationship with each other. Parents can stay out of the "rescuer" role by simply leaving the room. Taking a quiet moment elsewhere eliminates the audience—and sometimes, the struggle.

If the noise level and fear of mayhem is too strong to ignore, try giving both of the children a big hug. "What?" you say, "Reward them for fighting?" Not exactly. If your children are competing for your attention, try giving it in an unexpected way. While hugging them, say "I bet the two of you would like my attention right now. Next time, try telling me with your words instead of hurting one another." Acting in an unexpected way can cause children to pay more attention to your words—and it's always great to be hugged!

Since both children are involved, treat them the same way. Even toddlers can be placed in their rooms to "cool off." Don't try to be judge and jury; worry about "who dunnit" when you read a mystery, not when you raise a preschooler! When your children are ready to get along, they can come out. You have shifted the message from "who is loved more" to "hurting each other is not okay."

A parent with arguing children can use one of the following three options:

1. "Beat it." You can choose to leave the area. It is amazing how many children stop fighting when they lose their audience. Don't be surprised if they follow you. This is why Rudolf Dreikurs suggested that the bathroom is the most important room in the house—the only room with a lock on the door. If your children pound on the door, you may want to jump into the shower or stuff your ears with Kleenex while you read a good novel. If you choose these methods, it is a good idea to tell your children, in advance, that this is what you will do when they fight. Also, you may want to discuss fighting and problem solving at a family meeting.

2. "Bear it." This is the most difficult because it means staying in the same room without jumping in to stop the fight or fix the problem. When children are fighting in a car, "bear it" may mean pulling to the side of the road and reading for a while, telling your children "I'll drive as soon as you are ready to stop fighting." The hard part is keeping your mouth shut until they say they are ready.

3. "Boot 'em out." You can send both children to cool off somewhere, or they can go outside if they want to continue their fight. Or they can "end the bout," an option they have at any time.

Mr. Conners found another creative way to deal with fighting when he saw two five-year-olds wrestling with each other at their preschool. He grabbed a toy microphone, rushed up to the boys and said, "Excuse me. I'm a reporter for the six o'clock news. Would you each be willing to take 30 seconds to tell our listening audience your version of what this fight is all about?" He handed the microphone to one boy and told him to look into the make-believe camera. The boy caught the spirit of the game and started telling his story. When 30 seconds were up, Mr. Conners took the mike and handed it to the next boy. When his 30 seconds were up, Mr. Conners looked into the imaginary camera and said, "Well folks, only you can decide. Tune in tomorrow to find out how these boys solved their problem." Then Mr. Conners turned to the boys and said, "Would you boys be willing to come back tomorrow and tell our listening audience how you solved this problem?" With big grins on their faces, both boys agreed and went off together to work on a solution—which was reported the next day to the imaginary camera. Mr. Conners turned fight time into playtime that distracted the boys into learning some social skills.

Playtime

Children's play is actually a laboratory where intensive research about human relationships is taking place. Playing is an activity that will form the foundation of their future interactions with others—it definitely is not meaningless or wasted time.

Still, there will be rough spots, and most parents and care-givers can tell stories like this one. Four-year-old Sharon came home with a scraped and bleeding knee one afternoon; her "best friend," Jaimie, had pushed her off the swing. Her mother's first instinct was to call the preschool teacher and complain. After all, weren't they supposed to be watching the children?

But fortunately for Sharon, her mom was more interested in helping her learn life skills than in blaming others for social conflicts. She sat down next to Sharon and asked, "Honey, can you tell me what happened?"

"Jaimie got off the swing and I got on. She wasn't using it anymore," Sharon said.

Mom suppressed a smile, suddenly realizing where this story might be going. "Do you know why Jaimie got off the swing?"

"To get her jacket," was the calm response.

As Mom suspected, when Jaimie came back with her jacket she found Sharon on "her" swing and pushed her off. Mom took a moment to validate her daughter's feelings.

"I'll bet it was scary when Jaimie pushed you. Maybe you felt that she wasn't your friend anymore."

Sharon's lip quivered. "Uh huh," she said and burst into tears. When her crying had subsided and she felt better, Sharon and her mom explored what happened. Mom asked if Sharon might have done something other than get on the swing when Jaimie got off. Sharon thought for a moment and decided that she could have held the swing for Jaimie until she got back.

"What might have happened if you held the swing for Jaimie?" Mom asked.

"Jaimie would have gotten back on," Sharon said.

"Would Jaimie have pushed you off?"

Sharon shook her head. She could see that the results would have been different if she had behaved differently. Mom agreed that it was wrong of Jaimie to push Sharon and helped her daughter understand that she could have told Jaimie clearly, "No pushing." Mom has helped Sharon understand that she has choices that can affect the outcome of a situation. In other words, Sharon has power and influence. By talking this through with Sharon rather than rushing in to rescue her, Sharon's mother has helped her to feel capable.

"But Nobody Likes Me"

As we've mentioned, children's friendships are social skills laboratories—and not all of their experiments turn out well. Scraped knees and hurt feelings come with the territory. When we can help children learn from their mistakes and avoid playing "superparent" or "superteacher," we will be teaching them to feel capable and competent.

Marla, too, is four years old. She says she doesn't want to go to preschool because she has no friends and no one likes her. Marla's parents and teachers must figure out what is really happening. If, in fact, Marla does not have playmates, the adults in her life can help her understand why. A child who is hurting others or who refuses to cooperate in games is not a welcome playmate, but such children *can* be taught more effective ways of relating to their peers.

Children who are successful at social relationships often learn to watch a game in progress and then join in by creating a role for themselves. Angela, for instance, spends a few moments watching her playmates play "house," then offers to bake cookies for the others. She smoothly blends into the game in progress.

Erica is less skilled at doing this. She bounces over to a group of children and says, "Can I play?" She is often told "no" because the others don't want to be interrupted by having to create a role for Erica. Helping a child develop social skills can help her find success at belonging to her peer group, a need which, if not met, can result in the "mistaken goal" behaviors of attention, power, revenge, and inadequacy (more about these later).

A child like Marla may actually be a welcome playmate who simply does not see herself that way. Class meetings may be helpful in dealing with this situation at preschool; a parent confronted with this dilemma might try a different approach.

Try asking simple questions. Marla's dad might ask her "What makes you believe that the other children don't like you?" or "What do you think it means to be someone's friend?" Together they can explore Marla's perceptions of friendship and then examine her experiences. "I noticed that today Adrian asked you to play on the swings with him. Why do you think he did that?" Marla now has an opportunity to compare her perceptions with what has actually happened. Teachers may also be able to offer information about positive experiences that happened during the day.

Inviting a child over to play is often a way of establishing a connection between home and school. Children feel a greater sense of kinship when they share times together in different settings. Marla's parents can invite one of her schoolmates to go to the zoo with them, or perhaps to spend a Saturday afternoon playing with Marla's new Play-Doh set. The increased closeness that results will often translate itself into increased playing at the preschool as well.

The Less-Than-Lovable Friend

Sometimes your child will actively dislike another child—or you may not care for the way your own child behaves when with a particular playmate. If your child's friendship results in exceptionally rowdy behavior or aggressiveness, it is helpful to set clear expectations.

Ben just loved to play with Marty, who lived down the street. Marty was a wild little guy who was very physical. The two four-year-olds inevitably wound up running recklessly around the house or wrestling on the lawn, and more than once Ben returned scraped, bumped, and bruised.

Ben's mother wasn't very happy about this friendship, especially since Marty was the only child with whom this sort of play occurred. Ben's mom decided not to rescue Ben, but to establish clear guidelines about what she would allow when the boys played at her house.

One quiet morning, Mom sat down with Ben and explained her problem, and her concerns for the boys' safety. She then clearly explained her expectations to Ben, gently having him repeat them back to her to be sure he understood.

She established three rules:

1. No misuse of indoor things. This means no climbing on the furniture, jumping on the beds, swinging on the doors, or throwing things inside.

2. When Ben's mom asked him to stop, he would listen. This meant that if Mom asked Ben to stop running from room to room or to begin picking up toys, he would do what she asked.

3. No name calling or making rude faces or noises. This included no bad names, laughing at people, or sticking out tongues.

Mom and Ben agreed that when Ben chose not to follow the rules, Marty would have to go home. Marty would wait in the den and Ben would wait in his room until Marty's mother could come to get him.

The plan was discussed with Marty and his mother, who agreed with the rules. Now both moms needed to plan ways to follow through when necessary. It is the nature of learning (and young children) that Ben and Marty would need to check it out and see if the plan was for real. They might play nicely once or even twice, but eventually the rules would have to be tested.

Sure enough, the day came when Ben joined Marty in climbing on the countertop. Ben refused to get down when his mother asked him and threw in a "you're a butthead" for good measure.

Ben was given the choice of walking to his room or being carried there. Mom pointed kindly but firmly to the sofa, where Marty could wait for his mother. There was no reminder or warning necessary, since both boys knew the expectations and consequences. Marty's mom arrived at the front door quickly and escorted Marty home. Now both boys have learned that their parents really meant what they said and their behavior will have to change. If it doesn't, Ben and Marty will lose the opportunity to play at one another's houses.

It is especially important in group settings to provide opportunities for learning about social skills. Class meetings can be used to explore possible problems. Ask "What would you do if . . . " or describe a situation and ask the children what they think went wrong. Storytelling, flannel boards, and books are other ways to introduce skills. Help children identify the skills you are teaching, and take time to discuss what happened and why.

Special Friendships

Three-year-olds often focus on one special playmate with whom they have a special relationship. Sergio and Kenneth are best buddies. Each watches for the arrival of the other at the child care center in the morning. They greet each other by rolling around on the floor in mock combat, or quickly run off to begin a new Lego tower. They want to sit next to each other at group time, and their teacher sometimes has to remind them that if they can't sit together quietly, they will have to sit apart. Sergio and Kenneth are together all through the day; theirs is a wonderful and important early friendship.

Five-year-old children are at the peak of being social and love to play elaborate and complicated games, trying on dress-up clothes and many different roles. They may have one special friend or a special circle of friends.

Lauren, Erin, and Allie are all five-year-olds. They choose the same activities to do together each morning, and at play-time they are engaged in elaborate games of "let's pretend" with lots of dress-up props. Their friendship goes beyond indi-vidual play—they form a special group of their own. Erin runs up to the teacher with something in her fist. "I found a potato bug," she announces. "Lauren wanted me to find one for her and I did. Allie wanted me to find one for her, too, but it was nap time." This is typical of the older preschooler's "one for all and all for one" style of friendship.

Catastrophe often threatens when one member of a spe-cial group links up with another, excluding the third. Lauren's parents will hear anguish in her voice when she tells them that Erin and Allie are going swimming together; being left out is very painful. But by the next day, the hurt feelings are usually resolved and the friendship continues to thrive.

Hal, Aaron, and Shelley are also pals. They chase one an-other around the playground and are an inseparable team. Shel-ley is the clear leader of this threesome; she is frequently the one who chooses the game to be played and makes the rules.

The wise teacher knows that if he wants to get these three interested in a new activity, the one to convince is Shelley.

Such friendships form important foundations for many of life's relationships and provide a way for children to experiment with different roles. Just because Aaron chooses to follow Shelley's lead now, for instance, doesn't mean he will never be a leader. It's just one of the roles he's trying on for size.

Social skills do not come without practice and there will be many yelps of complaint and tearful faces. But if adults can focus on nurturing healthy children who feel influential and capable and who can achieve a sense of belonging rather than playing the rescuer or referee, they will be giving children the social skills they need to thrive in a world of relationships.

Social Interest

Alfred Adler described "social interest" as a real concern for others and a sincere desire to make a contribution to society. In addition to learning and perfecting the skills needed in social relationships, children learn about themselves and others through the social context of their experiences. As children enter into the lives of their families and schools, they want very much to feel that they belong. And one of the most powerful ways to achieve a sense of belonging is to make a meaningful contribution to the well-being of others in the family or group. When elderly people continue to feel needed, it can add years to their lives. From cradle to grave, belonging and significance are among our most basic human needs. In the family or preschool, a wonderful way to encourage social interest is by sharing chores or the work the family does together.

For young children there really is no difference between play and work. When a baby strives over and over again to grab a toy that is just out of reach, we say she is "playing," but actually she is hard at work, growing and developing new skills. Young children are usually eager to participate in whatever they see us doing, and the time to invite children to participate in the family is when they *want* to—not when they can do a task perfectly. Once you begin to see your youngster as an asset, he won't seem to be "underfoot" so much.

While Charlene Clark fixed the hamburger patties, three-year-old Sean happily unwrapped cheese slices and placed them on the buns. When the family sat down to dinner, imagine how pleased Sean felt when the family mentioned how good their cheeseburgers tasted, thanks to Sean's efforts.

Five-year-old Becky reminded her Grandma to use her eye drops every evening during her visit. When Grandma returned home, Becky wanted to call her every night so she could continue to remind her. That is social interest at work; it is meaningful involvement that benefits others.

What Can My Little One Do?

Children can do any number of things to contribute to their family's well-being. Here are some ideas, listed beside the earliest reasonable time a child might master them; you can use your own creativity to discover others. But be careful—these are just possibilities. Don't expect your child to do them all!

Working alongside your child can give both of you a great deal of pleasure as well as countless opportunities to learn. And helping your child feel competent, resourceful, and confident will help him succeed both in his relationships and in the challenges life brings to all of us.

Age-Appropriate Tasks

	Self Care	Food	Household
18 months	eat with a spoon	help self to finger foods drink from a cup	tasks involving water at the sink
2–3 years	undress self wash hands feed self put on coat take off shoes	wash vegetables pour milk (small pitcher) oil potatoes for baking peel and slice bananas (butter knife) stir batter slice hard-boiled eggs in special slicer	set table (napkins and silverware) serve fruit and cookies pick up toys put own clothes in hamper dig in garden
4 years	select clothes dress and undress self put on shoes	squeeze fruit for juice grate cheese butter toast scrub mushrooms scramble eggs knead dough measure water for juice	straighten bed-covers arrange cut flowers harvest berries and other garden produce stack newspapers and crush cans for recycling set table wash car sort laundry
5 years	help pack lunch comb/brush hair wash hair (with help)	slice fruit or vegetables roll out dough make a cake mix spread peanut butter and jam on crackers or bread "smash" cooked potatoes with masher	fold washcloths help care for pet put away laundry wash windows hep plan menus help grocery shop polish shoes

1. Lott, Lynn and Riki Intner. *The Family That Works Together*... Rocklin, CA: Prima Publishing, 1995.

CHAPTER 10

The Messages of Misbehavior

We hug them, laugh with them, buy them presents, brag about them, and celebrate them. And at times, we're exasperated with their behavior. Sometimes we resort to yelling or spanking; sometimes threats are hurled in both directions. Parents and teachers may respond to a child's behavior in ways that leave both child and adult feeling discouraged and miserable.

How can adults possibly hurt people they love so much? How can such a tiny and vulnerable person trigger such strong responses from others? Part of the answer is that adults tend to respond to a child's behavior as though it were the whole problem. And all too often, adults resort to punitive measures because they are the only tools with which they are equipped—they just don't know what else to do.

This chapter is about learning to see and interpret behavior in a new way. We will look at behavior as a message or code that reveals a child's underlying beliefs about himself and about life. When children misbehave they are communicating to us in code. When we look for the *message* behavior sends us—when we learn to decipher the code—we usually find that our responses change.

There is a parable that urges us to walk a mile in someone else's shoes before we condemn or criticize his actions. This parable can also apply to our children and their behavior. Another phrase for this is "getting into the child's world." An amazing thing happens when we decipher the code in our children's behavior and change our own responses: the child's behavior changes, too.

What Is Misbehavior?

When does a child's behavior become "*mis*behavior"? When we react without taking a moment to think about what might be going on from the child's perspective, we are likely to regard any atypical behaviors as "misbehaviors." Put yourself in your child's place for a moment; make an effort to get into his world.

Three-and-a-half-year-old Randy was at home with his mom, recuperating from the chicken pox. Mom had had to take a few days off from work and needed to spend some time on the phone keeping up with business. One afternoon, after a particularly long phone call, she walked into Randy's room and found him absorbed in using the permanent marking pens. The imaginative little boy had looked at his chicken pox spots and been reminded of his dot-to-dot coloring book. Randy had removed his clothes and was busily drawing lines from one spot to the next with the marking pen. Now, Randy was *covered* with red spots.

His mom was wise enough to realize that this was not misbehavior. Randy wasn't trying to get attention or make a mess; he was being wonderfully creative. His mom realized that Randy had discovered that his body looked like a large dot-to-dot drawing so he had simply "connected the dots!" What did his mom do? She let her sense of humor take over. She went and got the washable markers and finished connecting the dots with him.

It would have been easy for Mom to scold and humiliate Randy. The entire event could have disintegrated into tears and misery. Instead, Mom made room for one of childhood's trea-sured moments. When Randy is a dad himself, sitting with his children around Grandma's table telling "remember when . . . " stories, Randy and his mom will both laugh as they remember Randy's dot-to-dot chicken pox! And as they laugh, they can recreate that moment of fun and love shared long ago, passing it on to a new generation.

When two-year-old Elsie's dad picked her up from pre-school one evening, he immediately noticed that Elsie's hair was significantly shorter in the front than it had been that morning. "Did someone cut Elsie's hair today?" the perplexed father asked Elsie's teacher.

"No, she did that herself," the teacher replied. "Elsie has been practicing a lot with the safety scissors lately."

Was Elsie misbehaving? When Dad let himself get into Elsie's world, he realized that Elsie was actively exploring the wonders of using scissors. Today she had discovered that hair can be cut. Dad may not like his daughter's new hairstyle, and he will surely explain to Elsie that he would prefer that she not cut her own (or anyone else's) hair. He might also tell his intre-pid daughter, "Let's find some things you *can* cut."

This dad knows that Elsie's experiment was a learning ex-perience. Hair grows back. Elsie made a mistake, and her dad helped her to learn from it.

Both of these children were behaving in ways that are de-velopmentally normal—and quite creative. Yet many parents would have interpreted both situations as "misbehavior."

So, how do we know when a behavior is "misbehavior?" Randy's behavior might have been misbehavior if he had wanted his mother to play with him rather than talk on the phone. His behavior then might have been intended to get at-tention or power as a mistaken way to feel belonging. One of the primary human needs is the need to *belong*, to feel a sense of worth and significance. When we don't feel that sense of be-longing, we can become discouraged and we often look for ways to feel that we belong. When a child believes he doesn't belong, he feels discouraged. Out of that discouragement he chooses what Rudolf Dreikurs, author of *Children: The Challenge,* called a "mistaken goal of misbehavior." (The Four Mistaken Goals of Misbehavior—Undue Attention, Power, Revenge, and Assumed Inadequacy—will be discussed in more detail later in this chapter.) They are considered mistaken goals because the child mistakenly believes the behavior will help him regain a sense of belonging. It puts a new light on misbehavior when we can remember that a misbehaving child is simply a discouraged child who wants to belong and has a mistaken idea about how to achieve this goal.

Misbehavior or Message?

Three-year-old Mary is visiting her grandparents' house on Thanksgiving, with all the other aunts, cousins, and members of her family. When Mary is found tearing toilet paper to shreds, is she misbehaving? It would be understandable for her grandmother's first response to be anger.

Getting into a child's world is a bit like looking through a kaleidoscope. Pretend that you are Mary's grandmother. What do you see when you look through the kaleidoscope? You may see piles of shredded paper *everywhere,* tinged by the red glow of your own anger. Now turn the kaleidoscope slightly and look again.

Look at Mary, who has just been chased away from the kitchen because she was "underfoot." Look at Mary who just got told by her big sister Joan that she was "too little" to play Monopoly with Joan and her older cousins. Look at Mary who wanted to show Grandpa how to do the "Itsy Bitsy Spider," but was abandoned when he had to go and help move the table into the dining room. What might Mary really be saying with her toilet paper? What might stop Mary from further acts of destruction? The kaleidoscope reveals a lonely little girl surrounded by a discouraging grey haze.

How do you suppose most adults would react to Mary's behavior? What would you do? Does understanding what Mary's world feels like just now influence your response?

Understanding Mary's world does not mean that deliberately making a mess is okay. But understanding some of what Mary is experiencing is likely to affect how we respond. Mary will still have to pick up all the tiny bits of paper. But armed with love and understanding, Grandma may be more likely to help her do so, and maybe to invite her to help stuff the turkey afterward.

Misbehaving children are discouraged children, and encouragement is like rain to their parched souls. It is important to create opportunities to help children feel encouraged and valuable, to let them know they belong.

Let's turn the kaleidoscope together and take a look at the four coded messages of discouraged children.

Breaking the Code

If we can learn to read the code behind children's behavior in different situations, we can deal effectively with the *message* instead of just the behavior itself. There are three specific clues that will help us break the code to identify the message behind the behavior: our own *feelings,* our usual *reactions,* and the child's *response.*

1. Your feelings.   How you *feel* in response to a child's misbehavior is the first important clue to understanding the mistaken goal. For instance, when the child's mistaken goal is undue attention, adults feel annoyed, irritated, or guilty. When it's power a child is after, adults usually feel angry, challenged, or threatened. When the child's mistaken goal is revenge, adults feel hurt, disappointed, disbelieving, or disgusted. When a child has given up (the mistaken goal of assumed inadequacy), adults also feel inadequate, despairing, hopeless, or helpless. When you look at the Mistaken Goal Chart on page 138, you can usually find one set of feelings in the second column that best describes your feelings when faced with a misbehaving child.

2. Your reactions.   Adults often respond to the behavior of each mistaken goal in predictable ways. For instance, Dad and Ryan are constantly battling over something: whether it's time to brush teeth, what to wear, how much to eat, and how many stories there will be at bedtime. This constant struggle reveals an ongoing battle for power. Dad gives a command, Ryan resists, and Dad reacts by fighting with Ryan, thinking, "You can't get away with this; I'll make you do it." Some adults just give in. In either case there is an ongoing power struggle with a winner, a loser, or a slight pause while each gathers strength and ammunition to continue the battle. The third column of the Mistaken Goal Chart lists the common reactions of adults to each of the Four Mistaken Goals behaviors.

3. The child's response.   The third clue is how a child responds when the adult tries to stop the misbehavior with punitive or permissive methods (instead of the positive discipline methods).

When the teacher at his child care center tells four-year-old Matthew to stop misbehaving, he usually responds by damaging his toys or knocking over other children's blocks. Sometimes he even yells, "I hate you!" Matthew's mistaken goal is revenge. When the goal is revenge and a parent or teacher tries to stop the misbehavior, children react by hurting others, damaging property, or retaliating in some other way such as using insulting words. The fourth column of the Mistaken Goal Chart lists typical child responses to ineffective intervention by adults for each mistaken goal behavior.

Stick to the Spirit of the Principle

Sometimes it is hard to determine a child's mistaken goal. Don't be overly concerned about getting the "right" answer; and don't get hung up in the "paralysis of analysis." Observe carefully, and do the best you can. But remember, no one is perfect. Learn to see your mistakes as opportunities to learn and grow. After all, you are a scientist of sorts! Always remember that behavior never happens in a vacuum; there is a message behind the behavior, and the message involves some form of discouragement. No matter what the goal, it is always safe to use encouragement through unconditional love, hugs, patience, and letting children know you have faith in them.

Seeing the Possibilities

No matter how hard we try, we can't force someone to change his behavior, at least not more than superficially. And when behavior is tied to deeply held beliefs, those beliefs will have to change before the behavior will. You may be able to make a child stop banging his spoon against his cup by removing the cup, but if that child believes he is important only when he is getting attention, he will surely be banging his leg annoyingly against the chair within the next ten minutes.

Stopping a symptom provides only temporary relief from the condition. When the child's deep need to feel belonging is satisfied, his mistaken method of reaching that goal is no longer necessary. There are a number of ways to invite a child to form a new belief, depending upon the goal. Alternatives for responding to the mistaken goals are shown on the Mistaken Goal Chart in the sixth column. You may find this a useful addition to the front of your refrigerator!

Satisfaction

Misbehavior takes a lot of energy from both children and adults. That energy can generate some pretty intense feelings.

Mistaken Goals Chart

The CHILD'S GOAL is:	If the PARENT/ TEACHER feels:	And tends to REACT by:	And if the CHILD'S RESPONSE is:	The BELIEF behind the CHILD'S BEHAVIOR is:	PARENT/TEACHER PROACTIVE AND EMPOWERING RESPONSES include:
Undue Attention (to keep others busy or to get special service)	Annoyed Irritated Worried Guilty	Reminding. Coaxing. Doing things for the child he/she could do for him/herself.	Stops temporarily, but later resumes same or another disturbing behavior.	I count (belong) only when I'm being noticed or getting special service. I'm only important when I'm keeping you busy with me.	"I love you and ___." (Example: I care about you & will spend time with you later.) Give positive attention at other times. Avoid special service. Say it only once, then act. Plan special time. Set up routines. Take time for training. Use natural/logical consequences. Encourage. Redirect. Use family/class meetings. Touch without words. Ignore. Set up nonverbal signals.
Power (to be boss)	Angry Provoked Challenged Threatened Defeated	Fighting. Giving in. Thinking: "You can't get away with it." "I'll make you." Wanting to be right.	Intensifies behavior. Defiant compliance. Feels he's/she's won when parent/teachers are upset. Passive power.	I belong only when I'm boss or in control, or proving no one can boss me. "You can't make me."	Ask for help. Don't fight and don't give in. Withdraw from conflict. Do the unexpected. Be firm and kind. Act, don't talk. Decide what you will do. Let routines be the boss. Leave and calm down. Develop mutual respect. Give limited choices. Set reasonable and few limits. Prac-

Child's Goal	Feeling	Tendency to React By	Child's Response	The Belief Behind the Behavior	Suggestions
					tice follow through. Encourage. Redirect to positive power. Use family/class meetings.
Revenge (to get even)	Hurt Disappointed Disbelieving Disgusted	Retaliating. Getting even. Thinking: "How could you do this to me?"	Retaliates. Intensifies. Escalates the same behavior or chooses another weapon.	I don't think I belong so I'll hurt others as I feel hurt. I can't be liked or loved.	Deal with the hurt feelings. Avoid feeling hurt. Avoid punishment and retaliation. Build trust. Use reflective listening. Share your feelings. Make amends. Show you care. Act, don't talk. Encourage strengths. Put kids in same boat. Use family/class meetings.
Assumed Inadequacy (to give up and be left alone)	Despair Hopeless Helpless	Giving up. Doing for. Overhelping.	Retreats further. Passive. No improvement. No response.	I can't belong because I'm not perfect, so I'll convince others not to expect anything of me. I am helpless and unable; it's no use trying because I won't do it right.	Show faith. Take small steps. Stop all criticism. Encourage any positive attempt, no matter how small. Focus on assets. Don't pity. Don't give up. Set up opportunities for success. Teach skills/show how. Step back. Enjoy the child. Build on his/her interests. Encourage, encourage, encourage. Use family/class meetings.

And being chased around the playground or carried kicking and screaming to bed might just seem better to a discouraged child than feeling unimportant, unnoticed, and powerless.

Getting into the child's world can help us understand the meaning of behavior. Remember, not all behavior, even when it's somewhat inappropriate, is misbehavior. Children are still learning social skills. And they are natural explorers and scientists, looking for ways to investigate the world around them. It can be tremendously helpful when we approach situations during the preschool years to maintain this perspective—and to keep a good sense of humor handy!

In the following chapters we will explore examples of each of the four Mistaken Goals. We will see what they look like at home in our families, and what they look like in the preschool setting. When you understand the meaning behind a child's misbehavior, you are well on your way to dealing with it in a loving and truly effective way.

CHAPTER 11

Mistaken Goals
at Home

We've explored some of the reasons children occasionally misbehave. To understand the code behind our children's actions and to work with them effectively, we need to learn to recognize mistaken goals in "real life." What do the goals of misbehavior look like in our homes and families? Get out your kaleidoscope and we'll take a look.

Attention

Mom, Catherine (age seven), and Ann (age five) are in the doctor's office because Catherine has a fever and cough. Mom gets Catherine settled in the waiting room and gently tucks her coat around her. She feels her forehead for fever and generally tries to help her feel as comfortable as possible. Mom then sits down and begins to look through a magazine. Ann comes over with a children's book she has found and asks her mom to read it to her. Mom says, "Not right now." She reminds Ann that she was up most of the night with Catherine, and now she just wants to sit quietly and look at a magazine.

　　Ann wanders away, but a few minutes later she begins to bounce up and down on the couch. "Stop," Mom calls out.

141

"You need to sit quietly." Ann stops bouncing but within minutes is asking if she can sit on Mom's lap. Mom says, "No, of course not. You are much too big a girl for that!" Mom gets up and goes over to Catherine to check on her fever again.

Then they are called into the examining room. As the three of them are waiting for the doctor, Ann begins to complain of a stomachache. Mom looks at her anxiously and feels her forehead. When the doctor arrives to examine Catherine, Ann starts tugging on Mom's sleeve and saying she has to go to the bathroom. Mom sighs loudly, gets up, and takes Ann down the hall to the bathroom.

If we look through our kaleidoscope, we see that Ann has noticed Catherine getting a lot of attention. And Ann has decided that Mom loves Catherine more.

How do you think Mom is feeling right now? Annoyed? Irritated? Worried? She probably wishes she'd left Ann at home. How would Mom feel if she got into Ann's world? What might she do differently?

Ann's behavior is saying, "I want attention, too. I want to be noticed and to be a part of what is going on." Ann believes that she belongs or matters only when she is being noticed, or when Mom is busy with her. The first of the four messages (or mistaken goals) is *attention*.

Identifying the Goal of Attention

Ann's mother felt irritated and guilty. These feelings are significant because they are the first clue to what is going on in this situation.

When Mom and her daughters were at the doctor's office, what sorts of things were taking place? Mom *asked* Ann to sit quietly and stop bouncing on the sofa. Mom *coaxed* Ann out of sitting on her lap by *reminding* her that she is a "big" girl now. Finally she walked her down the hall to the bathroom, which Ann *may have been able to do on her own*. All of these were reactions to Ann's behavior. Children whose mistaken goal is attention successfully keep the adults in their lives busy with them most of the time. All children need their parents' attention, but they may not be receiving that attention in positive, encouraging ways.

What was Ann's response to her mother? Each time Ann stopped one behavior, she would go on to another behavior within a short time. Looking at the feelings and reactions of Ann's mother and Ann's responses to her mother, we can see that all three clues lead to the mistaken goal of attention.

"Notice Me"

The child who sends a coded message by seeking undue attention believes that the only way he is able to count or belong is to keep others busy with him. He is willing to accept any attention, even negative attention, to achieve this goal. He wants to be noticed and to receive special service from those around him. Focus your kaleidoscope; picture this child wearing a large sunbonnet covered with feathers, fruit, flowers, or flying dinosaurs. There is a colorful banner on this hat. It says, "Notice Me. Involve Me."

Ann came to the conclusion that Mom loved her less than Catherine because Catherine was receiving most of Mom's attention. Not surprisingly, Ann's behavior reflects this belief. Attention becomes the measuring cup for love in Ann's world.

Alternatives for Undue Attention

How can we give children the attention and feeling of belonging they need without giving in to an endless stream of small annoyances? Understanding the message or belief that prompts the mistaken goal of attention will help us decide how to respond in ways that will help children instead of reinforcing the mistaken belief.

Let's go back to the doctor's office. How else might Mom have responded to Ann? If Mom realizes that Ann is feeling neglected because Catherine is receiving so much of her attention, she can deal with Ann's belief rather than her behavior. She might tell Ann that she will read her one book if Ann will agree to look at another book quietly afterward and let her mother look at a magazine. By asking Ann to honor her need for some quiet time, mother has not just "given in" to Ann's demands for attention, but has understood Ann's needs and respectfully stated her own needs. Or Mom could ask for Ann's assistance in caring for her sick sister. (Do you remember the sign on the hat that said "Involve Me?") She might ask Ann how they might help Catherine feel more comfortable. By involving Ann in the process of caring for Catherine, Mother will be giving Ann a meaningful role and directly meeting Ann's need to feel necessary and valued.

A third choice might be to hug Ann and tell her that Mother loves her very much. Mother then might ask for Ann's support by explaining how tired she is. Ann might offer to give her mother a neck rub. When adults ask children for their help and cooperation, children can be remarkably thoughtful. Perhaps Ann could even suggest that she read her mother a story! This could become a much more peaceful and satisfying time for all.

Power

Two-year-old Beverly is standing in front of her mother's book shelf. Beverly's mom is a single parent and Beverly is her only child. The brightly colored books look interesting, and Beverly reaches out and pulls several down onto the floor. The crash brings Mom running. "No, No!" she says, while slapping Beverly's hand. No sooner has Mom turned away than Beverly grabs more books and flings them to the floor, this time staring defiantly at Mom. Mom is hooked. "Oh, no you don't! I won't let you get away with that!" she yells, and proceeds with the

"No, No!" and hand slapping routine again. This scene is re-played for the next ten minutes until Mom, exasperated beyond belief, picks Beverly up and puts her into her crib for a "time out." Beverly is outraged and launches into a major tantrum; Mom has stormed into the next room. Right now, Mom is not only feeling angry and provoked, she is also feeling defeated. And by a two-year-old!

What is the message behind Beverly's behavior? Beverly is saying, "I don't believe I am important unless I have power, or at least don't let you boss me."

Identifying the Goal of Power

When Beverly and her Mom were struggling over the books, her mom first *felt* provoked and finally, defeated. Beverly's Mom *reacted* with some powerful statements: "I won't let you get away with that!" and "Oh, no you don't!" Beverly's *response* to her mother's ineffective interventions was to intensify her own behavior. And so the battle rages on.

Power Struggle

A special aspect of the goal or message of power is that both participants, and *note that it takes two*, are very determined to "win." Neither is willing to give an inch. And when parent and child are locked in combat this way, the result is a power strug-gle. And the problem with power struggles is that "winning" always takes place at someone else's expense. When that some-one is a child you love, the victory may not be worth the price.

"Give Me Choices!"

If you have heard an impassioned "You're not the boss of me!" shouted by a child, you might well suspect that the goal involved is power. The child whose goal is power can be imagined wearing a bright red or orange hard hat. Printed in bold letters on this hat is the command: "Give me choices and ask for my help!"

Alternatives for Power Struggles

When two-year-old Beverly and her mom fought over the books, they began a pattern of determined power struggles that could have set the tone of their relationship for many years. Fortunately, Beverly's mom learned about her own responsibility in maintaining their power struggle. She then changed her behavior and thus opened the way for Beverly to change her belief system and *her* behavior.

Beverly's mom learned how to empower Beverly by giving her power in appropriate ways. She gave Beverly limited choices instead of demands. "Would you like to pick the books up by yourself, or would you like my help?" "Would you like to pick the books up just before dinner, or right after dinner?"

A power struggle is often diffused by asking a child for her help. Mom let Beverly know how much she needed her. "Honey, we are a family, and you are so important to me. I don't know what I would do without you. What do you think we could do about these books?" Asking for help often redirects the child and the parent away from power struggles and toward cooperation.

Another way to disengage from a power struggle is to be firm but kind. When Beverly threw the books onto the floor repeatedly, she was also throwing down the gauntlet, or challenge to fight. Instead of picking up the gauntlet, Mom can stop talking and *act*. She can kindly but firmly pick Beverly up and take her into another room. There need be no further mention of the books until after a cooling-off period, which is often necessary before a child will listen to a limited choice or an appeal for help. By not lecturing or shaming her daughter, mom does not invite further resistance. Even if Beverly chooses to have a tantrum, mom has defused the power struggle by refusing to become engaged.

Tantrums are less likely when children feel the energy of kindness along with firmness. It does not mean that tantrums can be entirely avoided, but avoiding a tantrum is not the goal. The goal is to kindly and firmly act upon what you have said.

Revenge

It is bedtime. Dad is getting three-year-old Alice ready for bed. Dad says it is time for "pj's," but Alice is having great fun playing with bubbles in the sink and doesn't want to stop. Just as Dad is becoming impatient, Alice spills a cup of water on the floor. Dad immediately becomes angry, thinking Alice spilled the water on purpose. He picks Alice up and spanks her on the bottom. Alice begins to cry and Dad has to wrestle her into the pajamas as she kicks and struggles.

When Alice is finally in her pajamas, Dad grumpily goes over to pick out a book for a bedtime story. Alice's lower lip puffs out. "I hate that book," she yells, "and I don't want you to read to me! I want Mommy!" What a blow! Dad feels terrible—his own daughter doesn't love him. He is hurt and disbelieving.

Alice may be saying "Daddy hurt me, so I'll hurt him back" in the only way she knows. The third of the Four Messages or Goals is *revenge*.

Identifying Revenge

Dad was shocked that Alice would deliberately spill water all over the kitchen floor. He was trying his best to get Alice to bed while his wife was working late and now, on top of everything else, his *feelings are hurt*. He feels badly that he spanked Alice. He didn't like doing it—but he didn't know how else to respond to her behavior.

First of all, did Alice deliberately spill the water? Young children spill a lot of things. Their muscle control is still developing. If Dad had understood the developmental nature of Alice's action, he might not have seen it as misbehavior. By getting into Alice's world, he would have understood that Alice simply had an accident or made a mistake. We all learn by making mistakes.

Even if Alice had deliberately spilled water, spanking is unlikely to help matters much. Spanking teaches children that "might makes right." It can invite many responses, and few of them are what parents intend. In this case a spanking invited revenge. Both Alice and her Dad wound up feeling hurt.

As we examine Dad's *feelings* and *reactions*, and Alice's *response*, we see the clues that indicate the mistaken goal of revenge. Whenever an adult feels hurt by the behavior of a child, it is likely that the child is feeling hurt, too. We will examine the way we form our beliefs about ourselves and life later on, but this probably was not the first time Alice had received a spanking. She knows it isn't fair because she didn't mean to spill the water, but she doesn't have the skill to speak up for herself. She is telling her Dad in the only way she knows (through the coded message of her behavior) that she feels hurt, both physically and emotionally. Others aren't fair to her so she will get revenge.

"Help Me, I'm Hurting"

When you picture the child whose goal is revenge, imagine a black baseball cap turned backward. On the back is written the plea "Help me, I'm hurting."

Alternatives for Revenge Cycles

When parents can begin to see a child who is hurtful as a "hurting" child, they often feel motivated to respond to that child differently. Instead of giving in to the instinctive desire for retaliation and punishment, they can choose to offer care and support. If a child is feeling hurt, does it make sense to make that child feel worse?

First of all, Dad can deal with Alice's hurt feelings. He can tell her that it was wrong of him to spank her; he may apologize. (It would be even better not to have spanked her, but he may still make mistakes as he learns new ways to respond.) Dad can reassure her that it is wrong for others to hurt her, and no matter what she does, she does not deserve to be hit. He can ask her how she is feeling. If she is too young to articulate her feelings, he can ask her if she thinks that Daddy doesn't love her. Alice will probably respond with a verbal (or nonverbal signal) that lets her dad know he has understood correctly.

When a child is feeling hurt, it is difficult for her to move beyond her emotions to solutions. Therefore it is very important to address the feelings first. Dad now has a chance to tell Alice how much he *does* love her, and how important she is to him. He can share how he felt. He can ask Alice why she threw water on the floor. She can explain that "it spilled" or "on accident." When Dad and Alice have this kind of conversation, they are developing a new sense of trust. When Dad can listen to and respect Alice's feelings and then explain his own, each will learn a great deal about the other.

If Dad tries these new ideas, he just might find himself snuggling close to his precious daughter as they read a bedtime story together. Even a painful and damaging experience can be healed when the message of love and caring gets through. And through her dad's example, Alice will be learning new tools herself, storing them up for the day she gets her own child ready for bed.

Assumed Inadequacy/Giving Up

It is Jean's birthday; she is turning five years old today. Jean lives with her grandparents. When she enters the kitchen, her grandparents eagerly watch for her reaction to the brand new bike, proudly displayed in the center of the room with a big red bow. Jean looks anxiously around and doesn't comment on the bike. Grandmother impatiently asks, "Well, what do you think? Do you like it?" Jean doesn't respond. Grandma then says in a coaxing voice, "Jean, look at your wonderful new bike."

Jean shakes her head and mumbles, "I can't ride a bike." Grandpa rushes over to reassure Jean. "That's no problem, sweetie, you'll learn in no time." Jean says nothing and does not go near the bike. Her grandparents look at one another in exasperation and shrug their shoulders. "What's the use?" they think to themselves and Grandpa dejectedly begins to pour Jean's cereal and milk for her.

Jean's grandparents have been successfully convinced to "give up" on her. They *feel* hopeless both about themselves and about Jean. Somehow Jean has come to believe that she is not "good enough," that she is truly helpless. She acts upon this belief by convincing others of her inadequacy. Jean's grandparents love her, but they mistakenly believe that the best way to show that love is to do things for her, such as pouring her cereal and milk, which she could easily do for herself.

Of all the four goals or messages, children displaying assumed inadequacy are often the most overlooked. Because they are so busy shrinking back, they don't create the havoc that children acting upon the other three goals do. Children communicating this message often become nearly invisible.

This goal is rarely found in children younger than age five unless they are given little or no opportunity to develop a sense of autonomy. It can be especially baffling when highly productive and goal-oriented parents see this behavior in their child. What parents value as personal drive and determination may overwhelm these children and convince them that they are truly incapable. The fourth and final of the Four Messages or Goals is called *assumed inadequacy* or *giving up*.

Identifying Assumed Inadequacy

Jean's grandparents try not to *feel* hopeless, but Jean looks so tiny and helpless. They do their best to protect her and to make up for the fact that her parents aren't around. Grandma and Grandpa *react* to Jean's helpless behavior by doing things for her. Grandpa pours her milk, a task she might take pride in learning to do for herself. They are there to supply her every need. They buy her endless "things" and make plans and choices in which she has no participation. Jean's *response* is to retreat further, to act passive, and to refuse to try anything new. The feelings, reactions, and responses all give clues that the behavior is assumed inadequacy.

"Believe in Me"

Children who develop a belief in their own inadequacy may have adopted the "perfection myth." They believe that because they cannot do things perfectly, they might as well give up. When children learn that mistakes are part of how everyone learns, they can break the power of the "perfection myth."

When a child is criticized for the mistakes she makes, it is easy to understand how she might develop the belief that she can't do anything right. As a toddler, Jean was always dressed in beautifully ironed, frilly dresses. She was admonished to "keep clean," and her grandmother would become very upset when Jean got paint or food on her clothing. Jean's perception was that messy was "bad"; because she was often messy, Jean eventually began to believe in her own inadequacy. It seemed that every time she tried to paint a picture or pour her own juice, she made a mess. Jean decided that she couldn't do anything well. Her action, based on this belief, has become inaction. The child who pursues this mistaken goal may be pictured wearing a drab-colored ski hat pulled far down over her face. What you will find stitched on the front (if you look closely enough) is "Believe in Me."

Alternatives for Assumed Inadequacy

"Inadequacy" or "giving up" is a very lonely place to be. Since their goal is to be left alone, these children are rarely much trouble to others. There are many things parents can do to meet this child's needs. The biggest one by far is to encourage and truly believe in this young person. Stop doing things for the child that the child can do for herself. Have patience and take time for training, then say, "I have faith that you can handle this task." Helping a child who believes that she is inadequate requires a great deal of patience, gentle perseverance, and faith in the child's abilities.

Of course, Jean does not know how to ride a bicycle; no one does without teaching and practice. Grandma might share a story about her own experiences learning to ride a bike. Perhaps she could tell about how foolish she felt the first time she fell and her brothers and sister laughed. When Grandma shares a story such as this, she is also telling Jean that feeling embarrassed is okay. Because Grandma felt that way, it is easier for Jean to express her own fears. Children don't know that it was ever hard for adults to learn new things unless they are told such stories. Staying on a pedestal may be good for your image, but it can cripple the growth of closeness and trust.

Children watch adults as we struggle to learn new things. They may watch us try something and meet with repeated failure. How we react will be giving them clues about their own experiences. What is our attitude toward our own mistakes? Remember, we learn much more from what we see than what we hear.

Criticism is difficult for most of us to accept. For a child who believes she is inadequate, criticism only reinforces her belief in her inadequacy. One of the healthiest things we can learn to do for such a child is to stop all criticism.

If Jean messes her dress up with paint or mud, Grandma may consider dressing her in more durable clothes. What a great message it would send if Grandma could learn to say, "Wow, you are covered with paint! You must have had a great time painting today."

Awareness of the Hidden Message

"Whew," you may be saying, "I had no idea there was so much going on in my child's head when he acted that way." It is important to understand that children do not consciously decide to pursue one of the mistaken goals; they are only rarely aware of their own beliefs and are not out to baffle their parents with a game of "guess my goal." But when parents can be aware of the message hidden in their child's behavior, when they can observe their own feelings and reactions, then they can take steps not only to stop undesired behavior but to celebrate a child's willingness to take risks and make mistakes. In so doing, parents nurture children who believe they are capable, lovable, and worthwhile.

CHAPTER 12

Mistaken Goals in the Preschool Setting

It should come as no surprise that where groups of children are gathered, the desire for undue attention appears. At the Tiny Treasures Child Care Center this morning there are 12 children in Miss Marcia's classroom, all four- and five-year-olds. Johnny is five. At about 10:00, he finds Marcia; his shoe is untied and he asks her to tie it for him. Marcia does so and Johnny goes off to play. Less than five minutes later he needs help sharpening a pencil. Marcia helps him do that, too, but no more than two minutes passes before she notices that Johnny has begun to mess around with Ben's blocks. Marcia reminds him that these are Ben's blocks and Johnny needs to choose something else to do. By 10:15, Johnny's shoe is again untied. . . .

Undue Attention in the Preschool

By now, Marcia is longing for recess time or her break. In addition to feeling annoyed by Johnny's constant demands, she is also feeling guilty that she doesn't enjoy being around this child very much. These feelings are the first clue that Johnny's behavior is motivated by the mistaken goal of attention.

155

Marcia's reactions to Johnny's behavior were fairly typical. She did things for Johnny that he could reasonably be expected to do for himself—or be learning to do on his own. She also spent a good deal of her time reminding Johnny to stop certain behaviors. The second clue that the goal was undue attention was that Johnny would stop for a short while when Marcia reprimanded him, but soon was off to seek more undue attention. Every teacher will recognize a child they have known in Johnny. These children successfully keep the adults in their lives busy with them most of the time. And isn't it remarkable that Johnny's shoes have an above-average capacity for coming untied?

The Belief Behind Attention

What are Johnny and other children like him really saying by their behavior? When a child's message is "notice me," he is acting on a deeply held belief that he can belong or count only by being noticed or by keeping adults busy with him.

When we know how to decode their mistaken goal messages, we understand that children who misbehave are really saying to us: "I'm a child and I just want to belong." But because we're human, too, it's hard to hear the plea for belonging when we survey the crayon damage on the living room wall or feel exhausted after a morning of Johnny's demands!

Alternatives for Teachers

Those of us who work in school settings are certainly familiar with children like Johnny. Even when his teacher is able to understand that Johnny's behavior is a cry for attention, it is not always possible to give one-on-one attention in group settings. Still, a number of things can be done routinely with all of the children that will greatly diminish constant bids for attention, such as Johnny's.

Children can be taught signals that will let the teacher know that they need her time or attention. Marcia might have taught the children in her class to gently place a hand on her arm to let her know that she is needed. Marcia's signal that she will honor that child's request for assistance is to make eye contact with the child, wink and say, "As soon as I'm free." This gives attention but in a reasonable way, while still allowing a child to feel acknowledged and important. Marcia can also take the time to greet all of the children in her classroom individually each morning, giving positive attention to each at a time when they have not used an inappropriate or annoying way of seeking it.

Marcia could comment on something that makes each child feel special. She might greet Johnny and tell him she found a spider's egg sac and brought it in to the science table. She knows that Johnny is fascinated by spiders. Her special attention and recognition of his interests might make him feel included and cared about in just a brief conversation.

Now, about Johnny's shoes. Marcia could create a training plan to help Johnny learn to tie his own shoes. After an adequate amount of demonstration and practice, it would be reasonable for Marcia to tell Johnny that she would love to watch him tie his own shoes. Eventually Johnny would be encouraged to tie his shoes and come back to show Marcia when he has been successful. Johnny is being given attention, but not in ways that reinforce the constant flow of small annoyances or demands for inappropriate special service.

Power Struggles in the Preschool

It is a lovely, sunny day at the Silverport Preschool. Over by the apple tree, three-year-old Sarah and her teacher, Julie, are glaring at each other. Julie says it's time to go inside. Sarah refuses to go. Julie explains that playtime is over and everyone else has gone inside and Sarah *must* come in right now. Sarah latches onto the side of the climber. Julie's face is turning pink and she begins to threaten her small pupil, "If you don't come in this minute, you won't be allowed to come outside the rest of the day."

Sarah sticks out her tongue. "You can't make me!" she taunts. Julie heads over to pick her up and carry her inside, but first she has to chase Sarah down.

Julie is really angry (and a little embarrassed—after all, this is a three-year-old) and feels that her authority has been challenged. As Julie carries the writhing, kicking, screaming child inside she says through clenched teeth, "When I say it's time to come inside, you will do what I say."

What do you think? Will Sarah meekly obey Julie next time? What is the message behind Sarah's behavior? She may be saying "I want to be the boss and have some power in my life. Don't tell me what to do. Give me choices!" Sarah's way of achieving power is by proving that "you can't make me!"

Identifying Power

This teacher felt angry; she also felt that her legitimate authority had been challenged. These are the typical feelings adults have when they are involved in a power struggle.

As we've mentioned before, a power struggle can't be staged alone. Sarah needed Julie's reactions to engage in the battle. Julie reacted to the situation by using her superior strength to overpower Sarah and carry her inside. She made Sarah do what she told her to do. But did Sarah ever give up her end of the fight?

Remember the way that Sarah grabbed onto the play equipment to fortify her position? An additional clue that the goal is power is that the behavior intensifies. Sarah's response is an *intensification* and is characteristic of the goal of *power.*

The Belief Behind Power

The child who acts upon the mistaken goal of power will spend a great deal of energy in finding ways not to cooperate. Sarah had to clutch the playground equipment fiercely to maintain a hold that her teacher couldn't loosen. In the heat of battle this ferocity may be described as "stubbornness." But when the same child is learning to do a complicated math problem or running those last few miles of the marathon, this same trait may be seen positively as "tenacity." The underlying belief of the mistaken goal of power is that "I belong only when I am in control. No one can make me do things."

Alternatives for Teachers

How might Sarah's teacher give her power in appropriate ways? There are several possibilities. As we've mentioned, one of the best ways to empower a child is to give her limited choices in which all alternatives are acceptable. Asking a child if she is ready to come inside now implies the hidden option of *not* being ready to come inside. If that is not an acceptable alternative, do not include it in your choices, stated or implied.

Sarah's teacher could ask Sarah whether she would like to lead the class inside at the end of playtime or hold the teacher's hand and follow the others. These are limited choices, both of which are acceptable. Staying outside is not one of the choices. If a child answers by naming an alternative that was not a choice given, such as "stay outside," simply respond, "That is not one of the choices." Another option might be to let Sarah choose which equipment to play on before going inside, and to say that the bell would ring in two more minutes. These approaches would both give Sarah time to consider her behavior and the opportunity to feel empowered, which might make her cooperative.

Giving choices is a respectful way to treat children, not a "gimmick" designed to trick a child into compliance. Choices empower a child, meeting the need for power and belonging in acceptable ways. And meeting the underlying need will address the real cause of the misbehavior, rather than the symptoms only.

If there is a pattern of power struggles between Julie and Sarah, Julie could work to break the cycle by asking for Sarah's help—which invites Sarah to use her power in productive ways. Julie might say, "Sarah, I need your help. Would you please tell the boys in the far corner that it is time to come in?"

Or Julie could do the unexpected. When Sarah refused to come inside Julie could have said, "I'll bet you can't catch me." Julie could then run away from Sarah. What a surprise that would be for someone who is clinging fiercely to the railing! What is the point of hanging on to the railing now? Sarah just might let go to chase her teacher and when she caught her, Julie could give her a big hug and walk peacefully inside with her. The standoff evaporates; both are winners.

The secret to dealing with power struggles is to seek "win/win" solutions. It is when both people involved remain committed to being the only winner that the power struggle escalates. Why assert our own power when it inevitably means a child must be the loser?

Revenge in the Preschool

It is a Tuesday afternoon and four-year-old Eric has been throwing the toy dinosaurs across the room. His teacher, John, comes over and removes the toy dinosaurs, telling Eric he cannot have them for the rest of the morning. Eric is furious. Eric remembers that when Zachary threw the blocks into the corner yesterday, nothing happened to him. This isn't *fair!* Eric stomps off.

A little while later, John makes the charming discovery that Eric has stuffed the toilet full of toilet paper and has clogged it up. John shows Eric the mess he has made and asks, "How could you do such a thing to our school?" Eric doesn't hesitate. "I hate this place," he says, "and I'm glad the toilet is broken."

John tells the little boy that he will have to write a note to Eric's parents about this, and Eric will also have to stay in at recess. Before the day is over, Eric has also managed to cut Sally's hair. . . .

Right at this moment, John is deciding to call in sick tomorrow. He just can't take another day of this child. Eric's message is, "I've been hurt, so I'm going to hurt others back. Life is unfair!"

Identifying Revenge

John is undoubtedly feeling pretty discouraged and hurt himself. He has devoted so much time and energy to becoming a teacher, and what's the use? John also feels disgusted and disbelieving, and he is baffled by Eric's disdain for the school's property.

Adults (and children) often cover their hurt feelings with anger. John's reaction to Eric's behavior was to hurt back through reprimands and punishment. This created a revenge cycle.

Eric's response was to escalate his behavior by stomping off to stuff the toilet full of paper, proclaiming his hatred of this place, and to cut Sally's hair. Children are very good at revenge cycles. They have many weapons to hurt adults who can't see the message behind the behavior and don't know how to get out of the revenge cycle.

The Belief Behind Revenge

Unfortunately, a child who has chosen the mistaken goal of revenge believes that maybe he can't belong (which must hurt a lot), but at least he can get even. Unfortunately, it is difficult for most adults to love and enjoy a child who is hurting others and destroying property. By acting upon his belief that he doesn't belong, this child behaves in ways that prove his point.

Alternatives for Teachers

It can be difficult to deal with a child like Eric. Once his teacher realizes that Eric feels he has been treated unfairly and is hurt, he can respond to Eric's real need. Eric wants to feel belonging, to be a real part of the group. How can that be achieved?

Before Eric's behavior can change, he must learn to trust. John can spend time with Eric and help him find acceptable ways to express his feelings of hurt. The best way to start the learning process is through modeling. John could say, "Eric, when you behave that way, I feel hurt. My guess is that you might be feeling hurt too. Can you let me know when you are ready to talk about our hurt feelings?" By spending this kind of time with Eric, his teacher can gain Eric's trust by showing that he accepts Eric, even when Eric is not feeling likable. In addition, when his hurt feelings are validated, Eric will feel understood.

Learning to name the feelings inside of himself gives a child a new tool. By learning to stop, acknowledge, and name his feelings, Eric can slow down and take time to think before he acts. Eric needs to learn that there is a difference between feeling hurt and *acting* on those hurt feelings. Remember, a child must deal with the hurt feelings before he can move forward to find solutions to the problems his behavior may have caused.

Eric can also be taught different ways to act when difficult feelings arise. John can let Eric know that the next time he is feeling hurt, he can come to John and practice naming the feeling. Eric may well need a little time to cool off before he is ready to discuss his feelings.

After John has taught his children about positive time out (see Chapter 15), he can suggest that Eric go to time out until he feels better. John could even ask Eric if he would like company in time out, or if he would like to go alone. If Eric wants company and John has a few minutes he could offer, "Would you like me to go with you, or would you like a buddy to go with you?" Children who feel they don't belong usually jump at the chance to have someone go with them—they can cool off and feel belonging at the same time.

Later, when Eric has cooled off and feels better, John and Eric can talk about why Eric is feeling hurt and look for ways to help him feel better again. Eric could tell John how he felt about John's reaction to the block throwing incident. Perhaps John could remind him that the consequence for throwing blocks was decided at the morning's class meeting. That would explain why another child had been treated differently the day before. Or John could ask Eric to suggest a solution that would feel more fair to him. By dealing with the hurt feelings, John and Eric can move on to problem solving together.

In addition, John can focus on ways to give Eric a sense of belonging in the classroom. It is important that John help Eric see the ways in which he is liked by others to help him feel a sense of belonging. During a class meeting or circle time, John could begin a discussion of how good we feel when others want to do things with us. John could then say that he has chosen Eric to pass out the morning snack. He could ask who would like to share this task with Eric. Several hands would go up and a helper would be chosen. By focusing on "sharing the task with Eric," John has sent a different message than if he'd simply asked, "Who else wants to serve the snack?"

Afterward, John could spend a moment with Eric and comment on how many children raised their hands to do something with him. Did Eric feel good when so many children raised their hands to pass the snack with him? In this way John would be helping Eric to be an important and contributing member of his class, as well as helping Eric perceive himself as a likable person with whom others want to share tasks. This sort of processing is a crucial piece in helping Eric to form different beliefs about his experiences.

What about Eric's destructive actions? Remember, making a child *feel* worse is unlikely to encourage that child to *act* better. Retaliation and punishment are typical adult reactions to destructive behavior, but they often provoke a child to respond with more revenge.

When a child destroys something, it is reasonable to expect him to take responsibility for replacing the damaged item or addressing the damage he's done. When Eric stuffs the toilet with paper and causes it to overflow, he can be expected to help clean up the mess, but it may be a good idea to talk first with Eric about what he is feeling. If Eric does not want to say anything, the teacher might tell about a time that he felt really hurt. John could tell about feeling hurt when he wasn't chosen for the baseball team, and that he took the ball after recess and hid it so that the other children could not find it. Eric will probably feel more willing to talk with John about his own hurt feelings after hearing John's story. When those hurt feelings have been acknowledged and admitted, Eric can begin to feel better.

Now Eric and John can discuss how Eric could help clean up the mess in the bathroom. Notice that the focus is on "the mess in the bathroom," rather than the mess Eric made. This is not the time for blaming but for working together to find a solution to the problem. It takes time, but this kind of respectful and caring approach is much more likely to lead to improvements in Eric's behavior.

Eric hasn't "gotten away with" anything; he will agree to a plan for repairing the damage he has done, and John will follow through and see that the plan is implemented. When the focus is on solutions, the result just may be a change in the behavior. The revenge cycle can be broken.

Assumed Inadequacy in the Preschool

For Paul, it is just another day at swim class. Paul is five years old, but he is still in the group with the three-year-olds. The instructor, Tom, is trying to get everyone to blow bubbles in the water. Paul hates to get his face wet and blows little puffs well above the surface. Tom comes over and suggests that Paul pretend to "blow out the birthday candle." Paul only folds his arms around himself, puts his chin into his chest, and gives a tiny shake of his head. After a minute or two Tom gives up and goes on to the next child.

A little while later, the other children are holding onto the edge of the pool and practicing kicking in the water. Paul sits on the side, refusing to get into the pool. Tom offers to hold Paul while he kicks, but Paul refuses and turns his body away from the pool. Eventually Tom gives up and leaves Paul alone.

Paul has successfully convinced his swimming instructor to leave him alone. Paul believes that because he is not "perfect," he must be hopeless. He acts upon this belief by convincing others to give up on him, demonstrating to perfection the mistaken goal of *assumed inadequacy*, or "giving up."

Identifying Assumed Inadequacy in the Preschool

Tom must stay alert to the needs of all of the children in his swim class—he can't spend all of his time with Paul. Tom feels hopeless when he can't convince Paul even to try the various activities. Tom's only choice (reaction) seems to be to leave Paul alone, to give up on him. What else can he do?

Paul's response to Tom's efforts is to retreat further. He isn't fighting or being aggressive. In fact, he makes it pretty easy to ignore him and leave him alone.

The Belief Behind Assumed Inadequacy

If Paul only tried, he might prove to be a terrific swimmer. Where did he acquire his belief in his own inadequacy? As it happens, Paul has very athletic parents who excel in most sports. They run, they rollerblade, and they bike. When Paul attempts to join them, it's difficult for his parents to hide their impatience at how much he slows them down. They love Paul very much; they just don't know how to adjust their activities to Paul's level.

Paul's believes that because he is not perfect, he might as well not try at all. He can't seem to do anything well enough—at least not as well as his parents. It is safer to be helpless. If Paul can convince others that they can't expect much from him, they will leave him alone.

Alternatives for Teachers

How might Tom encourage Paul when he is backing away from the pool? Tom might say, "Paul, I know it took a lot of courage for you to join in the bubble blowing. I want you to know I really appreciate that kind of effort." A simple message, but what a powerful one! Tom did not assume that learning to swim was easy; in fact, he acknowledged how hard it is for Paul. Tom took time to notice the small step that Paul *had* been willing to take. Over time, this kind of gentle encouragement may help Paul take additional risks.

Adults can learn to focus on what a child *can* do, to help him to see his own abilities first through others' eyes and eventually, through his own. All too often, teachers are occupied by the attention seekers or are busy waging power struggles with defiant children. Yet the child whose mistaken goal is assumed inadequacy or giving up is the one who can least afford to be ignored.

Adults who live and work with small children can learn to appreciate each small step a child takes towards success, and to have realistic expectations. Rudolf Dreikurs said, "Work for improvement, not perfection."[1] When Paul's parents learn to enjoy just being with their son, sharing their pleasure in the activity, and encouraging his enjoyment rather than achievement, Paul will feel much more capable and encouraged.

Paul's teachers, too, can be instrumental in helping him believe in himself. The key words for a child with this mistaken goal are "Believe in me!" and "Encourage, encourage, encourage!" When parents and teachers can work together to truly understand children's behavior and deal with it effectively, the results for children can be nothing short of miraculous!

1. Dreikurs, Rudolf, M.D., and Vicki Soltz, R.N. *Children: The Challenge.* New York: Penguin, 1990.

CHAPTER 13

Personality:
Yours and Theirs

It is bedtime at the Jasper house. Bedtime routines are too much bother for Mrs. Jasper; she would rather wait until the children fall asleep on the floor and carry them to bed than create stress for herself by arguing. She prefers avoiding emotional pain and hassles in life, and she thinks that letting her children "do their own thing" is one way to keep things comfortable.

Mr. Jasper, however, does not agree. He believes it is very important for the children to have a schedule, and he is willing to take responsibility for it. He walks the children through every step of their routine, making sure they are in their pajamas, have their teeth thoroughly brushed, and are in bed by 7:30 P.M. He believes that being in control of himself, situations, or others is a way to avoid humiliation and criticism.

Mrs. Jasper avoids situations that she believes will take her out of her comfort zone. We call this a *comfort lifestyle priority*. Mr. Jasper controls situations to avoid criticism and humiliation. His lifestyle priority is called *control*. The Jaspers act differently in situations that appear potentially stressful to them. What do we mean by lifestyle priority? Why were such different people attracted to each other? How will their lifestyle priorities affect their parenting and their relationship?

169

Before answering these questions, let's peek into the Sanchez home and look at two more lifestyle priorities. It's bedtime here, too. Mrs. Sanchez believes it is good for children to be in bed on time and tries to convince her children by lecturing them about their responsibility to do what is "right." She is constantly frustrated that the children find her lectures meaningless. They hardly listen while she talks. What an insult! Meaninglessness is the one thing in life she wants to avoid, and she believes doing things "right" is one way to make life meaningful.

Mr. Sanchez has a very different approach. He just wants his children to be happy and bedtime to be easy. To make things pleasant, he tries "loving" his children into bed. He plays games with them to get them into their pajamas and to brush their teeth. He reads them stories and hugs them a lot. He feels he can win their love and avoid rejection by making bedtime fun and by doing what he thinks will please the children.

Mrs. Sanchez has a *superiority lifestyle priority*. Mr. Sanchez has a *pleasing lifestyle priority*. They, too, are very different. What attracted them to each other? What problems are they having now that the honeymoon is over? How will their lifestyle priorities affect their parenting styles and influence the personality development of their children? What a challenge it can be to unravel all the actions and interactions of family members with very different personalities, beliefs, and private logic.

These are extreme examples. Few parents with a comfort lifestyle priority actually wait for their children to fall asleep on the floor (although one author admits she did that before she learned effective parenting skills). However, most parents can recognize a few of their tendencies in these examples, which illustrate the concept of lifestyle priorities.

Lifestyle Priorities

So far we've spent a great deal of time looking at how children grow and develop, and at the influences that shape their behavior. In this chapter we will focus on *parents'* behaviors originally defined by a theory called "Impasse\Priority" developed by Israeli psychologist Nira Kefir, which we have refined as "Lifestyle Priorities." It can be helpful for parents and teachers to know how their "priority" choices influence their parenting and teaching styles—and thus, the lifestyle choices of their children.

We will expand on the assets and liabilities of each style and discuss effects they might have on children. With understanding we can learn to build on the assets and avoid getting hooked into the liabilities of our style (at least some of the time). But the first step, as always, is to understand.

What Are Lifestyle Priorities?

Adults have accumulated a wealth of subconscious decisions from childhood that combine to form their lifestyle priorities. Lifesyle priorities do not describe "who you are." They do define your accumulation of decisions that affect the way you choose to *behave* in certain circumstances. The information in this chapter will help you identify your primary priority (what you may do when stressed) and your secondary priority (your usual method of operation when not under stress).

We have already identified the four Lifestyle Priorities: Control, Comfort, Superiority, and Pleasing (see chart, page 172). Each priority has both assets and liabilities. Most people want to claim the assets of each priority and reject the liabilities. For example, most people like to have some control of their life and dislike humiliation and criticism. However, humiliation and criticism are more difficult for a person with the control lifestyle priority to endure than they are for people with the other priorities. A person with a control lifestyle priority believes that the best way to avoid humiliation is to maintain control. Remember, this is a personal belief, not necessarily reality. Another person may laugh at a situation that would seem humiliating to someone with a control priority.

Lifestyle Priorities

Priority	Worst Fear	Believes the Way to Avoid Worst Fear is to:	Assets	Liabilities	Unknowingly Invites from Others	Creates then Complains About
Comfort	Emotional and physical pain and stress Expectations from others Being cornered by others	Seek comfort Ask for special service Make others comfortable Avoid confrontation Choose the easiest way	Easy going Few demands Minds own business Peacemaker Mellow Empathetic Predictable	Doesn't develop talents Limits productivity Avoids personal growth	Annoyance Irritation Boredom Impatience	Diminished productivity Impatience Lack of personal growth
Control	Humiliation Criticism The unexpected	Control self and/or others and/or situations	Leadership Organized Productive Persistent Assertive Follows rules	Rigid Doesn't develop creativity, spontaneity, or social closeness	Rebellion Resistance Challenge Frustration	Lack of friends and closeness Feeling uptight
Superiority	Meaninglessness Unimportance	Do more Be better than others Be right Be more useful Be more competent	Knowledgeable Idealistic Persistent Social interest Gets things done	Workaholic Overburdened Over responsible Overinvolved	Feelings of inadequacy and guilt "How can I measure up?" Lying to avoid judgments	Being overwhelmed Lack of time "I have to do everything"
Pleasing	Rejection Abandonment Hassles	Please others Active: Demand approval Passive: Evoke pity	Friendly Considerate Compromises Nonaggressive Volunteers	Doesn't check with others about what pleases them Doesn't take care of self	Pleasure at first and then annoyed by demands for approval and reciprocation	Lack of respect for self and others Resentment

Many people want superiority (in the form of excellence) and would be uncomfortable with meaninglessness and unimportance. However, meaninglessness and unimportance are to be avoided at all costs for a person with the superiority priority.

Just about everyone wants comfort in his or her life and wants to avoid emotional and physical pain and stress. However, trying to avoid pain and stress can be the concern that motivates the behavior of a person with the comfort priority. People with other priorities may have just as much difficulty with pain and stress, but they don't base their actions on trying to avoid them.

Few people enjoy rejection, hassles, and being left out. However, trying to avoid rejection and hassles is a primary theme and the basis for behavior when the person with the pleasing lifestyle priority feels stressed.

An interesting twist is that the behavior motivated by each priority often creates the opposite of what the individual intends. For example, the pleasing person may fail to please someone because he forgot to check out what the other person actually finds pleasing. He also creates hassles by trying to avoid them. The comfort person may create more stress by avoiding steps that seem uncomfortable at the time, but could create greater comfort in the future. Control people often invite criticism and humiliation when they attempt to control their feelings or the feelings of others, and superiority people may create meaninglessness by trying too hard and getting caught up in "busy work". Awareness and humor can help all of us get beyond our self-defeating beliefs and behaviors.

Discovering Your Primary Priority

As we've learned, when children perceive their world and make decisions about it, they come to some basic conclusions that include a "therefore, I must . . ." belief. The following examples illustrate the different decisions children might make based on the same circumstances.

"I'm little; others are big. Therefore, I 'must' get others to take
    care of me." (Comfort)
"I'm little; others are big. Therefore, I 'must' try harder to
    catch up, and even do better." (Superiority)
"I'm little; others are big. Therefore I 'must' please so I will be
    loved." (Pleasing)
"I'm little; others are big. Therefore, I 'must' maintain control
    of myself and situations so I don't feel humiliated. (Control)

These thought patterns represent different decisions life's
circumstances invite from individuals.

If you are still having trouble deciding which lifestyle priority is yours, choose the statement that fits you best:

1. I feel the best about myself when I and those around me
   are comfortable, and worst about myself when there is tension, pain, and stress. (Comfort)
2. I feel the best about myself when I can please other people
   and avoid hassles so that life is fun, not difficult. I feel
   worst about myself when I feel rejected, left out, or overwhelmed by the difficulties of situations. (Pleasing)
3. I feel the best about myself when I am the best, when I'm
   number one, or when I'm achieving, and worst about myself when I feel worthless, meaningless, and stupid. (Superiority)
4. I feel the best about myself when things are orderly and organized and I am in control of myself and the situation,
   and worst about myself when I feel embarrassed and humiliated, or criticized about something I think I should
   have known. (Control)

The statement that is truest of you in times of stress is
your primary priority. "In times of stress" is an important factor
in understanding Lifestyle Priorities. When not under stress, we
are not worried about humiliation, rejection, meaninglessness,
or pain. During peaceful times in our lives we are usually not

hooked into old childhood decisions and beliefs. It is only perceived stress that catapults us into priority lifestyle behaviors.

We say "perceived" stress, because that is what stress is. What is stressful to one person may not be stressful to another—only our *thinking* makes it so. You can find more information on this important concept in the book *Understanding: Eliminating Stress and Finding Serenity in Life and Relationships.*[1]

Discovering Your Secondary Priority (Operating Style)

You may say, "Well, I certainly want to avoid humiliation and embarrassment, but I don't think I try to control others or situations. In fact, I usually try very hard to please others." If that is the case, you have just identified your secondary priority. This means that your usual method of operation or "style" is pleasing. This is your secondary priority because it is what you usually do when you are feeling secure. It is only when you feel insecure or pressured that you may fall back into your "must have" beliefs. Then you may give up pleasing and use your control methods to avoid perceived humiliation.

Many of us choose one priority as our method of operation (or secondary priority), which we use on a daily basis when we feel secure. When we feel stressed or insecure, we tend to fall back on our primary priority.

All the priorities may serve as operating priorities to be chosen at various times under various conditions (for example, when we're happy and content as opposed to when we're frustrated and stressed). In other words, under different conditions and in different situations we will use behaviors from different priorities, but it is always for the purpose of maintaining our

---

1. Nelsen, Jane. *Understanding: Eliminating Stress and Finding Serenity in Life and Relationships.* Rocklin, CA: Prima, 1986.

"must have" priority. For example a control priority person may please others to obtain control, strive for excellence to obtain control, or make people or situations comfortable to obtain control.

Your priority identifies what you need in order to think well of yourself and maintain your self-esteem, and what you need to avoid feeling insignificant. Everyone strives for significance and belonging and, beginning early in our childhood we find a number of different ways to obtain it.

But How Does My Lifestyle Priority Affect My Parenting?

The many assets and liabilities of each priority affect how you behave as a parent. It is not our purpose to create stereotypes, but we have found that increased understanding and awareness help us make informed choices instead of being blind victims to perceptions we had and decisions we made as children then subsequently "forgot." When we understand the possible liabilities of our lifestyle priority, we can develop strategies to overcome them. We can take more responsibility for what we create with our choices and behavior instead of acting like victims. We can also enhance our assets with more confidence and purpose through increased awareness.

Control

On the asset side, control priority parents may be very good at helping their children learn organization skills, leadership skills, productive persistence, assertiveness, and respect for law and order. Positive Discipline parenting skills can help control priority parents curb their tendency to be too rigid and controlling of their children. Excessive control invites rebellion or resistance, instead of encouraging children to learn the skills these parents want to teach. Control priority parents may be more effective if they make an effort to recognize their need for excessive control and practice the skills of letting go, offering choices, asking "what" and "how" questions, and of getting their children more involved in decision making.

Mrs. Jones's lifestyle priority is control. She used to tell her children what to do, how to do it, and when to do it, and she certainly didn't allow any "back talk" from them. She truly believed that this was what responsible parents were supposed to do. Her controlling behavior was actually counterproductive to the goal of helping her children learn self-discipline, responsibility, cooperation, and problem-solving skills. Two of her three children were in constant rebellion, doing as little as they could get away with and always testing the limits until they were punished. This made Mrs. Jones feel "out of control"— the very thing she was trying to avoid. She was in a perpetual power struggle with these two children.

Her other child was becoming a "pleaser." He tried to live up to his mother's expectations and to gain her approval by pleasing her. However, instead of developing the life skills he needed to be a happy, successful citizen of the world, he was losing a sense of what pleased *him* and lived with the fear that he would never be able to make people happy enough. He was becoming an approval junkie.

Learning about priorities helped Mrs. Jones emphasize her assets instead of her liabilities. She started using family meetings with her children to involve them in solving problems. She learned to risk asking "what" and "how" questions to help both herself and her children discover the consequences of their decisions and to learn from their mistakes in an atmosphere of unconditional love. She stopped needing to be in charge of everything and invited suggestions and discussions about solving problems. She was grateful when she realized that as she let go of *her* need to be in control, she and the children *all* felt more in control.

Mrs. Jones also taught in a preschool. Her control style was sorely tested by the three-and four-year-olds in her classroom. Potty accidents, tears over a parent not waving goodbye, or the onset of an ear infection could sabotage her carefully orchestrated lesson plans. Mrs. Jones focused on the learning and activity portion of her teaching and felt annoyed when the children in her group forced her to deviate from her plan.

When Mrs. Jones began to understand her control priority, she realized that she found nurturing and dealing with the physical needs and limitations of the children the most challenging part of her job. She began to shift her focus by getting into the children's world more effectively. When she did this, she was able to feel compassion for the child with the spilled milk rather than impatience and a desire to take over. She began to see that learning life skills was the most important task of the children in her care. She became less concerned about completing the activities or games that she had prepared and more willing to let the children's needs set the pace for the day.

Pleasing

On the asset side, pleasing priority parents may be very good at helping their children learn friendly, considerate, non-aggressive behavior. They are often peacemakers because of their desire to make everyone happy. They are good at compromising and often volunteer to help others. They are champions of the underdog. Positive Discipline parenting skills can help these parents curb their tendency to please others at their own expense— and then feel resentful when others don't do the same for them. Excessive pleasing invites resentment and depression, and an occasional desire to reject people who refuse to be pleased.

Pleasing priority parents can be more effective when they quit trying to figure out what they can do to make everyone else happy and invite joint problem solving. They need to have faith in their children's ability to please themselves and teach them the skills of emotional honesty (more about that later). Both parent and child will benefit from learning to express what they think, feel, and want without expecting anyone else to think the same, feel the same, or to give them what they want—easily said, but not so easily done!

Mr. Smith's lifestyle priority is pleasing. He was committed to making his children be nice to each other, the neighbors, their grandparents, the members of their church, and their teachers. He was more concerned with how they treated others than with helping them with their own feelings. At other times he would give them too much special service when they whined or cried. For example, he would try to please them when they demanded drinks or more stories before bedtime. Then he would get angry when the drinks and stories didn't satisfy them enough to make them go to bed cheerfully. All too often, everyone went to bed upset. *No one* was pleased!

It was also important to Mr. Smith that his children like him and approve of him as their father. It seemed only logical to him that his children would also want to please him. He couldn't understand it when his children complained that he didn't care about their feelings. It was a vicious circle; he was sure they didn't care about *his* feelings, even after "all he did for them."

Mr. Smith wasn't sure whether or not he believed the information about lifestyle priorities. But when he started using family meetings with his children to involve them in joint problem solving, he couldn't help but notice the changed atmosphere in his family. Mr. Smith and his children learned to use emotional honesty to express their feelings. They discussed the idea of "separate realities" and the fact that different things pleased different people and that it was respectful to *ask* instead of to assume. He discovered that it was important to take his own needs into consideration—and the "needs of the situation." He learned to respond to his children's bedtime demands by kindly and firmly saying, "It is bedtime now." At first he had to repeat that simple statement several times. However, once his children learned he meant what he said, they gave up trying to manipulate him.

Mr. Smith eventually realized that when he tried to please his children without first discovering what pleased them, he wasn't really pleasing *any*one. This family began listening to each other, asking for what they wanted, and being honest about whether or not they would grant each other's wishes. When Mr. Smith learned about priorities and Positive Discipline parenting skills, his children began to enjoy being his children—and Mr. Smith began to truly enjoy being a parent. Everyone was pleased—at least most of the time.

Marnie also had a pleasing priority. She taught a group of five-year-olds in the Sunday school at her church. It was very important to her that the children learn how to behave correctly. She approached children in conflict by insisting that they apologize to one another. When the children forgot to say "please" or "thank you," Marnie rushed in to supply the correct words for them. Yet somehow the children in her class weren't "getting it." There were more and more fights and rudeness was rampant. When the pastor came to visit her class, Marnie was mortified when some of the children forgot to call him "Sir."

When Marnie learned about priorities, she also realized how much time she spent worrying about others' opinions, and how little time she spent actually enjoying herself. She began to allow herself to smile at the children's attempts at good manners and to feel encouraged by their small successes. She also started to ask the children what they were fighting about rather than insisting they offer each other insincere apologies. When they began to seek solutions together, much to her surprise Marnie found that the children were willing to apologize when they hurt another child—when an apology was their idea. The atmosphere in the classroom became much more pleasant and encouraging for everyone.

Comfort

On the asset side, comfort priority parents may model for their children the benefits of being easygoing, diplomatic, and predictable. Their children may truly learn to enjoy simple pleasures in life and take time to "smell the roses." Positive Discipline skills can help parents understand their tendency to be too permissive with their children because it seems easier at the time. Comfort-seeking parents often choose a laissez-faire, permissive parenting style which may translate into a tendency toward "spoiled brattiness." Comfort priority parents can become more effective when they get their children involved in creating routines, setting goals, and solving problems together.

Mrs. Carter's priority is comfort. She often left too many decisions to her children and was too quick to give in to their demands because it seemed "easier." But oddly enough, taking the easy way out didn't always make life easier. She began to suffer a great deal of stress and discomfort (as did her children) because the only way they knew to get along was through emotional tyranny (whining or throwing tantrums until their mom gave in). Instead of making them comfortable, Mrs. Carter had unwittingly created a family atmosphere of great tension.

Mrs. Carter was excited to learn how understanding priorities could help her emphasize her assets instead of her liabilities. She started taking time to teach her children life skills and providing opportunities for them to practice what they were learning. She gave them allowances, discussed saving and spending, and then allowed them to experience the consequences of their choices.

When the children made demands, she put their requests on the family meeting agenda to be discussed later. During the family meetings she invited discussion and brainstorming on various ways the children could get what they wanted through their own efforts. They created morning and bedtime routines, decided on plans to accomplish chores, and discussed goals and what they would need to do to accomplish them. Mrs. Carter was grateful to realize that she was more comfortable, there was less tension in the home, and the children were more comfortable, having learned respectful ways to get their needs met.

No one wanted their child to be in Miss Sheila's class at the child care center. She constantly looked exhausted, and no wonder—the toddlers in her class didn't do anything for themselves. She helped them eat, then she put on and buttoned everyone's coat carefully. She thought no one could put shoes on properly either, and every child seemed to constantly have a runny nose and no clue how to wipe it himself. If children objected to the snack that was served, Sheila would hurriedly offer several other items to prevent tantrums (she lived in terror of tantrums).

Learning about her comfort priority gave Sheila insight, and she realized that her unwillingness to deal with conflict was running her life. Sheila decided that she needed to pay some attention to her own comfort. When a child would demand yet another story or a different color Play-Doh, she learned to tell him that was all for now. She also instituted a training plan so that within a month all of the children had learned how to put on their own coats and shoes. What a relief it was not to be trying to do it all! Sheila found the children in her class began to show more and more interest in learning to do things on their own. And *she* went home with enough energy to go out to a movie in the evening. Not surprisingly, parents began to request Miss Sheila as their child's teacher!

Superiority

Superiority priority parents may be very good at modeling success and achievement. They are often able to assess quality and seem to have a knack for "motivating to excellence." Their children, however, sometimes see this as "badgering to perfection" and feel inadequate to meet the high expectations of their parents.

Positive Discipline parenting skills can help these parents curb their tendency to expect too much from their children. Excessive superiority often invites feelings of inadequacy instead of the desire for the achievement these parents want to inspire. Superiority priority parents will be more effective if they make an effort to let go of their need for things to be "right" and "best" (according to their own standards, of course) and practice the skills of "getting into their children's worlds" to discover what is important to them, always making sure the message of unconditional love gets through.

They can also learn to model and teach that mistakes are wonderful opportunities to learn, and listen to and accept their children's ideas for solving problems. Sometimes superiority parents are so focused on the final goal that they completely miss the joy of the process.

Mr. Lyndol's priority is superiority. He used to tell his children about all his wonderful accomplishments, as well as what he expected from them. He believed this would inspire and motivate them to follow in his footsteps, and he invested much of his self-worth in the expectation that they would surpass him.

This dad's superiority personality was actually counterproductive to the goal of helping his children achieve excellence. One of his children became a troublemaker at his preschool. (If he couldn't be the best of the best and live up to his dad's expectations, he could at least be the best of the worst.) This child also had developed a superiority priority, but was exercising it in opposition to his dad. His other child became a perfectionist who couldn't stand to lose, and who couldn't relax and enjoy his accomplishments when he won because he was constantly afraid of the embarrassment and humiliation of failure.

Mr. Lyndol was motivated to emphasize the assets of his superiority priority instead of his liabilities, and to be the sort of father he'd always intended. He and his family worked to cultivate a sense of humor when discussing mistakes and began projects they could work on together. Sometimes they would even make mistakes together, just to reassure themselves that it was okay. He learned to use family meetings to improve communication with his children. They worked at enjoying and cooperating on the process and not just emphasizing the excellence of the finished product.

Mr. Lyndol stopped lecturing and invited discussions about differences of opinions. He and his children decided on a community service project which they planned together. Mr. Lyndol was excited to discover that he was feeling better about his ability to communicate with his children and felt encouraged with what he was learning from and with them. The children began to exhibit signs that they, too, were encouraged: they were enthusiastic and willingly cooperated both at home and at preschool.

Mr. Lyndol also volunteered as a coach for a children's soccer team. At first, he had wanted only children who had strong skills and who wanted to practice hard—and especially, children who wanted to win. Mr. Lyndol's new insights helped him to see that all of the children had potential if he would only encourage them. He began to work with these children, to hone their kicking and running and passing. He taught them that it was more important to do their best than to win a game.

They won many games (and lost a few), but Mr. Lyndol found his greatest pleasure in the attitude his team displayed. They worked together and enjoyed the work. In sports, a superiority priority proved to be an asset. Mr. Lyndol brought his drive for excellence to helping a group of children become highly motivated to do their best. He had learned to find ways to encourage and include each member of his team.

Lifestyle Priorities in Adult Life

We have discussed what happens when parents learn about priority styles and Positive Discipline parenting skills. Remember the four couples we introduced in the beginning of this chapter? As Alfred Adler often said, "Opposites attract, but they have difficulty living together." An understanding of priority styles coupled with Positive Discipline parenting skills can help couples live together with fewer conflicts. Each is attracted to the other for possessing the assets he or she lacks. But sometimes what seemed cute and adorable at first becomes downright irritating after marriage. Take the case of Mr. and Mrs. Johnson.

David and Suzanne Johnson met on the ski slopes. There was an immediate attraction between the two and a relationship quickly developed. Suzanne was attracted to David because he was relaxed, easygoing, and really comfortable to be around. Even when he skied, he seemed to glide easily down the mountain.

For his part, David was attracted to Suzanne because she was bright, attractive, articulate, creative—just one of the best around. They had a lot in common. They both loved to ski. Little did they realize how the ups and downs of the ski slope would become a metaphor for their relationship, and for their parenting styles when their first child arrived.

David's priority was comfort, while Suzanne's priority was superiority. We are often attracted to someone who seems to have what we believe we lack. David never stood in the way of Suzanne's many activities; in fact, he encouraged her accomplishments. After all, her ambition and drive made life easy for him. David's easy charm and relaxed manner were a perfect foil for Suzanne's lofty goals and excessive energy.

Then their first baby arrived. Before long (and with absolutely no knowledge of lifestyle priorities), he seemed to have an uncanny ability to cause Dad discomfort and to make Mom feel less than superior. He also had an ability to get Mom and Dad arguing about parenting skills and styles, too. Dad was too easy, Mom too hard. Or at least, that's what David and Suzanne had to say about each other.

When a kind soul eventually explained lifestyle priorities to them, things began to turn around for David and Suzanne. They attended a parenting class together and made an effort to parent their youngster as a team. They focused on appreciating the attractive aspects of their priorities (which had brought them together in the first place). They agreed that each of them would work on his or her own liabilities, and that each would offer support and understanding rather than criticism. They were especially delighted to find that their new Positive Discipline parenting skills fit *both* their styles and helped them achieve what they most wanted to create: a happy family.

Growth happens when we learn to turn our liabilities into assets. As we gain insight and awareness, growth can be exciting and rewarding. Understanding our own priority and how it influences our relationships with our children can help us, with time and patience, learn to be the best parents we can be.

CHAPTER 14

Mistakes Are Wonderful Opportunities to Learn: The Fine Art of Encouragement

There—we said it again! But if there's one message parents and their children need to get firmly in mind early in the parenting process, it's this: if we can be human with each other, give each other room to learn and grow, trust one another to continue loving, and laugh together occasionally, we can survive just about anything. Allowing both children and parents the room to make mistakes and own up to them is one of the best ways to build a relationship based on trust, warmth, and closeness— and it begins in the earliest days of childhood.

Learning the fine art of encouragement is one of the most important skills of effective parenting. Experts who study human behavior and development tell us that a healthy sense of self-esteem is one of the greatest assets a child can have, and parents who know how to encourage, have faith, and teach have the best chance of helping their children develop self-esteem.

But what exactly *is* self-esteem? And where does it come from? Self-esteem is, quite simply, the confidence and self-satisfaction each one of us has in him- or herself. Self-esteem comes from having a sense of *belonging*, believing that we're capable and worthwhile. Self-esteem provides young people with their best defense against peer pressure.

And it is self-esteem that gives children the courage to take risks in life and the willingness to try new experiences—everything from being the first kid at day care to say "hello" today to trying out for the football team or honors orchestra later. Children who lack self-esteem fear failure and often don't believe in themselves even when they possess wonderful talents and abilities.

Self-esteem doesn't just "happen" in children—we have to help them grow it. But how?

Loving the Child You Have

Most of us have dreams of who our child will be. We may cherish visions of our child as a star athlete or musician, a Nobel-prize winning scientist, or even (yes, it's true) President of the United States. We may hope for a child who is quiet and dreamy, one who is energetic and outgoing, or one who possesses some other combination of qualities and talents. We may even want a child exactly like ourselves. (Parents and children do not necessarily come in matched pairs!)

For instance, Michael had dreamed of the day his son would be born. He proudly carried his newborn into a room decorated with pennants and some of Dad's own trophies, and placed a tiny blue football in the infant's crib. As little Kevin grew, he was signed up for every sport. His dad was never too busy to toss the football or to take some batting practice. Kevin played "tee-ball" with the other five-year-olds and soccer with the youngsters' league. He had a miniature basketball hoop and a perfectly oiled baseball glove. His dad never missed a practice or a game.

There was only one problem: Kevin hated sports. He did his best, but he had little natural ability and he loathed competition. Alone in his room, he dreamed of being an actor or a comedian, of standing on a stage before smiling, applauding people. He lined up his stuffed animals and told his favorite stories and jokes, hearing in his mind the enthusiastic response. He regaled his neighborhood buddies with tall tales.

As Michael talked eagerly to his son about the "majors," Kevin only sighed. Shattering his dad's dreams would take more courage than he possessed; he was afraid of losing his father's love and approval. So he played on, growing just a little more discouraged with every game, feeling disappointed that he would never be the son his father *really* wanted.

Janice, too, had dreamed of her child's babyhood. Janice had been delighted when her child was a little girl and had painstakingly furnished the nursery in pastel-colored lace and ruffles. She bought ribbons and bows for her daughter's almost-invisible hair; she filled drawers with adorable little dresses. She cleaned up her own favorite dolls and added several more, preparing herself to share all sorts of blissful times with her daughter.

The little girl in question, however, had other ideas. She never was a cuddly child, but squirmed and wriggled constantly. She crawled and walked early, and was always into something—much to her mother's dismay. She delighted in pulling the vacuum cleaner attachments apart and emptied the kitchen cabinets time and time again. The dainty dresses were a nuisance; the baby seemed to have a gift for tearing and staining them.

Things only got more difficult as she grew. She preferred to be called "Casey" rather than "Katy." She had no patience with dolls and tossed them into the darkest corner of her closet, or undressed them and scribbled on them with ink; she insisted on "borrowing" her older brother's trucks and guns. Her favorite game was "army," and as soon as she was able, she joined the older boys (despite their howls of protest) in their games, showing an astounding talent for street hockey and climbing trees. She even liked lizards and snakes. Janice tried ballet lessons and even gymnastics, but to no avail; Casey refused to be Katy.

Did Michael and Janice love their children? Undoubtedly they did. But one of the most beautiful ways of expressing love for a child is learning to love *that child*—not the child you wish you had. All parents have dreams for their children, and dreaming is not a bad thing. If we are to encourage our children, though, and build their sense of self-esteem and belonging, we should keep several things in mind.

Accept your children as they are.   As we have already seen, children have their own unique temperaments. They have abilities we didn't expect and dreams of their own that don't match ours, and sometimes their behavior is a real disappointment. It is terribly easy to compare our offspring with the children down the street, with their cousins, or even with their own siblings, and to find them lacking in some way.

We humans are not terribly good at unconditional love, yet children *need* to be loved unconditionally. We need to learn to love the child we have, which is sometimes easier said than done—and which takes time and patience.

Parents need to remember that even the youngest child has an amazing ability to sense her parents' true feelings and attitudes. If she knows she is loved and accepted—if she feels the sense of worth and belonging she craves—she will thrive. But if she senses that she *doesn't* belong, that she is a disappointment or a nuisance, her budding sense of self will wither, and her parents may never get to know the person she could have been.

We must try to teach our children to be the best people they can be—not to be someone they are not.

Be patient with your child's development.   Developmental charts are a wonderful way to keep track of the average time span during which children do certain things. The problem is that there are no average children! Children develop—crawl,

walk, talk—at their own pace, and many early childhood conflicts stem from parental impatience. Your child will walk and
learn toilet training when he's ready; after all, have you ever
seen a child crawl off to kindergarten in diapers? If you have serious concerns about your child's development, a word with
your pediatrician may set your mind at rest—and save both you
and your child a great deal of discouragement.

Provide your children with opportunities to succeed. Far
more powerful than even the most loving and appreciative
words are experiences that teach children they are capable, competent people. Begin early to look for your children's special gifts
and talents, their abilities and strengths, the things that make
them bubble inside. Then give them chances to try those things.

Provide opportunities, too, for them to help you and to
take on the little responsibilities they can handle. Early successes
and experiences that say "I can do this!" are powerful builders
of self-esteem.

Beware of self-fulfilling prophecies. It is interesting to
wonder just how "terrible" the twos would be if parents weren't
forever telling each other—and their children—about them.
Children have an uncanny ability to live up (or down) to their
parents' expectations. If you call your rambunctious toddler a
"little monster," don't be surprised if he does his best to be what
you expect. In the same way, we can build self-confidence in our
children by letting them know we love and accept them, and
believe in their ability to succeed.

It seemed that Rick and Carol were forever telling their
four-year-old daughter, Lizzie, to be careful. Lizzie, they often
told their friends and relatives, was "accident-prone." Each day,
as Carol sent Lizzie out to play, she called after her, "Be *careful*,
baby. You know you get hurt so easily." And over and over
again she sighed as she cleaned off the latest scrape or bump
and kissed away Lizzie's tears.

"I should buy stock in a bandage company," Rick joked as Lizzie played nearby. "We go through a case a week!"

It was after a parenting class one night that Carol and Rick sat down together and decided that something had to change.

"We need to do something different," Carol said. "Maybe if we don't make such a big deal out of things, Lizzie will stop having so many accidents."

"I don't see how that could help," Rick said, "but it's worth a try."

So the next time Lizzie appeared with a scrape, Carol said warmly, "Why, honey, that's not like you!" And after she'd calmly comforted her daughter, she gave her a hug and sent her off to play again.

Slowly but surely, Rick and Carol began to tell Lizzie by words and actions that she *wasn't* doomed to injuries, that she could do lots of things and take good care of herself. And unbelievable as it seemed, the day dawned when Rick and Carol realized that it had been several weeks since Lizzie had hurt herself.

Are our children always going to live out our predictions and expectations? No, of course not. But parents need to remember how powerful our words and opinions are to children. If we tell our children that they're bad, or lazy, or stupid, or clumsy, we shouldn't be surprised that we've reinforced the very behavior we dislike. By the same token, if we look for what's positive in our children, we can choose to reinforce those things—which leads us to one of the most powerful tools a parent has for building self-esteem in young children.

Encouragement: Looking for the Positive

The next time your toddler or preschooler is playing quietly, peek in for just a moment and watch. What do you see? You may notice your child's glowing smile, his ability to build tall towers with his blocks, or his wonderful creativity and imagination. Whatever it is that you see, make a note to share that observation with your child, and then watch what happens. Behavior that is appreciated is often repeated!

Preschool teachers, too, can make a practice of taking time each day to simply observe. Step back and watch the children in the housekeeping corner, draped in colorful scarves and vests, twirling merrily. In another corner, David is busy serving up pretend pizza, while Mary soothes the baby doll. Find a time to comment on what a caring and loving "mother" Mary is to her baby; tell David what a thoughtful host he is, and what a careful job he did of dividing up the pizza. These comments give names to the qualities we value and encourage, and help children not only learn but practice them.

All human beings long to be appreciated. And young children, who are just learning about their world and their place in it, have a special need to be encouraged, to have their progress noticed, and to feel they are valuable people.

It is easy in this world of ours to focus on what's *wrong*. We have no trouble making long lists of what we dislike about ourselves, our spouses, our jobs—and our children. Think for a moment about how you'd feel if your boss at work never did anything but point out your errors and shortcomings; how motivated would you feel to try harder?

Some young children hear a constant litany of "No, no, do it *this* way" or "How many times do I have to tell you?" or "Here, let me do it." It's no wonder they get discouraged; and as we've already learned, discouragement often leads to misbehavior.

Celebrate the Positive

Take a moment sometime soon to make a list of what you really like about your child. Hang the list someplace where you can see it (the refrigerator or the bathroom mirror work well) and add to it when you think of something new. Then find an opportunity each day to appreciate your child for something on the list. Children often bloom amazingly in the steady light of love and encouragement.

Encouragement means noticing progress, not just achievement. It means thanking your small son for picking up most of his cars, even though he missed a few in the corner. It means giving a hug for an attempt on the potty seat, whether or not there was a result. It means smiling with a child who has put on her shoes, even though they're on the wrong feet. Encouragement says to a child, "I see you trying, and I'm proud of you. Keep it up!"

Be sure to keep your encouragement specific. For instance, if a three-year-old at the child care center brings you his latest drawing and you tell him, "Oh, it's the most *gorgeous* picture I've ever seen—I'm going to frame it and hang it on the wall," you may not be encouraging him as much as you think. You may have taught him that the most important thing he can do is to please people, which can be a dangerous creed to live by. Telling that same child, "I see you really like red and yellow. Can you tell me about these shapes?" opens the door for talking and learning together.

Looking for the positive in your children and encouraging it is a skill that will serve you throughout childhood and adolescence, and will help your children to feel good about themselves.

"I Love You, But . . . "

We've all heard it before: the compliment that simply sets up the criticism. "You did a good job, but . . . " "Thanks for picking up your toys, but . . . " "I'm glad you dressed yourself today, but . . . " All too often, parents can't resist following a compliment with a helpful suggestion for doing even better. What we fail to realize is that whatever comes after the "but" is what sticks in the mind; what came before the "but" is minimized or even lost entirely.

Sometimes, too, children develop the "compliment flinch." They've learned that whenever Mom or Dad says something nice, it means something not-so-nice is sure to follow. When that happens, whatever power our encouragement and appreciations might have had is gone.

If what you truly want is to encourage your children and build their sense of worth and belonging, separate your suggestions for improvement from your encouragement. Let your smiles, thanks, and appreciations stand alone; find a quiet moment another time to give that helpful hint or suggestion. And most important of all, be sure you've provided your children with the skills and knowledge they need to do their best.

Take Time to Teach

It was a busy Sunday morning, and Anita Casper was in a rush. Church started in just an hour; breakfast still needed to be cleaned up, and the beds needed to be made. Keith was dressing the baby, but both Anita and her four-year-old daughter Lindy still had to get dressed. Suddenly Anita decided: it was time Lindy helped out a little. After all, she was four years old.

As Anita combed Lindy's hair, she asked, "Would you help me out, sweetie? While I get dressed and do the dishes, would you make your bed?"

Lindy looked up into her mother's harried face and smiled. "Okay, Mommy," she said. "I can do it."

But sheets and blankets are big, and four-year-old arms are short. Lindy wrestled valiantly with the covers, tucking and smoothing as best she could, but as she set her favorite teddy bear next to her pillow, she knew it didn't look *quite* like it did when Mommy made it. But she felt pleased; after all, it was her first time.

Anita didn't have a chance to check on her daughter's handiwork until after church and lunch. She took one look at the bunched covers and tangled sheets, sighed, and set about straightening things up. When she'd repaired Lindy's work, she went on to the next chore without a second thought.

She might have thought again if she'd seen Lindy's face a little later. The little girl stood looking at her tidy, perfectly made bed and felt her spirits sink. She'd done her very best, but obviously it hadn't been good enough: Mom had to fix it. The next time Anita asks her daughter to make the bed, she may receive a different, less willing response. After all, why try when you know you can't succeed?

The Magic of Teaching

Teaching children can take many forms, and surprisingly enough, it doesn't have to be unpleasant. Most young children have an inborn desire to imitate their parents, to do "grown-up" things—a desire parents sometimes unwittingly squelch. It's amazing how often we tell an enthusiastic three-year-old, "No, honey, you're too little," and then find ourselves wondering why she won't help out when she's seven or eight.

Taking the time to teach not only gives children the skills and abilities to succeed (an essential part of developing self-esteem), it can provide us with precious moments of closeness and even fun with our young children.

Teaching a young child has four basic steps.

1. **Let him watch you.** As your little one watches you set the table, feed the dog, or make a bed, explain in simple terms what you are doing and why.

2. **You do it with his help.** Next time there's an opportunity, encourage your child to help you do the task. Remind him of the things you told him before, and let him know you welcome his help.

3. **He does it with your help.** Now it's time for your child to try his hand at the task, with your occasional help—and lots of encouragement.

4. **You watch him.** By now, your child should feel confident enough to do the task on his own—with encouragement and loving support from you. Remember to keep your standards realistic; expecting perfection can cause both of you to become discouraged. And offer encouragement and appreciation for your child's efforts. Making "helping Mom and Dad" a pleasant adventure will take much of the hassle out of "chores" during the years ahead!

In the same way, you can let your children know how to deal with new situations by taking the time to prepare them for what will happen, which might make the experience much more pleasant for all concerned.

For example, Patsy Morgan was on her way home from picking up her two-year-old son Eric when she decided to stop in at the jewelry shop to get her watch, which had been repaired. She hurried in with Eric tagging along behind her and went straight to the counter to present her claim check.

Eric stood clinging to his mother's coat. He had never been in a shop like this before, and there was a lot to look at. He was gazing about him when suddenly an open display shelf near a window caught his eye and utterly dazzled him.

The late afternoon sunlight was glinting off a collection of the most fascinating objects Eric had ever seen. They were small crystal figures—little animals and people, and even a perfect, tiny castle atop its own crystal mountain, exactly like the one in Eric's favorite storybook—and every movement of Eric's head created rainbows of bright light.

Before Patsy had time to realize what was happening, Eric was off toward the shelf as fast as his short round legs could carry him. He reached for the wonderful castle, but his small fingers were only strong enough to drag the castle off its shelf and onto the tile floor, where it splintered into pieces.

Eric howled in fright; Patsy was embarrassed, apologetic, and angry—the crystal castle turned out to be shockingly expensive.

What are Patsy's options? Unfortunately, at this point she doesn't have many. She can pay for the broken castle and whisk her small son out to the car, vowing never to take him anywhere again. She can explore with Eric what happened and hope he remembers next time. (Notice that we haven't mentioned punishing Eric; it is doubtful a slap or a "time out" would make things any better, especially since Eric had received no guidelines beforehand.)

Or Patsy could have thought things through before entering the store and taken the time to teach. She could have gotten down on Eric's level, perhaps placing her hands gently on his shoulders or taking his hands in hers, and explained that there would be many pretty things in the store, but that touching and holding might break them. Eric could look, but not touch. Patsy could have made sure that Eric had something to occupy him while she was busy with the clerk. She probably should plan on holding his hand anyway, because it is too much to expect that a child not want to explore at that age, no matter how much teaching takes place. Or she could have decided that discretion was the better part of valor and picked up the watch sometime when Eric could be elsewhere.

Have Faith in Your Child's Ability to Learn

It is tempting to tell ourselves that our toddlers and preschoolers are just too young to understand or to do much for themselves, but young children often are more capable than their parents give them credit for. Even the youngest child can choose between two shirts to wear or two selections for breakfast; even a toddler can put napkins on the dinner table, one at each place (for a list of age-appropriate tasks, see page 129).

Giving children *reasonable* responsibilities provides them with opportunities to succeed, to be capable. And that is what self-esteem is all about.

Many parents complain that they have to do everything for their children, that they must nag and remind them to get things done, or that their children are lazy. Using the power of encouragement and appreciation, looking for the positive, and taking the time to teach appropriate skills can harness children's natural energy and desire to "help" and produce competent young people.

Is teaching children time-consuming? Undoubtedly. But letting children know what's expected, the best way to do things, and how to succeed in life is an investment of time that will more than pay you back as your children grow. Healthy, confident children who've learned they are capable of learning and doing often grow up to be healthy, confident adults. And isn't that worth the effort?

A Word About Child Care

If your child spends much of his or her time in a day care center or preschool, you may want to make sure that the staff shares your philosophy about encouragement and self-esteem. It may be a good idea to ask if you can observe for a few hours, just to see what the usual routine at your center is and how the staff and children relate.

Most child care workers genuinely love children and do their best to provide them with gentle, encouraging care. But if you discover that your child is spending hours in a discouraging atmosphere, you may want to consider changing child care arrangements. Or you might share this book with the staff and see what happens! We will discuss child care and preschools in more detail in Chapters 17–19.

Humor and Hope

Among the greatest gifts parents can bestow upon their children are the ability to laugh and the ability to hope and dream. From the earliest games of "peek-a-boo" with your infant, laughter is one of the closest bonds that bring parents and children together. Babies and young children are a wonderful source of joy; every day can be an adventure, a chance to laugh and love together. Learning to share a smile, to make funny faces, or to find the humor in situations can carry your family through many tough times.

Rules and limits have their place, and we couldn't function well without them. But there are also times for relaxing a bit, for allowing a child an extra hug or a few extra minutes of talk before bed; and there are times when the best medicine truly is laughter and play.

Roots and Wings

Your children will have their own dreams. Take time to explore your children's hopes and dreams with them; use these opportunities to learn about each other. A very wise person once said that good parents give their children two things: one is roots, and the other, wings. Loving your children as they are will give them roots; encouraging your children to believe in themselves and to dream will give them the wings to take risks, to try new things, and to live fully.

Will there be rough times along the way? Of course! Parents and children alike will make their share of mistakes. But remember what we've been saying all along: Mistakes are wonderful opportunities to learn!

CHAPTER 15

Discipline Versus Punishment: What's the Difference?

You may have noticed as you've read this book that the authors don't advocate spanking, slapping, yelling, or any of the other methods that pass so often for discipline in our society. You may have wondered why. Most people do. After all, weren't most of us raised with good "old-fashioned" discipline? And don't we often hear people saying that if kids today just got a bit more "discipline," we would have fewer problems?

It's important to look first at exactly what discipline is. As it turns out, when people talk about "discipline," they usually mean "punishment." Yet the two concepts aren't the same at all.

Most of us have absorbed our ideas about discipline from our own parents, our society, and years of tradition. We often approach discipline with one subtle, basic belief: children have to suffer (at least a little) or they won't learn anything.

"A good swat once in a while lets my kids know I mean business," a parent might say. Or, "My children lose all their privileges when they mess up. That's what teaches them not to disobey me." Or, "Punishing my kids teaches them to respect me." It is tempting to believe that we can control our children, especially when they're young and can easily be picked up, moved, or confined. But a wise parent (or teacher) realizes that total control is not only unwise, it's rarely even possible. (Can we ever completely control anyone's behavior—even our own?) Relying on control and the power of punishment turns parents and teachers into policemen, full-time enforcers who set the rules then watch constantly for violations. But what happens when the policeman isn't around? And how many parents and teachers want life with their children to become a constant power struggle?

True discipline is not about punishment or control. The word itself comes from the Latin word *disciplina,* which means "teaching." At its best, discipline is about guiding and teaching young people, helping them to make wise decisions about their behavior, and allowing them to gradually accept responsibility for their choices and actions—to choose (or not choose) a certain behavior because they understand its consequences, not because a policeman is lurking in the vicinity.

Many parents believe that punishment, especially spanking, is mandated by the Bible. The Bible *does* say, "He who spares the rod hates his son, but he who loves him is careful to discipline him" (Proverbs 13:24, New International Version). Many biblical scholars believe that the word "rod" has a number of meanings. It was a symbol of authority, and shepherds used a rod to guide and direct their sheep—not to beat them. The Bible also says, "Your rod and your staff they comfort me" (Psalms 23:4). How many children truly feel "comforted" by a good spanking?

The question of how we choose to discipline our children goes right to the heart of parenting. Most of us grew up accepting that punishment and spankings were normal, even necessary, parts of raising children. And often, at least in the short term, punishment seems to "work." But we need to beware of what seems to work for the moment, and consider instead the long-term effects of punitive discipline.

What Are Your Children Really Learning?

As we've discovered, children are constantly making decisions about life, how they feel, and how they will behave. Often the decisions they make after being punished are not those their parents intended.

A segment of the ABC television news show *20/20* took a close look at spanking, including studies of Murray Straus of the Family Research Laboratory at the University of New Hampshire. For this show, four families in which children are regularly spanked allowed the television cameras to follow them around and record the parents' interactions with their misbehaving children. Most parents who later viewed that show, including parents who had spanked their own children, found it painful to watch. Many agreed that the spankings they viewed didn't teach, but only punished a child for wrong choices or vented parental frustration and anger. There was no emphasis on problem solving or on preventing misbehavior in the future; the spankings alone were supposed to take care of that.

Yet these parents kept on having to spank their children regularly. There appeared to be no lasting changes in undesirable behavior. Perhaps more important, the show quoted research showing that spanking and similar punishments produce children who are discouraged, have lower self-esteem, are more likely to seek out abusive relationships later in life, and consider hitting an acceptable way to solve problems—results that these parents, who certainly loved their children, obviously didn't intend.

Punitive forms of discipline often teach children unintended lessons: to misbehave when the enforcer isn't around, to get even if possible, or to focus on the "mean old parent" rather than on the behavior that got them into trouble in the first place. Spanking, in particular, presents several hidden problems. It becomes less and less effective over time, and it eventually becomes physically impossible. It commonly creates feelings of guilt and regret in parents. Is it possible *not* to punish, yet still produce children who are responsible, well-behaved, and respectful (at least most of the time)?

Well-Prepared Parenting

It should be said that *nothing* works all of the time for all children and for all adults; after all, none of us are perfect. And there is simply no substitute for patience and the willingness to repeat yourself over and over when working with very young children—it's hard for children to learn things the first time through, even when they try.

But it *is* possible to provide discipline, in homes and in preschools, that teaches, guides, and encourages *without* spanking, yelling, or taking away privileges. Effective, consistent discipline takes a good deal of thought and preparation, but the benefits for your children and in your lives together will be well worth it.

The Beauty of Planning Ahead

An often-overlooked part of discipline is actually prevention, good old "thinking ahead" to the problems and situations that might occur. For instance, if you're about to take an airplane trip with a squirmy, active three-year-old, you can choose either to have a prolonged power struggle (with a curious captive audience) or you can prepare by packing a bag with snacks, story tapes, puzzles, and several small, new toys to keep your little traveler occupied and interested. You can even plan your trip for a time of day when your child is normally quiet or even sleepy, rather than a time when he's likely to be full of energy.

Let's take a close look at the familiar scene of many parent-child battles: the shopping trip. We've all seen it—the fussy, whining child and the anxious, irritated parent. If discipline is really about teaching, you may ask, how can a parent take a child along and prevent problems before they begin? There are several things to consider.

1. **Look for danger signals before you go.** Did your child skip a nap or a meal? Is she already tired and cranky? Are you? It is usually wisest to postpone errands and trips until both of you are rested and relatively cheerful. Don't plan to do a list of errands at the end of a tiring day—you and your child will probably regret it!

2. **Explain the rules and set the boundaries before entering the store.** If your child is old enough to understand, tell her gently but firmly what sort of behavior is acceptable in the store. Don't just ask if she understands (children always say they do); have her repeat the rules back to you. You may even want to play a game of "let's pretend." Be sure you talk together *in advance* about whining or begging for treats. And remember to encourage your child's cooperation by noticing when she behaves and follows the rules.

3. **Be prepared.** Most young children are fascinated by shopping for about five minutes. What will you do when the novelty wears off? It may help to bring a small bag of "things to do," especially if the bag can be tied to the handle of a shopping cart or stroller. Markers and paper for a child's own shopping list may provide some amusement; a favorite stuffed toy may help your child feel more secure. It may also be wise to bring along a snack, such as cut-up fruit or a bag of cereal.

4. **Make shopping a time to laugh and to learn.** See how creative you can be in keeping your child occupied as you shop. You may want to give him a stack of coupons and let him match the coupons to the items in your cart. Play "I spy" and see who can find a fruit that begins with "B" or a vegetable that is yellow. See if you can find all of the letters in the alphabet on signs and advertisements. Invite your child to plan a funny meal from items in your cart.

If your child is old enough, allow him to shop with you from a "list" with pictures of the items you need, perhaps even carrying his own basket. Show your child how to help you select the shiniest apples or to thump the watermelons (gently, of course). You can even begin to teach comparison shopping by seeing which price is lowest. Giving a child a job to do is an excellent way to help him feel needed and learn respectful, cooperative behavior.

Give your child an opportunity to make some of the choices. Even a very young child can choose between two cereals (preselected by mom or dad, of course), two flavors of ice cream, or striped or plain socks. It may all sound like a great deal of work—but it's undoubtedly easier than coping with a screaming toddler at the checkout stand! Even more important, you are teaching your child cooperation and life skills—and providing opportunities for building healthy self-esteem.

"My Kid Still Misbehaves—Now What?"

Even with the best preparation and training, it's unrealistic to expect perfect behavior. Sooner or later (usually sooner) it happens—a temper tantrum, a child crawling toward a forbidden object, a toy thrown in anger. How can a parent or teacher stop unacceptable behavior without resorting to punishment?

First of all, take the time to think carefully about the result rules, limits, and discipline should accomplish in your child's life. Keeping a few things in mind may help you avoid unnecessary conflict.

Be aware of your child's development, abilities, and limitations.   Remember that children develop differently, and have different strengths. Expecting from a child what he cannot give will only frustrate both of you. Your sister's children may be able to sit quietly in a restaurant for hours, while yours get twitchy after just a few minutes no matter how diligently you prepare. (Refer to Chapter 6 on temperament and Chapter 7 on developmentally-appropriate behavior for more discussion of this subject.) That being the case, you may decide to save that fancy meal out for a time when you can enjoy it in adult company—or for when your children have matured enough for all of you to enjoy it together.

Remember, too, that babies need love, not discipline. Babies in the first year of life don't need rules; they may not even understand what "no" means, and they rarely possess the will or understanding to *choose* misbehavior. A firm but gentle word and redirecting attention toward a more acceptable object is all the discipline your little one will need for a while.

Choose your battles.   *Everything* in family life can become a battle, if we let it. Take time to decide on the things that are important to you, and explore the issues about which you can afford to be flexible. Every family will be different. Some parents value church attendance, while it's not important to others. Messy rooms push some parents' buttons, while others couldn't care less. Be sure you save your energy for the things that really matter. When you've decided what matters most, communicate your expectations clearly and reinforce them with lots of training and appropriate action.

Think before you speak.   Most parents have had the uncomfortable experience of making a rule or a promise in the heat of anger (such as telling a child you will throw away all of his toys if he doesn't pick them up immediately) and realizing later that they couldn't follow through. One of the best pieces of child-rearing advice is also one of the oldest: "Say what you mean, and mean what you say." Don't tell your four-year-old that if she's not in the car "this minute" you'll leave for Grandma's house without her. She knows as well as you do that Grandma lives in the next state, and you're not about to drive away and leave her standing in the driveway.

If we constantly tell children things we don't mean or make promises we're not willing to live up to, we teach them that they only need to listen to some of what we say, and we run the risk of damaging their trust. Be sure you've thought about the possible consequences of your words; if you're not sure you mean them, don't say them.

One preschool teacher learned this lesson the hard way when she found herself warning a child, "If you don't come down from that tree right now, I'm going to come up and get you." Guess what? She did. But she was much more careful of what she said from then on!

Remember that children do what "works." Children are intelligent little people, and if a certain behavior (or misbehavior) gets the desired response, they will almost certainly repeat it. For instance, if your child throws a tantrum at the grocery store checkout and walks away with candy or a pack of gum, what do you suppose you'll see the next time you arrive at the checkout stand? If a desire to "talk," a few tears, and big blue eyes allow your child to delay bedtime, can you expect to see these behaviors every night? Try to avoid inadvertently reinforcing the wrong sorts of behavior.

Work toward consistency. No one is consistent all of the time. But as much as possible, try to make sure that your goals, your rules, and your approach stay the same from one day to the next. Children find frequent changes confusing and may resort to constantly testing the limits just to find out what they *are*. Making your rules *few, firm, and fair* will help you to be reasonably consistent and will let your children know what to expect, which may eliminate a great deal of misbehavior.

Focus on the belief behind the behavior. Human behavior (adults' *and* childrens') never happens in a vacuum; we behave as we do for a reason, whether we understand it consciously or not. Take time before you react to something your child has said or done to decipher the code hidden in her actions. Consider your child's feelings and reflect them (see Chapter 16). If you can figure out *why* a child is misbehaving, you're a giant step ahead, not only in stopping the behavior this time but in preventing it in the future. And isn't that what discipline is all about?

Learn to see mistakes—including your own—as opportunities to learn. Remember all those things we've just talked about? Most parents manage to forget them and get hooked into reacting to exasperating behavior. And that's okay. You can't be perfect either, so you will have many opportunities to demonstrate to your children that mistakes *are* wonderful opportunities to learn.

After you've had time to cool down, acknowledge your mistake to your children, apologize (children are so forgiving), and work on solutions with your children. Things often turn out better than if the mistake had never been made in the first place!

Nonpunitive Discipline for Young Children

As we've already learned, children misbehave most often when they're feeling discouraged. They may choose one of the four coded messages in the mistaken belief that it will help them feel better. A wise parent or teacher will work toward helping a child feel encouraged, invite cooperation, and practice mutual respect. Adults can use a number of effective tools to deal with young children's misbehavior in ways that teach, that focus on solutions to problems, and that help both adults and children feel better.

Time Out

Jean had absolutely *had* it. Three-year-old Paul would not stop teasing his eighteen-month-old sister, and the incessant fussing and crying had frayed Jean's nerves. "That's it, Paul," she finally exploded, "you're in time out."

Jean dragged her kicking son to his room and closed the door. "I'm setting the egg timer for three minutes," she said firmly, following the rule she had always heard. Paul answered his mother by kicking the door and throwing a toy—and by opening the door as soon as his mom was out of sight.

Jean heard the door open behind her and sighed, "I must be doing something wrong."

Believe it or not, time out need not be a punishing confinement or a battle of wills between parent (or teacher) and child. Time out, effectively used, is an opportunity for children to feel better. (Thinking of it as a "cool off" rather than a "time out" may help.) And when children *feel* better, they usually choose to behave better.

Picture the following scenario . . . . The "time out corner" at Willy's preschool was a special place. All of the children had worked together to set it up, and it boasted an old-fashioned claw-footed bathtub filled with soft pillows, several teddy bears, and a stack of inviting books. At the moment, Willy was busily engaged in tripping the unsuspecting children who passed his spot on the floor. This amusing game came to a sudden end, however, when he tried to trip the teacher.

"Willy," the teacher said, "I thought we talked about tripping. Someone could fall and get hurt."

Willy looked a bit sheepish—they *had* discussed this habit of his several times recently—but his only response was a sullen silence.

The teacher smiled. "Perhaps you'd feel better if you visited the time out corner. Go curl up and look at the books for a little while, and you can come back and play with us when you feel better and can change your behavior."

Willy spent almost ten minutes curled up in the old tub, looking at books and watching his classmates play. When he returned to the group, the teacher asked, "Feeling better, kiddo? No more tripping?"

Willy nodded and offered a tentative smile. "Come and join us, then," the teacher offered, and Willy moved to join the group.

Some parents and teachers believe that making a time out corner inviting and pleasant rewards children for misbehavior. However, wise adults realize that all people have moments when they just can't seem to get along. A few moments in time out (when it's not shaming or punishing) provides a cooling-off period, and children know they're welcome to return when they can get along and behave properly. If you still have doubts, ask yourself whether you'd rather be Willy's teacher or Paul's mother!

We invite you to see for yourself. Help your children set up a cozy corner in their rooms for time out. You may want to include favorite stuffed toys, books, music, or coloring books and markers. Then, when you sense that your child needs a moment to cool off, suggest a time out. Tell your child that he or she can return when he feels better *and* is able to follow the rules. Notice that the end result is to "return when he is able to change his behavior."

Punitive time out is "past-oriented." It may make children suffer for what they have done, but parents and teachers might be surprised if they checked out the decisions (conscious or unconscious) that children are making for the future. Positive time out is "future-oriented" and encourages children to make positive decisions about self-control and responsibility—training that will benefit both of you as your child grows.

Distraction and Redirection

Thirteen-month-old Ellen was crawling rapidly toward the stereo system—one of her favorite "toys"—when her dad spotted her.

"Ellen," he called out firmly. Ellen paused and looked back over her shoulder. Her dad scooped her up and carried her across the room to where her barnyard set was waiting.

"Here, sweetie," he said with a tickle, "see what the pigs and cows are up to."

If Ellen chooses to head for the stereo again, her dad can intercept her again and direct her towards a more acceptable object. Acting without lecturing or shaming avoids a power struggle and lets Ellen know that Dad won't let her play with the stereo.

What if Ellen keeps returning to the forbidden stereo? How many times must a parent distract or redirect a child's attention? Well, as many times as it takes. As we've mentioned before, it takes patience and perseverance to train a young child. If Ellen's dad slapped her hand or spanked her, would she still want to play with the stereo? Probably so. And even if spankings stop the behavior, what is the cost in self-esteem, doubt and shame? What are the lessons about violence? Kindly but firmly directing Ellen toward acceptable objects, and continuing to do so until she gets the message, guides her behavior without punishing or shaming, and without inviting a battle of wills.

Ignoring

Marcy is an expert at throwing temper tantrums; she considers it her specialty. She has learned that when she throws herself down on the floor, kicks her feet, and howls, she's pushing Mom and Dad's "buttons" in a very effective way. They come running to see what's wrong, and she gets all sorts of attention.

Today, however, something is drastically wrong. She pitches her very best tantrum, but Mom, who is fixing dinner in the kitchen, only smiles. Marcy throws her doll for added effect, but after a quick glance to make sure Marcy is in no danger of hurting herself, Mom leaves the room! Marcy hears her go into her bathroom and begin running water for a bath.

Marcy steps up her tantrum, screaming even louder and pounding on the carpet with her fists, but there is no response. After a while Marcy begins to feel rather silly. She gets up and trots down the hall to see what Mom is up to.

If Marcy throws a tantrum in Mom's room, Mom can simply return to the kitchen. Eventually Marcy will get the message that her tantrum isn't working, and Mom will be able to deal with the situation in a calm, effective manner.

Ignoring misbehavior works well when the misbehavior is designed primarily to get our *attention*. Of course, you never want to leave your child in a situation where he or someone else could get hurt; but ignoring misbehavior, even if you remain in the room, can teach children with surprising speed that they can't manipulate you.

Consequences and Follow-Through

Consequences teach children by allowing them to experience the results of their choices. *Natural* consequences, for example, are things that happen without parental intervention. If you go out in the rain, you get wet. If you don't eat, you get hungry. If you make snowballs without gloves, your hands get very cold. If you throw your lunch on the floor, there's nothing for you to eat. Children can learn from these experiences if parents resist the urge to lecture and rescue.

Sometimes, however, natural consequences either don't exist or aren't acceptable. The natural consequence of playing in the street, for example, is a lesson we can't afford to have our children learn. In these instances, parents can intervene with *logical* consequences.

Parents and teachers often get hung up in trying to determine what the consequence should be for a certain action. It's important to remember that consequences when misused can easily *feel* like good old-fashioned punishment. The best consequences are those that children have a hand in designing and which focus on preventing problems in the future.

For instance, if a child draws on the wall with marker, it is appropriate to have the child help you wash the wall (and it may be a good reminder never to buy a young child permanent markers!) You may then want to sit down with the child and discuss what will happen if the child chooses to draw on the wall again. Remember, if a consequence isn't obvious, it isn't logical, and a child probably won't learn much from it. You may agree that drawing on the wall means that a child isn't ready for the privilege of owning markers and will have to give his up for a while. It isn't helpful to say unnecessary, hurtful things like "Maybe this will teach you to obey me" as you take the markers. Such comments only shame and humiliate, and will not encourage your child to do better. Be sure you provide for a time to try again when the child is ready.

Consequences work best with children who are old enough to think logically and understand the connection between their behavior and the consequence. This doesn't happen as young as you might think. Take time to be sure that your child understands what has happened, why you feel the way you do, and what will happen if the behavior is repeated. Remember, effective discipline is teaching for the future.

Follow-through means that parents and teachers decide what *they* are going to do and then follow through with kind and firm action instead of punishments and lectures. As psychologist Rudolf Dreikurs has said, follow-through means you "shut your mouth and act." Follow-through with young children is relatively simple: you do what you have said you would.

The fewer words spoken, the better; many parents talk too much, and children learn they can safely ignore about half of what they hear.

Consider the following scenes.

SCENE I. Five-year-old Alex is having a wonderful time with his Legos in the middle of the living room floor. His mother pokes her head into the room and says cheerfully, "It's bedtime, honey. Pick up your Legos and put on your pajamas."

Alex appears to have developed a hearing problem; he ignores his mother and continues building his tower. Now Mom's voice gets a bit tense. "Did you hear me, Alex? I said it's time for bed. Put away the Legos now."

Still Alex doesn't move. And now Mom's voice sounds like an elastic band that is stretched to the breaking point. "If you don't pick up those toys and get ready for bed this instant, you're going to get a spanking. I'm counting to three . . . ."

Alex keeps playing, but when Mom moves toward him he is galvanized into action. He scrambles to pick up his Legos, but Mom delivers the spanking anyway and drags him off to his room, where she tells him, "It serves you right. You can just go without your story now. Maybe next time you'll obey me."

Alex gets into bed and screams for 15 minutes. Mom returns to the kitchen, wishing fervently she were *anywhere* but home.

What might this encounter look like if Mom used follow-through?

SCENE II. It's bedtime. Five-year-old Heather is sitting on the floor playing with her Barbie dolls. Her mother cheerfully says, "It's bedtime, honey. Time to put away your dolls and get ready for bed."

Heather keeps dressing her doll. After giving her daughter a minute or two to comply, Mom walks over to Heather and gently but firmly takes her hand. Heather tries to pull her hand away. "Come on, Mom," she says, "just let me dress Barbie."

Mom smiles, but doesn't say a word. She gently pulls Heather up from the floor. When Heather begins to whine, Mom says, "Do you want to pick out your bedtime story, or shall I do it?"

Heather's voice is sulky as she replies, "I want to."

Mom says, "Fine. Call me when you've brushed your teeth and put on your jammies and I'll come read as much as I can before 8:00. You'd better hustle if you want to read the whole book!"

By this time Heather has figured out that Mom means what she says. She still isn't entirely happy, but she gets ready as quickly as she can; she really does love reading with Mom.

After the story is finished, Mom tells Heather, "You didn't pick up your Barbies tonight. You can do it tomorrow before kindergarten or I'll do it and put them on the high shelf."

Heather and her mom have already agreed that toys go on the high shelf when Heather doesn't pick them up. Heather must show that she's ready to have them back by picking up her things for two days.

As children grow older, follow-through teaches more sophisticated skills. The difference between logical consequences and follow-through (and between follow-through with younger and increasingly older children) is that follow-through has more to do with what parents decide they will do instead of what they will "make" their children do.

For example, a parent may decide to go sit in the car for a while if a child is misbehaving. Dotty loved using follow-through because she always had a good novel with her. When her children misbehaved in the grocery store, she would kindly and firmly take them by the hand and walk to the car. Then she would sit in the car and calmly read her novel until they wound themselves down and said, "Okay, we'll behave."

She had discussed what would happen in advance with her children so they knew what she would do—and what they would need to do—before they could leave the car and continue their shopping. And Dotty was smart enough to shop for frozen foods last because she might have to leave the cart, full of groceries, with the manager while they sat in the car.

When the children misbehaved while they were driving, Dotty would pull over to the side of the road and whip out her novel to read until the children said, "Okay, we'll stop fighting."

As with all Positive Discipline methods, follow-through is effective only when the parent is kind *and* firm. When parents decide to go sit in the car for a while, they can say to their children, "Let me know when you are ready to go back and behave respectfully in the store." This is more effective if you have role-played the difference between respectful and disrespectful grocery store behavior. Parents may feel that *they* are the ones who suffer from sitting in the car, but fussing, fighting children, and angry stares in public places are no fun either. When your children learn that you will follow through with kind, firm action, such behavior usually diminishes. After all, it isn't nearly as much fun to push mom's buttons when she just settles down to enjoy a good book!

As children grow older, it is most effective to involve them in discussing the problem and brainstorming solutions. As we'll see later on, preschool classes can set rules and consequences in class meetings and teachers can follow through with firmness and kindness. Solutions don't always (or even usually) need to include consequences or follow-through. It is amazing how creative children can be when they are invited to use their considerable wisdom to solve problems—and how cooperative they can be when they feel listened to and taken seriously.

It is helpful to remember, however, that children simply don't have the same priorities adults do—they're usually perfectly content to have toys everywhere and bedtime whenever they like it. If you haven't discussed a problem or set a rule, it isn't fair to blame a child when he or she doesn't live up to your expectations. And honest mistakes should always be handled differently than willful misbehavior.

Remember that by the way you interact with your children, you will be teaching them mutual respect, dignity, and responsibility—gifts that will benefit them the rest of their lives.

Laughter Is the Best Medicine

Contrary to popular belief, it isn't permissive or sloppy parenting to have fun along the way. Sometimes the ability to laugh together, or to find a creative and funny solution to a problem, works better than all the other techniques put together. Humor can be a weapon if it's used to tease or humiliate children, but humor that allows parents and children to laugh and learn together will help create an atmosphere of warmth and openness in your home.

Beth was watering the petunias when she heard it: the sound she had grown to dread. Three-year-old Nathan had an unfortunate tendency to whine, and Beth was at her wit's end. She had tried talking, explaining, and ignoring, but nothing seemed to have any effect on Nathan, who continued to whine whenever he wanted something.

Beth turned, hose in hand, as her small son came toward her, and what happened next was probably more desperation than inspiration. As Nathan told her in his high-pitched voice that he wanted some juice, Beth turned off the water with a funny look on her face.

"Nathan," she said to the little boy, who was looking up at her with a perplexed expression, "something is wrong with Mommy's ears. When you whine, I can't hear you at all!"

Beth started toward the front door, with Nathan right behind her. Again Nathan whined for juice, but this time Beth only shook her head and tapped her ear, looking around as if a mosquito were buzzing near her head.

Nathan tried again, but again Beth only shook her head. By the time they reached the kitchen and Nathan opened his mouth to ask for juice, Beth heard something different. The little boy took a deep breath and said in a low, serious voice, "Mommy, can I have some juice?" When Beth turned to look at him, he added "please?" for good measure.

Beth laughed and scooped Nathan up for a hug before heading to the refrigerator. "I can hear you perfectly when you ask so nicely," she said.

From that time on, all Beth had to do when Nathan began to whine was tap her ear and shake her head. Nathan would draw an exasperated breath and begin again, in a nicer tone of voice.

It is amazing how many children who resist a direct order will respond with enthusiasm when that order becomes an invitation to play. Try telling your toddler, "I bet you can't pick up all your little cars before I count to ten," or "I bet Dad can brush his teeth and get into his pajamas before you can." Activities that might easily have become power struggles and battles can become opportunities for laughter and closeness if we use our instincts and our creativity.

Not everything can become a game, of course, nor should it; but rules become less difficult to follow when children know that a spontaneous tickling match or pillow battle might erupt at any moment. Taking time to enjoy your children works where discipline is concerned, too, and can make family life far more pleasant for everyone.

Going Too Far

It's a subject no one wants to look at. It's ugly and it's frightening, and it happens far too often in our homes and our communities. We're talking about child abuse and neglect. "I would never hurt my child," you may be saying. "Why talk about abuse in a book on positive discipline?"

Few parents *intend* to injure their children. Yet every year thousands of children are beaten, burned, molested, neglected, even killed—and the vast majority of those children are under the age of five.

Child abuse in all its forms—emotional, sexual, verbal, physical—is a complex subject with many contributing factors. Parents are often under stress, possess too few coping skills, or have unrealistic expectations of their children. And when we rely on spanking or other forms of physical punishment, it's dangerously easy to injure a small child, to shake an infant, to break a little bone.

All parents feel frustrated and overwhelmed occasionally. Some parents never experienced loving, effective parenting themselves and literally don't know what to do. It is important to get help if you feel you need it. Take a parenting class to learn better skills or get counseling to work through your own emotional problems. Take care of yourself (see Chapter 21). Learn to recognize your own "triggers" and deal with anger and frustration before they reach the boiling point. Talk to friends, a pastor, a teacher, or a counselor.

What should you do if you see someone else hurting or threatening a child? Most of us feel reluctant to "get involved," yet we could save the life or mental health of a child by doing so. There are things you can do that won't make the situation worse or direct the parent's hostility toward you. Distracting the parent's attention from the child without challenging or shaming is one effective way to intervene:

- **Sympathize with the parent.** Say something kind, like "I remember when my children were that age—they can be a real handful." Or, "Isn't it amazing how children think they can get their way by screaming?"
- **Offer to help.** If you know the parent, offer to watch the child for a while so he or she can take a break, get a drink of water, or calm down. Say, "You seem to be having a tough time. Is there anything I can do to help?"
- **Find something positive to say about the child.** Try, "Your little girl is beautiful" or "What wonderful blue eyes he has."

- **Take action if necessary.** If you feel the child's safety is in danger, speak to a store manager or other responsible person, or call your local Children's Protective Services. Such calls are kept confidential and anonymous in most states, and may offer a family an opportunity to get help and make changes they otherwise might not have had. If you know the struggling parent well enough, you may want to give him or her a copy of this book, or offer to go along to a parenting class. You may, in a very real way, be saving the life of a child. And because abusive patterns tend to repeat themselves through successive generations, you may change the lives of children you will never meet for the better.

Long-Term Parenting

Your own knowledge of your children's strengths and needs will help you guide and teach them. Remember the list of qualities you wanted your children to possess as adults? Each conversation, every crisis, every act of discipline should foster those qualities in them. And in order to do that, you have to know your child.

The best part of discipline is something you may never have thought of as discipline before. It's the time you spend together talking and playing and learning. Babies, toddlers, and preschoolers are learning every minute of every day; we can either consider those learning experiences a challenge, or we can join with our children in exploring their world, helping them to learn about life and their own capabilities by sharing experiences with them. Warmth and trust, closeness and understanding are tools of discipline, too. And with enough of these gentle tools, you may need the other sort far less often.

CHAPTER 16

"Don't Talk to Me in That Tone of Voice!": Feelings and the Art of Communication

Feelings can be such bewildering things. Take a moment sometime and watch a toddler or preschooler try to deal with frustration or anger. She may throw a toy across the room, stamp her foot, fall over backward in a tantrum, or collapse in a flood of tears. Or she may do all of the above, often within the span of a few minutes.

It is difficult enough for adults to cope with emotions, but for young children there is an added wrinkle: they haven't yet learned what feelings *are,* how to identify and talk about them, or what each one feels like, let alone how to cope with them in a controlled and effective manner. Communicating with young children means deciphering their nonverbal clues, understanding what they are feeling, and helping them to understand as well. Learning to recognize and deal with children's feelings is a vitally important step in handling children's behavior.

What Is a Feeling?

Just as they learn so many other things in life, children learn to cope with their feelings by watching their parents. And all too often, parents deal with difficult feelings either through emotional displays—dumping their stronger emotions on the people around them—or by squelching them entirely. The feelings we refuse to express don't go away, however; they simply go underground. And when they're finally released, the results are often far more damaging than if the feelings had been expressed early on.

Emotional displays and "squelching" give feelings a bad reputation, but the truth is that feelings themselves don't cause problems. Certain actions (or a failure to act at all) may cause problems. People often put feelings in the same category as emotional displays. A temper tantrum is an emotional display; acting depressed may be an emotional display. A feeling, though, is simply a feeling. And everyone, whatever his or her age, has feelings.

Feelings are our barometer, our way of keeping tuned in to how we're doing. Our feelings are intended to give us valuable information; in fact, some of them, like fear, help keep us safe and protect us from foolish actions. Paying attention to our feelings can help us decide what to do, or let us know that we need to make changes. We access useful information when we tune in to the deeper message our feelings have for us instead of squelching them or reacting to them.

It's important to help children deal with their feelings and to express them in ways that don't involve hurting themselves or others. Children (and adults) need to learn that feelings are different from actions. Feelings are always okay—they're never right or wrong. On the other hand, our actions—the ways we choose to express our feelings—might be either appropriate or inappropriate.

Many adults struggle with acknowledging and expressing their feelings. It often seems easier—or more "polite"—to simply repress feelings (although those feelings often leak out in the form of anger or depression). This mistaken pattern of denying feelings may then be passed on to children. How many times have you heard this exchange? An angry child says, "I hate my brother!" An adult responds, "No, you don't. You know you love your brother." It would be healthier to say to a child, "I can see how angry or hurt you feel right now. I can't let you kick your brother, but maybe we can find a way to help you feel better."

Young children often choose inappropriate ways to express their feelings, not because they're "bad" or malicious, but because they're still learning what to do with those tidal waves of emotion that wash over them. How can we teach children to accept and understand their feelings, and to express emotions in ways that will not only help them feel better, but teach them to use their feelings to help them find solutions to the problems they encounter in life?

Learning to Feel

Have you ever watched a mom or dad cradle an infant, gaze down into the baby's face, and coo words of love? What does it all mean to the baby? He can't understand the words—how does he learn to recognize the feeling?

Babies generally do not begin to understand the meanings of words until they are six or seven months of age. Long before that time, however, a baby will turn toward a familiar voice, smile into a parent's face, or reach with delight for favorite people. A bond of love and trust obviously exists, but how has an infant learned to respond to love with pleasure?

Babies and very young children read *nonverbal* signals and cues to learn about the world of feelings. While an infant may not understand all the complex meanings and concepts contained in the word "love," she *does* know the hands that touch and soothe her are gentle and caressing, mom or dad looks into her eyes and holds her attention, and the voice that coos and speaks to her is warm and soft. These things convey a feeling of "love" to a young child, and she responds with similar feelings and behavior.

Most young children remain acutely sensitive to nonverbal communication. In fact, the nonverbal signals we send our children are often far more powerful than our words.

For instance, three-year-old Kyle scampers into the kitchen where his mother, late for a meeting, is preparing dinner.

"Look, Mommy, look—I drew an airplane!" Kyle bubbles, waving his paper excitedly.

"That's great, sweetie. You're quite an artist," his harried mother replies quickly.

Mommy undoubtedly means well and there is certainly nothing wrong with her words; but Kyle notices that her hands never stop grating cheese for the casserole and her eyes never quite *look* at his airplane. What message has Kyle really received?

Five-year-old Wendy is helping Dad make lunch. Wendy's little brother is cranky, and Dad is trying to watch the football game on television while he makes the grilled cheese sandwiches. Wendy is valiantly pouring milk when the heavy carton slips from her grasp, sending a half-gallon of foamy liquid across the kitchen floor.

Wendy looks up timidly into her father's face. "I'm sorry, Daddy," she says. "Are you mad?"

Dad's eyebrows lower ominously, his jaw tightens, and when he speaks his voice is thin and tense. "No, I'm not mad," he says. When Wendy bursts into tears, he wonders why.

Ms. Santos is reading a nap-time story to her class of three-year-olds. She hasn't had a break because her replacement didn't show up and no substitute teacher is available. Little Allie looks at her teacher and asks, "Do you like this story?"

Ms. Santos looks at Allie in surprise and answers, "Yes, of course I do. Why?"

Allie answers, "Because your face is all wrinkled up and you look mad."

The Power of Nonverbal Communication

As our children grow and develop we need to be constantly aware of the messages we are sending them—and how frequently our words and our actions don't agree. A number of studies, for instance, have shown that saying "I love you" *isn't* the best way to communicate that important message to our children.

"Well then," you may wonder, "what *is* the best way?"

Saying the words often (and meaning them) is important, but that infant we began our chapter with has already experienced several more effective ways.

Eye contact. Try an experiment sometime. Stand back-to-back with someone and try to tell him about something that happened to you, or explain how you're feeling. If you're like most people, you'll find yourself wanting to crane your neck and turn around to look the other in the eye.

Eye contact signals attention. A good public speaker will catch the gaze of audience members, and by doing so, will involve them in what she is saying. In the same way, making eye contact with our children signals to them that they are important, captures their attention, and increases the effectiveness of our message.

Unfortunately, most of us reserve eye contact primarily for certain occasions. Can you guess what those are? Parents tend to make direct eye contact with their children most often when they are angry or lecturing them. We sometimes save our most powerful communication for our most negative messages.

Posture and position. If we want to make eye contact with our children, we are responsible for making it possible. Remember that without help, young children tend to look us right in the knees! If you want to communicate to your child, get down on her level. Kneel next to her, sit beside her on the sofa, or (as long as you hold on to her) set her on a counter where her eyes can meet yours comfortably. Now you can not only maintain eye contact while you speak to her, but you've eliminated the often overpowering difference in size and height. And watch out for the signals your posture sends: crossed arms or legs, for example, can indicate resistance or hostility. Your child will be quick to notice.

Susan was trying to coax her daughter, Michele, into sharing what was upsetting her.

Michele hesitated, then said, "I'm afraid you'll get mad at me."

Susan replied, "Honey, I promise I won't get mad. I care about you, and I want you to be able to tell me anything."

Michele thought for a moment, then looked up into her mother's face. "I'll tell you if you promise not to look at me with those tight lips you get when you're trying to pretend you aren't mad."

Poor Susan—she was trying hard to be unconditionally accepting and loving. Her daughter, however, was able to "read" the body language that betrayed her true feelings. When Susan's words and her expression match, Michele will feel far more comfortable sharing her problems with her mother.

Tone of voice.   Your tone of voice may be the most powerful nonverbal tool of all. Try saying a simple sentence, such as "I can't help you," emphasizing a different word each time. How does the meaning change? Even inoffensive phrases like "have a nice day" can become poisonous if we choose a particularly cold tone of voice. It is often the *way* we say something, rather than the words we use, that carries the message. Children are especially sensitive to these nonverbal communications.

Facial expression and touch.   When you're feeling particularly blue, does it help when a friend smiles and gives you a pat on the shoulder or a friendly hug? Why? The way we look and the way we use our hands can often communicate very effectively without a single word being spoken.

Tommy is curled up on the couch under a blanket, suffering from a bad case of the flu. Dad walks by, adjusts the blanket, and gently ruffles Tommy's hair. Has anything been communicated? Chances are Tommy knows without words that Dad cares about him, wants to help, and hopes he'll soon feel better.

Let's go back to where we started. How might you say "I love you" now? Imagine how powerful it might feel to your child if you knelt in front of him, looked him directly in the eye, smiled, and in your warmest tone of voice said, "I love you, honey." Now the words and the nonverbal cues match up, and a hug might be on the way! Nonverbal communication, which most of us take for granted, constantly teaches our children about communication, words, and the feelings that go with them.

The Art of Reflective Listening

Children, too, constantly send nonverbal messages. Their facial expressions, gestures, and behavior provide clues to vigilant adults about what they are feeling. An eighteen-month-old child cannot tell you, "I'm feeling tired, confused, and a bit frustrated that I can't reach the cookie jar"; he doesn't have the words to express such a complicated sequence of thoughts and feelings. What you might hear are wails and shrieks accompanied by a toy thrown to the ground, a crumpled-up face, and a small body collapsing on the floor.

A parent might react with understandable frustration of her own, possibly including harsh words. Or she can choose to help her child understand his feelings, give them a label that will help him to identify them in the future, and open the door to a way of dealing with the situation at hand.

Mom might respond, "Pumpkin, I can see that you feel angry because you can't reach the cookie jar. I feel angry when I can't do something, too. I'll bet we could figure out a way to solve this problem. What do you think?"

Once a child's feelings are validated and understood, he feels better and is more willing to work on solutions. In this instance, Mom helped her son figure out that he could push a chair over to the counter so he could reach the cookie jar. They also decided to fill the cookie jar with healthy snacks such as graham crackers or raisins so he could help himself any time.

Reflective (or "active") listening is another effective tool of communication that you possess, one that will serve you well as your children grow toward adolescence and adulthood. Reflective listening is the art of observing and listening to *feelings*, then reflecting them back. Reflective listening does not require that parents agree with their children, but it allows children to feel understood—something all people need—and provides an opportunity to explore and clarify those mysterious impulses known as feelings.

Four-year-old Chrissy ran through the front door, slamming it so forcefully that the pictures rattled on the wall, and promptly burst into tears.

"Tammy took my ball," she wailed. "I *hate* her!" Then Chrissy threw herself onto the sofa in a storm of tears.

Her mom, Diane, looked up from the bills she was paying. "You seem pretty angry, honey."

Chrissy pondered for a moment, sobbing fitfully. "Mom," she said plaintively, sniffling a little, "Tammy is bigger than me. It isn't fair for her to take away my stuff."

"It must be pretty frustrating to be picked on by a big girl, Chrissy," Diane said gently, still reflecting her daughter's feelings.

"Yeah. I feel bad," the little girl said firmly. She sat quietly for a moment, watching as Diane licked a few stamps. "Mom, can I go play out in the backyard?"

Diane gave her daughter a hug—and a great deal more. By responding with reflective listening, Diane refrained from lecturing, rescuing, or explaining, and allowed Chrissy the opportunity to explore what was going on for her. In the process, Chrissy discovered a solution to her own problem. Some other time, Diane might be able to talk with Chrissy about avoiding the problem in the future—and, perhaps, ask her what she could do to express her anger instead of slamming the door.

Diane also showed respect for her daughter's feelings. Parents often do not agree with (or completely understand) their children's emotions, but reflective listening does not require you to agree or completely understand. It invites children to feel heard and lets them know it's okay to feel whatever they feel. Validating a child's feelings with love and understanding opens the door for real communication and problem solving and works toward building a lifelong relationship of love and trust.

Pretend these statements are made by a child. How would you respond?

"No! I *won't* take a nap!"
"I want a bottle like the baby has."
"I hate going to the doctor."
"Nobody will let me play with them."

Parents can choose to respond with "adultisms" like "how come you never . . . ?" "when will you ever . . . ?" or "how many times do I have to tell you . . . ?" Or they can respond with reflective listening, which might sound something like this:

You look disappointed that you have to stop playing with your toys.
Sounds like you're feeling a little left out in all the fuss over your new baby sister. Is there more you can tell me?
Sometimes I feel a little afraid of going to the doctor, too.
You seem pretty sad at being ignored by the older kids.

These responses make no judgments and open the door for children to go further in exploring their feelings. Asking "is there more?" indicates a willingness to listen and may help a child discover deeper, buried feelings.

Like most adults, sometimes all children *really* need is for someone to listen and understand. Reflective listening will help your child learn about his own feelings (and the appropriate ways to express them) and will help you focus on what's really important.

What About Anger?
Dealing with Difficult Feelings

It is amazing how quickly some children learn that certain emotions aren't acceptable—that they must be softened somehow, or buried completely. Yet as we've already discovered, our feelings don't always go away on command; sometimes they linger in dark corners, waiting to erupt in a moment when our guard is down. It is generally better for parents *and* children to find acceptable, positive ways of dealing with feelings—even the difficult ones.

Young children often express anger in ways their parents find highly alarming: temper tantrums, throwing objects, yelling, hitting, kicking, even biting. (Biting is a common way for children who aren't yet verbally skilled to express anger or frustration.)

Does this mean parents should tolerate these behaviors as acceptable expressions of anger? Of course not. Actions that harm others are not acceptable ways of expressing feelings. Parents and teachers *can* make an effort to get into the young child's world and understand it; they can practice reflective listening to validate and clarify feelings; and they can then help children express their anger (which may be completely justified) in acceptable ways.

Mark was a bright and charming two-year-old. He was also about to become extremely angry. Mark, an explorer, had stumbled upon a bit of luck: his older brother, Luke, had gone outside to play and Luke's room—a veritable treasure trove of toys and other forbidden delights—was temporarily unguarded. Mark's dad was busy with a business phone call, and Mark dove headfirst into Luke's closet with a squeal of joy, emerging with a handful of toy action figures. He was busily investigating their anatomy by removing their arms and legs when Luke burst into the room. Not surprisingly, total chaos erupted.

The boys' father, Pete, heard the commotion, rushed into the room, and managed to separate the two combatants. "What's going on here?" he said.

"Mark got into my stuff," Luke said heatedly, snatching a toy from his little brother, "and he wrecked all my action guys." Luke gave Mark a hard shove, toppling the little boy over.

Mark searched his limited vocabulary for words to express his anger and disappointment and failed utterly. He looked at the one figure still in his possession and, with a thrust of his chin, pulled off its head and threw it at his big brother.

This brought a howl of rage from Luke and an exasperated sigh from their dad.

"Luke, can you wait here a moment? I need to talk to Mark, then I'll come back and we'll see what we can do about your toys."

Pete took Mark, now wailing in frustration, to his own room. He sat on Mark's bed, drawing a deep breath to help master his own annoyance, and waited a moment until he could speak calmly.

"Marky," he said gently, "I know it's fun to play with your brother's stuff. And I'm sure you felt disappointed when we took the figures away from you and angry when Luke pushed you."

Pete gently lifted his small son's chin so he could look into his eyes. "I can understand how you're feeling, but it's not okay

to break Luke's toys. I think he's feeling pretty angry, too."
Mark sniffled sullenly.

Pete thought for a moment, then smiled. "What do you
think T. Rex does when he's feeling angry?" he said, drawing
on Mark's love of dinosaurs.

Mark was intrigued, and momentarily distracted from the
lost action figures.

"He woars," the little boy said firmly.

"Can you roar like T. Rex?" his dad asked.

Mark blinked a bit at this unexpected question, then let
out a rather feeble roar.

"Oh, I think he'd roar louder than that," Pete said, "if he
was *really* mad."

Mark began to enter into the spirit of the game. He got
down on his knees, holding his arms up in front of him, and
emitted a truly frightening roar.

"That's right—now he sounds angry. I bet all the smaller
dinosaurs are running away."

Mark roared some more then suddenly began to giggle.
His smile faded a bit when Luke, wearing a quizzical expression, peered around the corner.

"You was mad, too, Luke," Mark said. "Wanta woar with
me?"

Luke wasn't ready to forgive Mark for his decapitated toy,
but he watched from the doorway then eventually came in to
sit on the bed beside his father.

When the rush of emotions had subsided and the boys felt
a little better, Pete approached solving the problem. He acknowledged Luke's grievance against his little brother, dealt
with the shove, discussed ways Mark could compensate his big
brother for the broken toys, helped the boys find ways to make
up to one another for their behavior, and helped them set limits
to prevent another raid on Luke's closet.

"Wait a moment," you may be thinking, "didn't Pete reward Mark for breaking his brother's toys? Shouldn't he have
been disciplined?"

It is tempting to respond to anger with anger—to join in the yelling, send kids off to a punitive time out, or otherwise try to "fix" the situation at hand. But these responses often escalate the conflict and destroy any opportunity there might have been to teach, to understand, or to find a workable solution to the problem. By reflecting Mark's feelings and helping him to express them in a way that didn't harm himself or his brother, Pete taught his boys that anger in itself isn't wrong, but shoving or destroying toys *is*. And when the boys felt understood and could sort out their feelings, the door was opened to preventing similar occurrences in the future.

Dealing with children's strong emotions can be a great opportunity to get into a child's world and to build closeness, understanding, and trust. Here are a few other ways you might help a young child explore and express strong emotions:

Invite the child to draw a picture of how the emotion feels. Does it have a color? A sound?

Ask the child to talk through rather than act out what he or she is feeling. If the child is too young to possess the verbal skills to do this, you might try asking simple "yes" or "no" questions about the feelings. Children usually understand a great deal more than they can actually *say*.

Redirect the behavior in a more appropriate way, as Pete did with Mark. You might purchase a "bop bag" that a child can punch when angry (it helps to stay nearby to talk through those strong feelings as your child expresses them). Some preschools have an "anger box," a knee-high cardboard box where an angry child can go to stand, jump, or yell when upset. Sometimes the teachers use it, too! Screaming into a pillow, running a race around the playground, or playing with water or Play-Doh can also help vent emotions and restore calm.

Invite the child to take a cooling-off "time out" period before acting on his or her strong emotions.

Anger isn't the only difficult emotion young children must learn to deal with. By practicing reflective listening, taking time to understand, and using some of the ideas above, adults can also help children deal honestly with jealousy, fear, sadness, and the other emotions that are a part of our human existence.

Preschools can have a "time out corner" where children can go when anger or other strong emotions threaten the peace, or a "cool-off basket" filled with soothing items such as a koosh ball or silky soft stuffed toys. These items are calming and have sensory characteristics that help a child regain his equilibrium.

Conflicts have a way of escalating quickly when many small children are involved. Teachers may find it helpful to practice ways of defusing anger or to allow groups of children to play "let's pretend" about what can happen when they feel angry. Talking *in advance* about what to do when we feel upset can give everyone—children and teachers alike—a plan to follow when strong feelings erupt.

Practicing Emotional Honesty

Parents (and teachers) often wonder how much of their own feelings they should share with children. It can help to remember that, as with so many things in life, children learn best by watching their adult role models. If you deal with anger by yelling, you shouldn't be surprised if the young ones in your life do, too. If, on the other hand, you can find positive ways of expressing your own feelings, you will not only reduce the chance of conflict, you will provide children with a wonderful example of how to deal with feelings appropriately.

As you have probably already discovered, sharing your world with a young child can stimulate all sorts of interesting emotions in you. In the course of a single day, a parent or teacher can feel love, warmth, frustration, anger, irritation, weariness, hope, and despair (see Chapter 21 for hints on taking care of yourself). Children are amazingly sensitive to the emotional state of those around them; their innate "antenna" and ability to read nonverbal cues often let them know what we're feeling even when we think we're acting "normal." (For instance, have you ever noticed what happens when you're feeling tense and stressed, and you pick up an infant?) So, how should adults explain and express their feelings to children?

Emotional honesty is often the best policy. It is not only okay, it may be real wisdom to tell a child, "I'm feeling really angry right now." Blaming or shaming statements aren't necessary; simply explaining to your children what you're feeling and why can help you deal with your own feelings and teach your children about possible results of their behavior. Remember, too, that children often assume that whatever you're feeling is about them. Explaining your feelings and the reasons for them may save you and your children a great deal of misunderstanding and confusion.

One helpful way of expressing feelings is by using "I statements." An "I statement" is a simple formula (formulas come in handy when we're too emotional to think straight) that allows us to explain what we're feeling and why.

An "I statement" might look something like this:

"I feel worried when you throw blocks in the playroom because one of the other children might get hurt. Perhaps you should have a 'time out' until you feel better."

"I feel angry when you dump your cereal on the floor because I'm tired and I don't want to clean up the mess. If you dump your cereal on the floor again, I'll know you've decided not to eat, and you can help me clean it up."

"I feel upset and frustrated because the car has a flat tire, and now I'm going to be late to work."

"I'm so angry right now that I need some time out until I can feel better, so I don't do something I'll regret later."

Parents and teachers can also practice separating children from their behavior, reassuring children about their place in our affections and encouraging their efforts to understand their world while still telling them that certain behaviors or actions are not acceptable.

For example:

"I love you *and* I can't allow you to kick me when you're angry."

"I glad you want to learn about the kitchen *and* you can't melt your crayons on the stove."

"I appreciate your help *and* you're not quite old enough to fix the vacuum cleaner."

How Much Honesty Is Too Much?

Adults often want to shield children from sadness, loss, and the other unpleasant realities of life, but it is usually best to be as honest with your children as you *reasonably* can be. As we've mentioned before, children's emotional "antennas" usually let them know when something in the family is amiss, and without enough information, they may assume they have done something wrong. Children shouldn't be asked to shoulder burdens too heavy for them or to take responsibility for their parents' problems; they should be given an opportunity to understand and share in whatever is going on. This draws children into the family circle and helps build in them a sense of belonging.

If a family member or loved pet has died, for example, it is best to include children and to provide them with information that will help them make sense of what has happened. It is tempting to tell a young child that Grandpa is "sleeping" or has "gone away," but that may lead a child to fear going to bed, or wonder whether Mom or Dad will also "go away" the next time they're out of sight.

Death can be explained in simple but honest terms and children can be helped to grieve, and to heal. You might choose to tell a child that when we die, we go to another, special place that some people call "heaven." Just as we can't see someone who is in another city, we can't see someone who has gone to heaven. Remember that it isn't necessary to tell children more than they can comprehend. You may want to explain that many adults also have difficulty understanding death and have different beliefs about what it means, and what happens after. Including children in the rituals surrounding death, such as funerals, may actually be less frightening for them than being left out. Death is part of the cycle of life; treating it as such will make coping with death easier for parents and children alike.

In the same way, if the family is undergoing financial strain or other stresses, parents can give children simple facts to help them understand, and then use reflective listening to explore and deal with their feelings. Be aware that children will have strong feelings and reactions to traumatic events in the family, such as divorce, and it is unwise to simply assume that they'll be "fine."

Take time to explain, without blaming or judging, what has happened and how it will affect your child. Be sure she knows that it wasn't her fault and that she is still loved and cherished. And stay tuned in; use reflective listening to check your child's perceptions and allow her to express her fears and feelings openly. (For more information on helping children cope with death or divorce, see *Positive Discipline for Single Parents*.) By including young children in the life of the family, parents help them learn about feelings and what it means to be human.

By exploring and respecting your children's feelings and by being honest about your own, you will build communication and problem-solving skills that will last a lifetime.

A Word About "Blankies" and Other Security Objects

Closely tied to a child's feelings of trust and security is one accessory of young childhood that has passed into folklore: the security blanket. Linus, in the cartoon strip "Peanuts," carries his everywhere, even using it to zap his obnoxious older sister. Children the world over rely on scraps of blanket, favorite stuffed animals, or imaginary friends to help them feel secure—and parents the world over often wonder if it's healthy to allow them to do so.

With a little thought, it's easy to understand how intimidating a place this world of ours can be to a very young child. A child's attachment to his "blankie" can be very strong; it often has its own feel and taste, and a child can usually tell if an attempt is made to replace or switch the favorite object. Many parents have had the alarming experience of leaving a teddy or "blankie" at the grocery store or in a motel, then having to make an emergency return trip with a hysterical child.

Feelings of insecurity and fear, while they can be upsetting for parents, are like all other emotions: they are just feelings and can be handled with reflective listening, warmth, and understanding. If sleeping with a special blanket or a stuffed animal helps a child relax and feel cozy, is there truly any harm?

Some children never adopt a "blankie" or stuffed animal, preferring instead to suck on their thumbs or on a pacifier. Pacifiers can be a wonderful way to help an infant satisfy her need to suck and can provide security (and peace) during times of upset or stress. In fact, children who appear to have given up their thumb or pacifier often resume the habit if the family moves, if they change preschools, or if there is some other upheaval in their lives. Most parents eventually wonder if thumbsucking or using a pacifier is wise, especially as a child grows older, but the problem is more the adult's attitude than the child's well-being. If you have concerns about sucking needs, especially where teeth and orthodontia are concerned, you may be able to put your fears at rest by talking to a pediatric dentist. As a general rule, the less fuss adults make, the sooner the issue tends to be resolved. As they grow older, children often are willing to restrict use of their security objects to bedtime or naptime, especially if they have experienced understanding and acceptance from their parents. Most children, left to themselves, eventually give up their "blankies" or pacifiers of their own free will, usually by the age of six. It is amazing how many parents who lamented their child's attachment to a blanket keep a small scrap as a memento long after their child has abandoned it!

Language Skills and Communication

It can be frustrating to try to communicate with and understand a young child who can't yet express his feelings and ideas—and it must be frustrating to *be* that child as well! Like most other developmental skills, the acquisition of language takes place at different rates for different children, and how comfortable your children are with using words will affect the way they behave and express their feelings.

As we've already mentioned, biting in young children is often an expression of frustration that can't be vented any other way. A child may be subconsciously thinking, "If I can't use my mouth to speak, I'll use it to communicate another way!"

Biting that occurs for this reason will diminish as a child learns the verbal skills to express his feelings in more appropriate ways. Helping your child to express himself verbally, providing carrot sticks to chew when frustration threatens, or holding a child's chin gently when he appears ready to bite may help resolve the problem. And no, biting the child back, washing out the mouth with soap, or placing Tabasco sauce on the tongue *doesn't* help; such responses are far more likely to escalate conflict than resolve it and may become abusive. If a child continues to bite after the age of three, it may be helpful to get a speech and hearing evaluation to ensure that language skills are developing appropriately.

Most parents eagerly await their children's first words, sharing them with friends and family and recording them for posterity in baby books and journals. We smile over their innocent mispronunciations and other manglings of the language, and rejoice when they can make themselves understood consistently.

By the age of seven or eight months, most babies understand the meanings of a few words. By three years of age, most children *understand* ordinary, conversational language, although they may not be able to produce it themselves. Children often understand five or six words by the age of one year, but they they may not *say* five or six words until they are two years old, despite endless coaching from mom and dad.[1] If your child seems alert and responds well to you, chances are that all is well, even if she hasn't got much to say—yet!

It is worth knowing that children learn language best by being spoken to often. And sharing books with your children is a wonderful way to not only learn language, but to build warmth and closeness, and to develop a love of reading that may last your child a lifetime. Even babies can be propped in your lap to look at a brightly colored "board book" (the kind with relatively indestructible cardboard pages). Point to the objects and name them, label colors, and talk about feelings. Your child will be learning simply by the sound of your voice.

Barbara was thirteen months old when her favorite aunt sat down to read a book about flowers with her. Barbara gazed intently at the picture, pulled the book into her hands, and put

---

1. White, Burton. *The First Three Years of Life*. New York: Fireside (Simon & Schuster), 1993, p. 231.

her nose against the page for a long sniff. Her aunt was amazed at this demonstration of just how well Barbara understood the connection between the printed page and the real object it represented.

As your child grows older, share with her the books you loved or check with friends for titles their children have enjoyed. Make reading together, a chapter or two a night, part of your bedtime routine. Many parents find that this cozy ritual lasts far beyond toddlerhood and provides a time of warmth and closeness for years to come.

It is also worth knowing that children do *not* learn language by being propped in front of the television, no matter how much time they spend there. *Sesame Street* and *Barney* are wonderful entertainment and may be valuable educational tools, but they are no substitute for real human contact. Children will learn best—and respond most—to conversation that includes and involves them, especially when it contains lots of eye contact and love.

It often seems that the first word many children learn is "why?"—or its cousin, "how come?" It can be frustrating to be endlessly bombarded by the questions of a curious three-year-old (or an entire roomful, if you're a preschool teacher), but do try to be patient. Thoughtful answers to questions teach children more than simple facts; they teach that the world is a wonderful place to explore, and that adults can be trusted as guides and teachers.

It's Never Too Soon to Begin

"My parents just don't understand me."

"I want to talk to my kid about sex and drugs, but I don't know how."

"I worry that my teenagers are getting into trouble, but they don't seem to trust me . . . I just don't get it."

"I would never tell my parents what my friends and I do—
   they'd only lose it. We just never talk at all."

Many teenagers—and many parents of teenagers—wish
things could be different, wish they could understand and trust
each other enough to talk openly about the choices and issues
that face them. Yet regardless of how much they may love one
another, they simply can't *talk*. They can't trust each other;
they don't understand each other. While it's never too late to
change, it certainly is harder the longer you wait.

If you're fortunate enough to be the parent of a young
child, you have a golden opportunity. The best time to begin
building a relationship of trust and openness isn't after your
children have become adolescents and you suddenly realize you
need to be able to talk; the time is *now*, while they're young.
Time spent talking to your children, listening to their day-
dreams and thoughts and feelings, teaching them about life,
and simply being human together is an investment in the future
you will never regret.

Pay attention to their feelings and help them to understand and express them; teach them to respect and understand
yours. Take time to solve problems together, to learn, and to
grow; discover together that being a family means making an
occasional mistake, but it also means learning to value and respect the worth and uniqueness of each member.

If you are a preschool teacher, remember that the time
your young students spend with you can shape the way they
view their world—you truly do touch the future when you
teach young ones. For parents and teachers alike, taking the
time to understand feelings and to express them in positive
ways will help you build relationships where love and trust can
flourish.

CHAPTER 17

Your Child and Child Care: What You Should Know

Your husband has two more years of graduate school to finish. You have just discovered that an unexpected baby is on the way. The income your family is living on is yours . . .

You have two children. The oldest is four and the youngest is eighteen months old. Your marriage just ended in divorce and you are unwilling to give up a career that provides stimulation as well as a good paycheck.

You are the director of research, midway through a ten-year project. If your research produces the results you expect, it may mean a cure for a type of cancer that has been considered hopeless. You just turned thirty-four, and you and your husband have decided that you can wait no longer to begin your own family . . .

Your neighborhood has no children. Your daughter is three now; she is lonely and wants playmates. You do not want her to watch television half of the day. A preschool has opened on the next block, but you're not sure if it's the best thing for your child . . .

You were such a devoted parent that you didn't leave your first baby until he was six months old. Then you left him with a sitter

for only two hours and called at least twice to make sure everything was all right. The baby slept soundly the entire time, but
you're still not comfortable leaving him . . .

These stories and their variations are endless. Whatever the
underlying issues, the reality is that many parents work and
many children are in child care or preschool. And leaving a
young child in someone else's care can be agonizing for parents. Most wrestle at least occasionally with guilt and doubts:
"Am I being a neglectful parent if I don't stay home with my
child?" "I don't have a choice—I have to work—but will my
child be scarred for life? Or will it be good for my child to experience a good preschool or daycare center?" And perhaps most
important of all, "How do I find quality child care?"

Once a decision is made, there are still feelings of sadness
and anxiety about leaving a child in any kind of child care
arrangement. Several things may help. The first step is to recognize that this is a necessary choice for you and your child.
When a parent can accept the need for (or see the value of)
child care in the life of the family, other concerns begin to fall
into place.

The next step is to deal with the many questions you may
have about handling the details of daily life when child care is
part of your family's routine. "How can I handle leaving my
child in the morning?" "What about pick-up time in the
evening? How do our home routines change or alter when we
are away from our child all day?" "What about my child's
friends?" "Will my child be safe?" "Will my child be loved and
feel loved?" "What can we do to make it all work?" Many of
these questions will be resolved once you feel confident that
you have selected a quality child care situation. In this chapter
we will discuss criteria you can use to evaluate the child care
you are considering or have selected.

One of the most important criteria is to find a center or
home that welcomes parents any time. These centers have
nothing to hide and will treat you as a respected partner in your

child's care. If you feel like an intruder when you visit your child's preschool, child care center, or licensed home, find another where you feel welcome.

The New Extended Family

Child care today often takes the place of the extended family of aunts, uncles, grandparents, and cousins that past generations grew up with. These days there may be no sister or cousin to compare notes with when Mary pulls a neighbor's hair or Jeff wakes up with a fever in the middle of the night. Parents need other adults as their own support system when raising a child. Today's child care center should be such a resource. It is a place to meet other parents, share concerns, and learn from one another.

Your child's caregivers should be knowledgeable and ready to answer your questions. In truth, a quality child care center needs to be a place for *families,* not just for young children.

Parents can work with centers to sponsor parenting classes, speakers, and parenting groups. Most parents have similar concerns and are reassured to simply know that other children behave in some of the same ways.

Today, for instance, Steve felt at his wit's end. He had been working overtime, his wife was out of town with their older son (at her sister's wedding), and it was all he could do to get three-year-old Rebecca up and ready for child care. And when he rushed in the door at the center, he realized that he had forgotten to pack Rebecca a lunch.

Mrs. Ball, the caregiver, came over to greet Rebecca. She noticed Steve's harried look and gave him her full attention as he told her how overwhelming the week had been. "And," he added sheepishly, "I forgot Rebecca's lunch today."

Mrs. Ball reassured him that what he was doing was very stressful and his feelings were understandable; she also offered to give Rebecca some crackers and peanut butter, milk, and fruit for lunch.

A child care center or preschool should be part of a family's support system. Sometimes having another adult there to listen means everything to a frazzled parent. Maybe things aren't like the "old days," but there are lots of ways that today's realities can be turned into opportunities. A good preschool can actually enhance life for you and your children.

There is a saying that "it takes a village to raise a child." Make your child care part of that village. Empower yourself to find quality care, or make it happen through your efforts to improve and enhance what is available.

Separation

Parents often feel not only sad but guilty when they leave their children in child care. (Working parents, please do not claim all the guilt for yourselves! The opportunities to feel inadequate and torn by separation from children are many and varied. Every parent experiences some degree of pain.)

Although the children are doing the crying in the morning at child care, the most important aspect of dealing with those tears is how *parents* handle the separation. The parent who, though sad, believes that her child will be well cared for and secure while she is absent communicates that confidence to her child. It is well worth the investment of time to get to know the adults who will be caring for your child and to have a clear picture of what your child's day will be like.

Choosing a Child Care Center

It is extremely important not to "bargain hunt" for a child care facility. Although cost must be considered, it should not be the

most important factor in your decision. Many extremely important hours of your child's life will be spent in the child care that
you choose.

Simply put, find the best care possible. If quality care is
unavailable, make what you find into quality care by putting the
caregivers in touch with information such as *Positive Discipline
for Preschoolers*. Actively work to bring training to your area if it
is lacking. First, though, it may help to know what a good child
care facility *is*.

The Environment

Is the space where your child will be spending her time clean
and well-maintained? Look for toys and equipment placed at
the child's eye level, easily accessible. There should be places to
climb safely and that encourage movement. A room designed
for infants should have child-safe, unbreakable mirrors at the
floor level, as well as rails or small, sturdy furniture that a child
can use to pull herself up as she learns to walk. Balls and rolling
toys on the floor will help your child with eye-hand coordina-
tion and encourage him to move and crawl.

Whenever possible, there should be child-sized equipment. Small pitchers, drinking cups, and tables and chairs are
very helpful for young children. If child-size items aren't available, then some adaptation of adult-size equipment will help.
An example would be to make sinks or toilets more accessible
by providing sturdy step stools.

Safety

Find out the local requirements for licensing by health and
fire authorities, then find out if the center has met those requirements. Is the center's license current? Check for safety
yourself, just as you would in your own home. Are electrical
outlets protected? Do cords hang within children's reach? Are

cooking surfaces or pan handles dangerously available to little hands?

The National Association for the Education of Young Children (NAEYC) has developed a very thorough accreditation system for early childhood programs across the country. Ask if the center has been accredited by NAEYC, and if so, when. (Accreditation must be renewed every two years.) Other sources of accreditation are also available. Try to educate yourself on the standards in your area. If those standards are insufficient, work to see that some form of licensing or accreditation is brought to your area. You will be helping many children as well as your own.

Nutrition

What will your child eat each day? A child in a full-day program will consume most of her daily food intake in your absence. It is very important to know what types of food will be offered to your child. Some programs will have you bring in your own food. If this is not the case, look for a daily menu or other listing that tells what your child will be offered to eat. Most licensing programs require that centers meet certain nutritional requirements.

Be aware of the regular dietary practices at your child's center. It may help you at home to know that your child has tried various foods—and you can encourage him by serving those foods at home as well.

Training and Continuity

Caregivers must deal with many demands on their time and a fair amount of stress. (If you doubt that for an instant, volunteer to help out for a day!) It helps to ascertain what kind of training the staff has. Are they experienced? How long have staff members been employed at this center? The longer staff stay in a center, the more stable the care given to your child is likely to be. Staff longevity indicates a center that is being run well. If it is a pleasant place for adults, it is more likely to be pleasant for children as well.

Are there regularly scheduled staff meetings? How often? (Once a month should be a minimum). What kind of ongoing training is the staff receiving? Parents might offer to raise funds for scholarship money to send caregivers to special training. Gifts of books and training tapes to a center are usually welcomed. Both are effective ways for parents to improve the quality of the care their child will receive.

The more the home and child care center work as a team, the better care your child will experience. Your peace of mind depends upon the trust you feel in the people who are with your child throughout the day.

Discipline

This is a big one! How will your child be treated? Is there a great deal of time spent dealing with misbehaving children? In addition to how the children are being treated, the level of misbehavior can tell you how well the children's needs for belonging and significance are being met. If spanking is allowed, yelling by the adults seems common, orders are frequently shouted at children, or time out is used in a humiliating, punitive way, don't stay there!

Mrs. Adams was visiting a child care center and noticed that in the hour she spent there, the staff always remained standing while speaking with the children. The children had to crane their necks to see the caregiver's face or address their remarks to kneecaps. Imagine how little and unimportant you might feel if you could never look into another person's eyes when you spoke! Find a place where caregivers know how to get down to the children's level when talking with them.

What type of atmosphere do you sense when you visit? Happy, peaceful children are a good sign. (Please note: that doesn't necessarily mean *quiet* children!) The level of activity should indicate that the children are involved in and enjoying whatever they are doing.

The Child Care Day

Your daily routines will be influenced and altered by the schedule, commute, and details of your child's care. Some families will have to include food preparation time if they must bring in all or part of their child's food. Getting dressed and out of the house, coping with nap time, establishing departure routines, and keeping up with your child's budding and shifting friendships are all common issues that overtake the whole family.

Even the most effective and smoothly functioning lifestyle can be derailed by a two-week bout with the chicken pox! Remember that everyone has a bad day now and then, and how smoothly your day goes depends on many different elements. These include the mood and condition of parents or a parent, a child or children, other children not your own, caregivers, traffic, and maybe even whether anyone remembered to put the milk back in the fridge the night before. With so many opportunities for disaster, make it a daily habit to celebrate what goes right.

It can be difficult to remember in the midst of rushing out the door, but even though two-year-old Nick insisted on wearing one purple sock and one orange sock and five-year-old Susan dropped the jar of honey on the kitchen floor, *do* take a moment to rejoice in the fact that Nick dressed himself at all and that Susan was helping set out breakfast things without being asked. There will always be imperfections: use your energy to focus on the daily victories.

Morning Hassles

Routines are critical for getting out of the house in the morning. We've discussed children's differing perceptions about time. We also discussed the process versus product thinking that prevails in early childhood. These traits sometimes work against a smoothly flowing morning. What *will* work in your favor with young children is their attachment to routines. They love to have the events in their lives predictable. Establishing clear routines for getting the little ones to child care can prove to be the difference between a calm or a hectic morning.

The Jasper family has four members. Dad has to be at work by 8:30 A.M., Mom begins work at 9:00 A.M., and their twin daughters, who are three years old, must be taken to child care. Since they only have one car, the family commutes together and both parents deliver the girls to child care each morning. They have found several things that work well for them.

Each evening the twins help pick out the clothes they will wear the next day. The family discovered that this wasn't quite enough for Amy, because she hated to take off her warm nightgown in the chilly mornings. After a number of frustrating mornings, Amy and her mom agreed that Amy could sleep in the shirt she would wear the next morning. This satisfied Amy; she was willing to get up and dress since she already had on a warm T-shirt.

The next part of the routine involved lunches. Since the child care did not provide lunches, either Mom or Dad would pack them the night before, with occasional "help" from the twins. (At a family meeting they had agreed that Mom and Dad would alternate weekly the jobs of packing lunches and helping the twins lay out their clothes and take baths.) Whoever packed the lunches also made sure that all coats and shoes had been located and were laid out near the door so there would be no last-minute panic over missing items.

Advanced planning and preparation the night before eliminated a lot of decisions (and opportunities to get into struggles) in the morning; the established routines kept things running smoothly. Some mornings Dad would begin breakfast and give everyone wake-up calls while Mom showered, then he would shower while she finished preparing breakfast. They would trade duties on alternate mornings.

The twins knew that they had to be dressed before they could have breakfast. Mom or Dad was available to help with difficult buttons or shoe tying, but the girls usually did a good job of getting their clothes on each morning. Both Mom and Dad had begun training and encouraging their daughters' efforts at dressing themselves when the twins were two years old.

Amy liked to pour the milk each morning. Her parents kept a small pitcher in the refrigerator that she could manage. (There was a sponge by the sink that the girls had been trained to use when the occasional spill occurred.) Both Angie and Amy were given things to do each morning to help with breakfast. Setting out napkins, putting salt and pepper on the table, and mixing the juice were among the jobs they could do. Angie and Amy felt good about the contributions they made each day. While the twins helped one parent clear up the breakfast things, the other got the car out and everyone's gear loaded up. Then, relaxed and smiling, out the door they went.

Does this sound like a fairy tale? Yes and no. It *is* possible to set up careful routines and achieve this kind of morning harmony. It did *not* happen overnight. First Mom and Dad hassled with each other over who should be doing what each morning. When they finally worked things out, they clearly understood each other's expectations and weren't spending lots of energy bickering.

Then Amy and Angie had to conduct a few tests to see if their parents really meant that they had to be dressed before they could come to breakfast. This meant that once or twice Amy and Angie did not have time to eat before leaving in the morning. Their parents knew that they could survive an hour or two until morning snack.

It also meant that on at least one occasion, one or both of the twins arrived at their child care in pajamas with Mom or Dad carrying a paper bag of clothing. Amy and Angie's parents did not mistreat their daughters; they gave them the opportunity to become responsible in ways that were respectful by learning from the results of their own choices. It also meant that Angie and Amy soon believed that their parents meant what they said, and both girls peacefully participated in the morning routines.

Usually the result was a hassle-free morning routine in the Jasper household. Notice the word "usually." There was not always a smooth beginning to the day. Sometimes Mom or Dad overslept and got a late start, or was just plain grouchy in the morning. Other times, no amount of routine would get Amy into her clothes. They learned to celebrate improvement instead of looking for perfection.

Another family, Susan and her son Jeffrey, also devised a working morning routine. Susan and Jeffrey had the additional stress of a bus to catch. Susan was enrolled in the community college, so missing a bus could mean missing a class, which would hurt her final grade. Jeffrey was four years old and attended a child care about three blocks from his mother's college.

Susan and Jeffrey also began their routine the night before. Jeffrey was in charge of picking out his clothes. Because the child care provided meals, Susan had only her own lunch to pack. She took the extra precautions of stacking the things she needed the next morning in a box by the back door; she also checked to be sure she had change for the bus and a change of clothes for Jeffrey so there would be no last-minute panic looking for missing items in the morning.

After tucking Jeffrey in at night, Susan still had studying to do. Jeffrey had had to learn that there were limits to their bedtime preparations. In the summer, when school was out, Susan worked on establishing a clear and consistent bedtime routine. Jeffrey then knew what to expect at bedtime and everything went smoothly.

In the morning Jeffrey also had to get dressed before breakfast and do the job of setting out bowls for cereal as his mother finished dressing. They had to be at the bus stop by 8:05, so at 7:30 Susan set the stove timer to buzz in twenty minutes. When it went off, Jeffrey and Susan knew it was time to gather their things and head to the bus stop. This left only about five minutes for last minute emergencies such as an urgent trip to the toilet or changing the shirt that got milk spilled on it.

Although their morning is hectic, Jeffrey is learning that he is an important part of a team. Because he and Mom have worked out these details at their family meetings, he feels involved and willing to help in the morning. When problems arise, the two work out new solutions. Once, when Jeffrey complained that he was sick of cereal, they agreed to make time for scrambled eggs once each week, but that would mean getting up ten minutes earlier and Jeffrey would help scramble the eggs. Instead of feeling deprived or burdened, Susan communicated to Jeffrey how much she loves him and made him feel valuable and capable.

No morning routine works perfectly all the time. With training, thoughtful planning, and respect—both for one another and for agreed-upon rules—mornings can proceed much more smoothly—at least most of the time!

Arrival

No matter what happened before you got there, the moment arrives when you and your child are at the child care center. Some things will help both of you to feel better about the day ahead. Take a moment to look around the center with your child. Find out what the teacher is planning for the day. Prepare your child if you find out there is a substitute; meet the substitute and make sure you introduce your child to any new person she will be with that day.

Notice any changes in the environment. If a new toy or climber is out, explore it with your child. Sometimes you may have time to read a story or do a puzzle with your child before you leave. If time does not allow that, ask him what he will play with when you leave. This will allow you to feel more con- nected, and you and your child can visualize what he will be doing after you have gone.

When it is time to leave, *go* (dragging out the farewell leaves you, your child, and the caregiver emotionally drained), but never just disappear. Tell your child that you are leaving. Tears may follow your announcement, but if you are respectful and honest, your child will learn that she can trust you. If your child clings to you, gently hand her into the caregiver's arms so that she can be held and comforted as you leave. It helps to have a special place for children to stand or be held to wave to parents as they leave.

Even when parents leave in a respectful and loving way, children may still cry. The important thing to remember is that your child will learn that she can trust the adults in her life. This is reaffirmed every day by the fact that you do, in fact, return. Eventually the tears will disappear and the routine of morning departure for parents and children will be smooth and happy. (If you feel the need, call the center mid-morning to reassure yourself that the tears were brief and all is going smoothly. Your peace of mind will be worth it.)

Departure/Evening Pick-up Time

When you arrive to take your child home, allow time for a friendly greeting and a bit of reentry. You are both about to begin a new segment of your day.

When Mrs. White arrives at closing to take her three-year- old daughter Anna home, she finds her playing with some dress-up clothes. Mrs. White gives Anna a hug and comments solemnly on the orange wig and flowered purse that Anna has chosen. Mrs. White then tells Anna that she may play for five more minutes.

During that time Mrs. White gathers the notes about Anna's day that have been left by the morning teacher. She also signs up to bring a casserole to next week's potluck. When she returns to the dress-up area, Anna is still wearing the orange wig. Mrs. White comments on how much Anna must enjoy that wig; perhaps she will be able to wear it again tomorrow. She then tells Anna that it is time to leave. Anna reluctantly leaves her toys and takes her mother's hand. Anna gets her coat and together they hunt down her missing shoe. Mrs. White signs Anna out for the day and mother and daughter leave the center together. Mrs. White feels comforted that her daughter is so happy at her preschool that she doesn't want to leave.

By taking time to reconnect with her daughter and giving Anna time to conclude her play, Mrs. Smith has set the stage for a calm departure. Anna may fuss anyway—after all, she was having a lot of fun—but she is likely to fuss less than a child who is dragged away from her play.

The school staff has contributed to a smooth departure by taking time half an hour before departure to have the children find everything they need to go home—coats, lunch boxes, art projects, notices for parents about an upcoming potluck. In spite of all this preparation some children may not be as cheerful as Anna when their parents arrive to pick them up.

There is a good reason for children to be fussy at the end of their day. An important element of child care is that young children must cope with a highly social environment all day. That means that a certain amount of tension and stress may have built up in your child. When a child falls apart at her parent's arrival, it may be her way of saying that you are the person she can trust to love and accept her, no matter what side of herself she shows to you. Social expectations can be relaxed in the warmth of a parent's arrival.

A major transition in a child's day takes place when he is about to leave the child care setting and young children need some gentleness to get them through this transition. Devoting

time to him and his needs at this moment will ultimately benefit
you both.

Family Support

Whether your child stays at home with you or goes to child
care, the type of child care that is available will affect you both.
In truth, child care affects everyone, either directly or indirectly.
The environment and the teachers who work with your children help shape their future—and the future of our society.
Quality care is a must. Child care centers should be safe, pleasant, nurturing places for children to be.

CHAPTER 18

Class Meetings
for Preschoolers

It is time for a class meeting at the ABC Preschool. As the group of youngsters settles into their seats, Mr. Scott, the teacher, begins.

"It sounds like we've had a problem on the playground with people throwing wood chips at one another. Does anyone have something to say about this problem, or can someone offer a suggestion of how we might solve it?"

Five-year-old Girard raises his hand. "Whoever throws wood chips could take a time out!" Four-year-old Natalie waves her hand, and when called upon, offers, "We could not have wood chips anymore and have grass instead."

The teacher looks toward two-and-a-half-year-old Cristina, whose little hand has been patiently held aloft and calls on her. "Guess what?" Cristina says with a bright smile.

"What, Cristina?" Mr. Scott asks.

"I had bananas in my cereal today."

"Mmmm, that must have tasted good." Mr. Scott smiles and thanks Cristina for her comment, then asks for more suggestions about the wood chip problem. Although Cristina was clearly not thinking about wood chips, she was still a valued member of the group. When children are old enough to participate actively in group or circle time activities (usually around the age of two and a half), they are ready for class meetings.

What Is a Class Meeting?

Class meetings are far more than group problem-solving sessions. In a class meeting, children gather on a regular basis to help each other, encourage each other, learn communication skills, and develop their judgment and wisdom. By far the most powerful effect of class meetings, though, whatever the age of the child, is to create a sense of belonging. Because it is the need for belonging that lies at the heart of all Mistaken Goal behavior, it makes sense that addressing this need will have the greatest long-range effect on the behavior of children in the group.

Class meetings emphasize four things:

1. children helping each other find solutions to problems
2. learning and practicing mutual respect for the needs and ideas of other group members
3. learning to encourage and support others in the group
4. that there is time for planning and sharing fun times together

Class meetings provide many opportunities to learn and strengthen skills. They aid in the acquisition of social skills and promote language development. The meetings foster a sense of both group and individual responsibility, and empower young children with positive attitudes about their own capabilities and significance—attitudes that not only help shape their behavior, but build their self-esteem.

"I can see the value of class meetings for elementary school children," you may be saying, "but aren't preschoolers a bit young?" Even the youngest members of your preschool group can begin to cultivate the attitudes nurtured by the class meeting process. We will take a look at ways you can begin class meetings for the preschool set. (For a broader discussion of class meetings, see *Positive Discipline in the Classroom* by Jane Nelsen and Lynn Lott.) Parents, having family meetings at home can develop the same skills and attitudes. To learn more, refer to *Positive Discipline* by Jane Nelsen.

Family Meetings with Preschoolers

If you have older children, you may have already discovered the many benefits of having family meetings. If your children are all preschoolers, the concept may be new; you may even question the value of having family meetings with young children. You may wonder, "What can my preschooler possibly learn? Will she be able to sit still? How can a little child solve problems?"

Very little effort is required to adapt the material presented here on class meetings to allow you to begin family meetings—and the benefits and blessings are well worth the time and energy you spend. Family meetings teach children that they are valuable, capable members of the family, and you may be amazed at your preschooler's resourcefulness and creativity. Preschoolers can offer compliments, help solve problems, plan family fun, and learn to express their needs and get help in positive (and, surprisingly often, fun) ways. Regular family meetings will help you and your children build a sense of mutual respect, trust, understanding, and love—and that can lay the foundation for the many years that lie ahead.

Here are a few ideas to keep in mind when beginning family meetings with preschoolers:

1. **Be realistic.** You can have worthwhile, entertaining family meetings with children as young as three years old, but remember that the younger the child, the shorter the attention span is likely to be. Keep your meetings short and to the point; that way, no one will get tired of them.

2. **Make family meetings a priority.** Our busy lives have a tendency to get in the way of even our best intentions. If you want your family meetings to work, set a regular time to get together and *stick to it.* Don't allow telephone calls, chores, or other distractions to get in the way. Making the time you spend as a family a priority will help you build a sense of unity and will let your young children know that you value them and the time you spend together.

3. **Begin each meeting with compliments and appreciations.** This can feel awkward at first, especially if you have siblings who are more comfortable putting each other down, but looking for and commenting on the positive will encourage everyone and will get your meeting off to a friendly start.

4. **Post an agenda board in a handy place and help your preschoolers use it.** As we will learn later, even young children can "write" their problems and concerns on an agenda board, or make a mark to indicate they have something to talk about. Taking these concerns seriously (and being careful not to quench your little one's sometimes unrealistic ideas) will show your children that you value them—and the mere act of writing down a problem can be the first step to finding a peaceful, effective solution.

5. **Leave time for fun.** Make sure part of your meeting is devoted to just enjoying each other, perhaps by playing a game, watching a video together, planning a family activity, sharing a special dessert, or reading a favorite story. Some families like to alternate "business" meetings with family meetings that are "just for fun."

However you decide to do them, family meetings are one of the best habits you and your children can get into and will help you stay tuned in throughout the increasingly busy years ahead. For more information on family meetings with children of all ages, refer to *Positive Discipline.*

You will also find the information on preschool class meetings helpful in planning and holding your family meetings.

How Young Is Too Young?

Just like parents, preschool teachers may be wondering how valuable class meetings can be for young children. Two-and-a-half-year-olds like Cristina will certainly have different contributions to make than will older children. Still, there is real value in including the little ones, the greatest being that their sense of belonging to the group is established.

Children ranging from two-and-a-half to five years old can work together in a productive and encouraging class meeting. The younger children can learn from their older role models, and the older children learn to consider and include the needs of the younger ones.

Even if your entire class consists of two- or three-year-olds, you can still enjoy class meetings together. The teacher becomes the role model when older children are not present; he may need to generate most of the suggestions and help the children learn to make choices. Even toddlers can get into the act, although the main purpose of meetings for them may simply be planning an outing or fun activity together rather than solving problems. Taking into consideration the social and language skills of the children you work with will help you know how much you can expect to accomplish.

The Four Elements of Classroom Meetings in Preschool

A classroom meeting has four main elements:

1. to give compliments and appreciation;
2. to empower children to help each other;
3. to solve problems that affect the group; and
4. to plan future activities.

Young children learn the elements of class meetings by jumping right in and participating. For example, the concept of "helping others" can be taught by finding someone to help.

(Young children often need to experience something before they can put a name to it.)

It may be helpful to list the four elements of class meetings on a chart, perhaps in bright colors, and to follow them in order. Even for children who can't read, seeing that there is a plan can help focus their attention.

"Put It on the Agenda!"

An agenda is a list of topics and tasks simply written on a piece of paper or a corner of the chalkboard that everyone can reach. Children and adults list things they wish to discuss at the next meeting. Effective class meetings follow an agenda. In addition to providing a list of things to discuss, an agenda can serve as a "cool off" device as well.

When Jon comes stomping over in a rage to tell the teacher that "Ben just killed a beetle," the teacher can share his concern and suggest that "how insects should be treated" would make a very good topic for their class meeting. She asks Jon if he would like to put it on the agenda. He readily agrees and together they write "bugs" on the agenda. The teacher sounds out the word "bugs" with Jon and he writes his name next to it. If Jon is very young, the teacher may write down "bug" and Jon's name. Or she may encourage Jon to draw a picture of a bug and either trace over his own name or make his own mark. Involving Jon in some way is respectful and creates a sense of responsibility and influence.

When it's time for problem solving, the teacher will look at the agenda and ask Jon to explain the problem of "bugs" to the others. Because Jon felt listened to when he was angry and placed his item on the agenda, he can now discuss the problem calmly.

Jon's teacher will watch to see that the group focuses on the treatment of insects—not on who killed the beetle or how he should be punished. Class meetings are for solving problems together and for nurturing care and respect; they aren't intended to serve as judge and jury. Teachers love class meetings because they don't have to solve every problem themselves—and can delay solutions until everyone can be involved.

Compliments and Appreciations

Compliments are clearly affected by the age of the children offering them. Four- and five-year-olds may say things like "I compliment Jane for being my friend" or "I compliment Eddie because he played dress-up with me." You may even hear an occasional "She pushed me off the swing!" (Well, they don't have it completely perfected yet!)

Two- and three-year-olds don't always understand the concept of compliments. They are more likely to say "I love my mommy," "I have a teddy bear at home," or "I get to go to McDonald's for dinner." These little ones usually say whatever is on their minds, but teachers can smile and thank them for their comments. The feeling of having contributed is no less because the "compliment" was a bit off target!

Teachers can ask some helpful questions to guide children in learning how to give compliments. "What is something that you like about the school?" for instance, or "Is there someone who helped you feel good today?" They can also model giving compliments. "I want to compliment all of you on the delicious cake you made yesterday. And I loved how all of the tables were washed and cleaned up after we finished mixing the batter." "Mary, I want to compliment you on letting us help you with the problem you were having about not liking your lunch. I appreciated the ideas that I heard because I can use some of them too."

Kid of the Week

A special preschool variation on compliments is what has been dubbed "Kid of the Week" at one child care center. (You could call yours "Child of the Week," if you prefer.)

Each week there is a special "Kid of the Week" circle time, and every child in the class will be selected at least once during each year. The teacher brings a large sheet of paper and an assortment of colored pens to the circle. At the top of the page she writes the child's name.

Today Maureen is "Kid of the Week." The teacher has written "I like Maureen because . . . " at the top of the paper. And just to get everybody in the mood, everyone sings the following words to the tune of "Camptown Races" while Maureen grins with pleasure.

> "We like Maureen , Yes we do . . .
> Doodah! Doodah!
> We like Maureen, Yes we do . . .
> Oh, yes we do.
> Gonna like her all day . . .
> Gonna like her all year . . .
> Thank her for the things she does
> We like her because . . . "

Then each of the children take turns saying what it is they like or appreciate about Maureen while the teacher writes their comments on the sheet of paper. Maureen's classmates have this to say about her:

> "I like her because she's my friend."
> "She plays with me."
> "She has a sparkle in her eye." (Wow!)
> "She jumps like Tigger."

Toward the end, two-and-a-half-year-old David says, "She is like a mommy." What a beautiful and heartfelt tribute.

If the children seem to be a bit stuck about what to say (or if they resort to comments like "I like her shoes"), the teacher can offer some guidance by asking questions. "Who wants to say that Maureen can come to their birthday party?" "Who remembers a game you played in the dress-up area with Maureen this week?" The teacher can also add comments to show appreciation for the child and to model the skill of complimenting others.

If some of the children still have trouble thinking of something to say (or are just a bit shy), the teacher can ask "Who would like to have his name written on the paper as one of Maureen's friends?" Even the youngest child can make this contribution. And when all who want a turn have finished, the teacher rolls up the paper and ties it with a bright ribbon. Another child is chosen to present the scroll to Maureen and the circle finishes with another song, perhaps a variation on "For He (or She)'s a Jolly Good Fellow."

Not a bad way to start a child's day, is it? For the rest of the week Maureen is the teacher's special helper. She is invited to dismiss the others from circle, help set out lunch boxes, and ring the bell at the end of playtime. The scroll goes home with Maureen's parents that night. Many families report that for months the scroll remains showcased on their refrigerator doors. Children frequently request that the scroll be read to them each day. Can you feel the tremendous value of this paper? It represents a warm outpouring of love and caring for Maureen from her peers.

Helping Each Other

Next up at the class meeting is "helping each other." This time in your class meeting is an opportunity for children to ask for help with something that is a problem for them.

It is Tuesday morning at the Hill Harbor Child Care Center. The class of three- and four-year-olds is just beginning their class meeting with their teacher, Mr. Silk. He asks if anyone needs help from the group today.

Matthias raises his hand and announces, "I can't wake up in the morning." Many of the other children agree that it's hard for them, too. Mr. Silk asks if anyone has a suggestion for

Matthias. The children offer all sorts of helpful ideas: "Go to bed earlier," "Get up anyway," and "Come to school in pajamas," they say.

Mr. Silk turns to Matthias. "Do you think any of these ideas will help you or should the group think of some more?" Matthias pauses to consider then says he is going to "get up anyway."

Next Julian raises his hand and says he needs help because "My mom doesn't have enough money." After sympathizing with Julian, other children volunteer that they have that problem, too. And Julian's friends are eager to help. Some of the children offer to bring in money. Bobby suggests that Julian could do some jobs to get money. Katie says, "My mom will help." Devon recommends that, "Your mom can get a job that makes more money."

It is unlikely that Julian's mom will have more money as a result of this discussion. But Julian was genuinely concerned about money and his concern was treated respectfully. He has also learned that his classmates care about his needs, and that some of them share similar worries. "Helping each other" can become a very powerful part of class meetings.

Parents may be invited to place items on the agenda too, and to visit and join in the class meeting. Seeing firsthand the experience their child is enjoying may encourage them to try similar meetings at home.

Solving Problems

It may come as a surprise, but even young children can be remarkably creative when it comes to solving problems. One afternoon the following note appeared near the sign-out sheet at the Mountain View Preschool:

"We are having a small bake sale this Thursday afternoon. We are learning to be responsible by replacing a ripped-up library book. We will bake cookies at school and sell them for twenty-five cents each. The children would also like to earn twenty-five cents at home by doing a special job. The bake sale idea came out of our class meeting discussion about a damaged book. We also discussed and demonstrated how to carry books and how to turn pages at the edge."

Over the course of the next week, the children prepared several batches of cookies during class time, learning new skills (and having a great time) in the process. On Thursday the sale took place and was so successful that even after subtracting the cost of the cookie ingredients, the children had raised enough to both replace the damaged book and to purchase a new one. They spent time at the next class meeting discussing what type of new book they wanted for their classroom.

Class meetings can provide valuable opportunities to learn social skills. One morning at meeting time Candace, who is four, said that another child had called her friend Eric a bad name. The teacher asked Eric if this was a problem he would like the group to address. (It is important that children learn to be responsible for their own needs.)

When Eric had told his story, the teacher asked whether anyone else had ever been called names. "How does it make you feel?" she asked. Others in the group had had the same experience, and lively discussion followed. The children agreed that it hurt to be called names. They then came up with a list of possible solutions, which the teacher wrote down for them on the board.

1. Maybe the name-calling person could control himself.
2. Walk away.
3. Say, "Don't say that!"
4. Get a teacher to help.
5. Tell them you don't like it.
6. Ask them to take a cool-off time out.
7. Say, "Stop!"
8. All walk away and discuss it somewhere else.

The suggestions may be similar, but all are honored and written down. Eric and his classmates can now talk about the possible results of each choice (with some gentle help from their teacher) and decide ways they might respond to name-calling in the future. Remember, preschoolers are still refining their social skills; suggestions like "call him a worse name" or "punch his lights out" would provide opportunities to learn about acceptable responses!

Planning Fun Activities

"We could all go to Disneyland."
"I suggest we go to the beach." (Never mind the snow out-side.)
"We can go on an airplane trip. My Daddy will take us with him."

When young children are asked about fun activities they might do as a group, not all of the suggestions will be practical. Once children start offering improbable suggestions they tend to "get on a roll," so it is helpful for the teacher to guide them by offering some practical, fun ideas for activities and outings.

There are dozens of ideas. Trips to the police station, fire station, zoo, and park may be possible field trips, depending on your program. Remember that a field trip can be a wonderful opportunity to invite the children to solve problems *in advance*. Ask them what problems they had on their last field trip, or what they think some good rules for the group would be. If the children can't think of anything, the teacher can make sugges-tions, such as crossing streets, pushing and shoving, running around, or not listening quietly and respectfully when the fire chief talks. The children can then brainstorm solutions. Chil-dren are far more willing to follow rules when they've had a part in making them!

More immediate activities can also be planned. Classroom treats such as ice cream or popcorn are fun and easy to provide. If an expenditure of money is involved, the children can work out plans to raise the needed funds. They can earn money at home through special tasks or do so at school as a group. One bunch of enterprising youngsters decided to sell baked potatoes at the end of the day to tired and hungry parents. The aroma as parents entered the school was wonderful, and needless to say, this fund-raiser was a rousing success.

The group may set a goal, such as throwing a pizza party when all of the shelves and toys have been washed. The teacher can provide buckets and sponges, and the children can pitch in. One program has an occasional floor-scrubbing day when the furniture is cleared away and there are buckets and scrub brushes for all. The children love the water play, training, and social interest all rolled up into one activity. Remember that involving children in planning an activity, whether in art or cooking or play, will make that activity more successful. When children are invited to feel capable and creative, they almost always respond with enthusiasm.

Special Tips

1. **Timing.** Class meetings for preschoolers may require that you be flexible. Depending on your children's mood, abilities, and attention span, you may need to keep meetings short or do only one element each time. Your meetings don't need to be lengthy to cultivate belonging and encouragement. Many pre-schools find that one meeting each week is ample. Others like to have a short meeting every day. Trial and error will help you find just the right balance.

2. **Signals.** Young children love special signals, such as the same song being sung each day to signal cleanup time. A ringing bell could mean that everyone should freeze and listen to an announcement from the teacher.

It works well to develop a special signal to open and close class meetings. In one class, everyone sits on the floor in a circle and places his arms together with the elbows bent. To begin the meeting they slowly move their arms apart, like opening a book, and announce "Class meeting is *open!*" At the end of the meeting they reverse the process while saying "Class meeting is *closed!*"

3. **Voting.** In preschool, children can vote when the choice involves everyone, such as a having a popcorn party or a pizza party. At this early age children can learn that people think and want different things, and they can learn to give and take. It is not appropriate to allow children to vote on a "solution" for another person. The person with the problem should be allowed to choose the solution she thinks will be most helpful for her.

4. **Minutes.** Keeping track of what happens in a meeting can be helpful, especially when your class needs to remember just what it was they decided! Because most preschoolers can't write, an adult probably will need to take the minutes. Preschoolers can take turns running the meeting when they have learned the process. They love to call the meeting to order, call on people who have their names on the agenda (sometimes with a little prompting from the teacher), ask for suggestions to solve problems, and close the meeting.

At the beginning of each meeting, you can review the previous meeting's notes and see how your plans and decisions are working out. If a problem persists, give it precedence over new agenda items. Evaluate what did not work about the solution that was tried. Look over the other suggestions that were not used and come up with new ideas as well.

A Learning Opportunity

Preschool class meetings are astonishingly productive, teaching many life skills while helping children develop a strong sense of belonging. Adults sometimes underestimate the ability of young children to be creative and responsible, and class meetings allow this learning opportunity for everyone. You may discover that the youngsters in your care not only learn self-esteem and cooperation, but have a marvelous time as well!

As we have learned, parents can begin family meetings using the same format when their first child is about three years old. And if your child is participating in class meetings at preschool, you will be amazed at how quickly he applies his new abilities at home. Class meetings are a wonderful way for children and adults to experience just how much fun learning can be!

CHAPTER 19

When Your Child Needs Special Help

Why do some children need special help? Countless parents spend sleepless nights wrestling with that question. "If only I was a better parent . . . ." "If the teacher would only . . . ." "I've tried everything and I'm at my wit's end . . . ." It seems as though *everyone* has suggestions or knows what you "should" be doing. Even though you try many different ways of guiding and encouraging your children, sometimes nothing seems to work.

Most parents look for ways to do a better job; in fact, the POSITIVE DISCIPLINE series of books exist for exactly that reason. Yet despite the information and advice, there are still children for whom life just seems *harder.* They struggle in school; they have trouble making friends. Some bounce off the walls while others don't seem interested in much of anything. These children (and families) may need more than improved parenting skills. How can you tell when your child needs special help?

Taking a Closer Look

It's usually best to start at the beginning. Take a moment to think about the information already presented in this book.

Consider your child's age and developmental level. Evaluate your own parenting style, lifestyle priority, and expectations. Carefully evaluate all the aspects of your child's temperament, and his individual needs and abilities. And consider the possibility of coded messages in his behavior.

Most parents will find the answers to understanding their child somewhere in all this information. But if you've carefully considered these things and you still find that you don't know where to begin to help your child, it may be time to look deeper.

When All Else Fails

Tony struggles and writhes when he puts on some types of clothing; the tag on his shirt collar causes him great distress. Johnny seems startled by the sound of the gerbil moving in its cage, even when he's sitting across the room and coloring. Kim just can't sit still or pay attention for more than five minutes, no matter how hard she tries. These children may not be misbehaving; they may be struggling with things that are genuinely difficult for them because of certain chemical imbalances. Such imbalances can result in the combination of characteristics known as "ADD" or "ADHD," attention deficit disorder without or with hyperactivity.

Five to ten percent of all children in the United States are believed to experience the combination of traits that indicate this disorder, which is responsible for about half of all referrals to child guidance counselors—and for a lot of frustrated, burned- out parents. Although this chapter will focus on ADHD, much of the information also applies to many other illnesses or difficulties children may encounter. Parents of children with virtually any chronic condition experience a sense of frustration, sadness and grief, anxiety, and the need to develop specialized skills. Knowing that you're not alone works wonders; so does information about finding help and support.

Labels

No one wants his child to be labeled. Labels such as "clever," "clumsy," "shy," or "cute" all define who a child is in others' eyes, creating an image that may prevent that child from being appreciated and experienced for who she *really* is. On the other hand, some labels simply describe what is obvious. Labeling a child who wears glasses as "the little girl with glasses" doesn't necessarily cause people to prejudge her behavior.

Sometimes a child's cluster or pattern of behaviors is equally obvious. Diagnosing such a child as having ADHD or ADD *can* be helpful. Most parents and teachers find it easier to encourage and support a child who has ADHD than one who has been labeled "disruptive," "squirmy," or "a trouble-maker."

Adults often must struggle with their own attitudes and expectations about children who are different or special. When Mrs. Corelli was told that her four-month-old daughter was going to need glasses, she went home and cried, grieving that her "poor" tiny baby was going to be "disfigured" with glasses. Abruptly, she stopped and listened to what she had just told herself. She had described her baby as "poor" and the glasses as "disfiguring." Mrs. Corelli asked herself whose problem this was. Her four-month-old had no concept of how glasses would make her "look." In fact, the glasses would help her to see better and would enable her to grow and develop normally.

Mrs. Corelli realized that the real problem was her own attitude. If she wanted to provide her daughter with the help she needed, Mrs. Corelli had to recognize the value of that help. From that moment on, she chose to support her daughter and obtain whatever care she might need, including glasses. Her daughter's "disability" had existed only in Mrs. Corelli's own mind.

In the same way, a learning difference or the diagnosis of a disorder such as ADHD does *not* define who the child is. It is simply a convenient word for a child's uniqueness and special abilities. Because most learning differences also result in a certain amount of distress, we usually hear a great deal about the many associated problems. But it is equally important (if not more so) to look at the *assets* and *attributes* a child possesses. When a child lacks one ability, growth is likely to occur in other areas. A person who cannot see often develops acute hearing. Everyone has both strengths and weaknesses. What are your child's special gifts? A gentle spirit, a lively sense of humor, or a tender heart often will outweigh the liabilities that accompany "differentness"—if we choose to let them.

Denial

A fear of "labels" or denying a child's special needs does not help anyone. Sometimes we feel more concerned about our own ego (or what people will think) than about what is best for our child. It requires a brave step to accept and parent your children as they really are, to give them what they really need.

Mrs. Avery taught parenting classes in churches and schools and was well respected as an educator in her community. She was also a skillful and effective parent who had raised three children. Imagine how embarrassed and despairing she felt when her fourth child came along and reacted differently to everything her mom did. By the time Grace was five, things were getting out of control. Three out of five days each week, Mrs. Avery would carry a screaming child who was throwing a wild tantrum out of the preschool, trying to ignore the knowing glances and stares of the other parents. She tried everything she knew, but nothing seemed to work with Grace.

Finally she decided that she simply had to accept Grace for the child she was. When Grace threw a tantrum at the preschool, Mrs. Avery took her to the car and read a book until the tantrum was over. Then she drove home. She didn't lecture. Grace still wasn't able to control her behavior, but Mrs. Avery quit worrying about what others were thinking and put her child's needs first.

Learning to Accept

It is often easier for adults to respond to children who have a highly visible disorder or who behave in extreme ways rather than children whose disorder may be less obvious. If Sally, whose limbs are contorted with cerebral palsy, accidentally bumps into a classmate while struggling to maneuver the stairs, a teacher probably will not tell Sally that she must stay in from recess for pushing her classmate.

Nor will Sally's mother be called in for a conference and told that if she would just improve her parenting skills and be more firm, Sally would not have to struggle so to feed herself or learn to walk. Unfair as it seems, parents of children with ADHD often receive such criticism and advice because ADHD is not as obvious or as well understood as cerebral palsy and other physical disabilities.

Because children with ADHD are often impulsive and find it difficult to sit quietly, their behavior is typically labeled "misbehavior" and others are quick to suggest remedies. Parents often find themselves accused of ineffective parenting; they also feel considerable guilt and may believe they have failed as parents. Perhaps most difficult of all, they are living with a child whom they love dearly, but with whom they must struggle a great deal of the time.

When accurate, a diagnosis of ADHD can be an enormously healing step for both parents and child. It establishes that this child is *not* merely disruptive, fidgety, or defiant. Difficult behavior can be understood as a symptom to be overcome, rather than a series of intentional misdeeds. Your ADD child is not a troublemaker, even when her behavior gets her into trouble.

Invisible Differences

The variability of behavior associated with disorders such as ADD and ADHD makes it difficult for most people to understand children who have these disorders. We can accept that a woman who has just given birth may experience wide mood swings; we know that her emotional highs and lows are due to fluctuating levels of hormones, and we're willing to be patient and supportive because we understand.

But imagine that you are a small child and sometimes, for reasons you don't comprehend, you become terribly upset and begin to scream and kick. Wouldn't your loss of control be frightening? Your parents might decide your tantrum occurred because you couldn't have a toy when you wanted it, or you didn't want to turn off the TV when you were told to, or you thought the teacher had scolded you unfairly. They might also imply that you are somehow at fault or "bad." It's not hard to understand why a child may begin to see *herself* as "bad." The reality—that she has little ability to control her behavior regardless of the circumstances—is scary.

Learning to understand the difficulties a child may face does not mean we condone inappropriate behavior. In fact, having clear, reasonable expectations and following through with kindness and firmness is essential. Parents and teachers can learn to respond in ways that are productive and do not reinforce a child's image of himself as a "bad kid." Children with ADHD and other differences need love and encouragement just as much (if not more) than other children do.

Still, if a new mother yells and hurls verbal abuse at her family, she will need to make amends and try to heal the damage her behavior has caused, regardless of the reason. Children also need to take responsibility for the results of their behavior, even when they lack the ability to bring that behavior under control. Real understanding will help adults stop punishing, blaming, and feeling guilty (which almost never make a situation better) and will empower them to choose different responses.

"Getting Away with" Misbehavior

Mrs. Harris has two daughters. The youngest, Megan, is five years old and has been identified as having ADHD. Sheila, her older sister, is seven and does not have ADD or ADHD. Before they go shopping, Mrs. Harris takes the time to discuss her expectations with her two daughters. She has found this especially helpful for Megan, who has difficulty with transitions. They discuss the behavior that is expected as well as what is on the shopping agenda. The girls are often allotted a small amount of money to spend on items for themselves.

Late one Friday afternoon, Mrs. Harris follows the usual pre-shopping routine with her daughters. Megan remembers their agreement that this is *not* the day they will get ice cream cones, and she proudly reminds her mother of this fact.

At the store, however, Megan sees a child happily licking an ice cream cone. In Megan's mind, seeing another child with an ice cream cone means she wants one herself; immediately, Megan believes that she *must* have an ice cream cone. Soon a tantrum is under way. What happened to Megan's agreement that there would be no ice cream today?

One of the characteristics of ADHD is an impulsiveness that translates "wants" almost immediately into "needs." All children behave impulsively at times, and most show other traits symptomatic to ADHD on occasion. But ADHD is suspected when the traits show up consistently, the child can't control them, and there is no psychological cause for them.[1]

---

1. Taylor, John F. *Helping Your Hyperactive Child, Revised 2nd Edition.* Rocklin, CA: Prima, 1994, p. 14.

Mrs. Harris stops shopping and asks Megan if she can regain control by herself or whether they should leave the store. The tantrum continues, so mother and daughters leave the store, with Megan hitting and screaming. The tantrum continues in the car; when they arrive home, Megan runs into her room and slams the door. By now Mrs. Harris is struggling to maintain her own control. She is angry, discouraged, and exhausted. Sheila, hurt and disappointed, is thinking, "I didn't do anything to spoil the shopping trip. Why did I have to miss out on the fun?" It's hard not to resent a little sister who behaves this way.

It's important to note that Mrs. Harris does not spoil either of her daughters. She does not respond to unreasonable or demanding behavior by abandoning agreements she has made. There was nothing wrong with Mrs. Harris' parenting.

"Well," some parents might say, "if *my* child acted that way in a public place, I'd sure let her know how I felt about it. That mother should have spanked her daughter, or refused to let her have ice cream for a month!" But think for a moment. Has Megan "gotten away" with misbehavior? Will punishment or humiliation help her to change her behavior in the future? And did Megan *want* to lose control? Did she *intend* to misbehave? It may be hard for her mother, who is experiencing a seething (and very human) mixture of anger, guilt, and blame to remember, but Megan may not have consciously chosen to defy her mother. She was proud of remembering her agreement with her mother and she knows that her mother follows through on those agreements. Dealing effectively with Megan's behavior means recognizing her special needs.

What can Mrs. Harris do? When she and Megan have calmed down, they can discuss what happened in the store. They might also discuss ways Megan could help her sister feel better. Maybe Megan could offer to do one of Sheila's chores or play a game with her. Sheila, too, has needs that should not be ignored.

Megan almost always feels terrible when she loses control of her behavior; she can feel her mother's exasperation and disappointment and it's hard for her to bear. Perhaps the most important thing Mrs. Harris and Megan can do now is to work on ways Megan can cope with those out-of-control feelings. ADHD is something they can acknowledge and face together; they can choose to be a family, loving and supporting one another.

It would be easy to allow Megan to feel that she is "bad" or "difficult," and because her mother is human, Mrs. Harris will sometimes make mistakes and say or do things she later regrets. But as we've seen before, mistakes aren't fatal. And Megan's behavior may not change anytime soon. Facing reality, learning coping skills, and getting support will help both mother and daughter survive the difficult times.

Despair or Pride

Labels and diagnoses are usually negative. (Even seemingly positive labels can be negative: "She's *too* nice.") The diagnosis of any type of learning or behavioral difference often focuses on undesirable behaviors.

Finding out that your child is anything but perfect comes as an emotional blow. But once adults move beyond their fear of labels and their own denial, they can stretch their horizons wider to see the wonderful gifts their child has, not always in spite of learning or behavioral differences, but sometimes because of them! Some behaviors that are undesirable in civilized society show skills that may be highly valued in a different environment.

Think of a person living in a hunting civilization. An ability to pick up on all extraneous noise and movement would make this person extremely important to the community. But place that same person in a modern classroom. Tuning in when a visitor knocks at the door or the class hamster moves in its cage means this child is not concentrating on his math assignment. What a difference context can make!

It undoubtedly takes time and determination, but you *can* learn to celebrate the very things that make your child require special help. Children with ADHD can be tremendously creative. The ability to perceive unusual links between divergent ideas has brought some of society's greatest concepts to life. Thomas Edison was though to have had ADHD. What would the world be like without his invention of electricity?

What About Medication?

Mr. Adams had struggled with his son Charles to the point of desperation. When Charles was five years old, his teacher suspected Charles might have some "borderline" ADHD characteristics. Mr. Adams was horrified, and not a little offended by this suggestion. He signed up for parenting classes, bought piles of books, and did his best to be a better father.

But Charles' problems continued. By the age of seven he was having trouble with schoolwork and friendships, and his difficulties were affecting the entire family. Everyone seemed tense and touchy; arguments were frequent. Finally Mr. Adams decided it was time to look for help.

This time Charles' doctor made a clear diagnosis of ADHD. After months of counseling and trying various approaches, Mr. Adams agreed to try medication. Within a week Charles' behavior was much improved. It was difficult for Mr. Adams to believe that those tiny pills could have such an influence on behavior—and equally difficult to admit that his son might need this kind of help. But whenever Charles missed his medication over the next few months, his behavior deteriorated dramatically. Mr. Adams began to see Charles in a different light, and to enjoy the calm, interesting child he saw emerging. Charles, too, was changing; finally he could be himself, rather than a desperate little person always struggling with the effects ADHD had on his daily life.

Medication is *not* a cure-all, nor is it the answer for all children. It is simply a *part* of what worked for this family. Equally important were the healing and understanding that came from focusing on Charles' needs and accepting the boy for who he really was. Charles also needed the firm, clear guidelines that Mr. Adams learned about in parenting classes. And Mr. Adams benefited from examining his own expectations, priorities, and approach to discipline.

Occasionally well-meaning teachers or other adults will suggest medication to "calm a child down." It is essential that parents first consider the individual needs of their child. Medication is not appropriate for a child who simply has a high level of distractibility, a high energy level, or a short attention span. Medication *can* be part of a comprehensive and loving approach to helping a child with ADHD.

We are not diagnosticians; diagnosis of ADD and ADHD is a controversial issue beyond the scope of this book. Parents interested in learning more can refer to Dr. John F. Taylor's *Helping Your Hyperactive Child, Revised 2nd Edition.* Dr. Taylor offers a screening checklist and a wealth of information and possible solutions in his book.

Positive Discipline parenting skills do help with ADD and ADHD children. Working toward consistency and taking the time to evaluate your child's individual needs and abilities are particularly important with these special children. If you suspect ADD or ADHD, seek a proper diagnosis from a qualified health care professional. Be sure that person conducts a *thorough* physical examination of your child. It may be wise to wait until a child is five years old to seek an evaluation. Prior to that age, immaturity is the most likely cause of difficult behavior. Because you may find you and your child need additional help and support, find out if your community has a support group for parents of ADD children. If not, consider starting one yourself.

Sharing experiences with others who understand and knowing you're not alone can help tremendously.

Look for the Positive

Whether your child has ADHD or a different physical or emotional challenge, focusing on your inadequacies as a parent will help neither you nor your child. Instead, find support for yourself, take care of your own needs, accept and learn from your mistakes, practice humor and hope, and get help for your child when you need it. Above all, make every effort to discover and celebrate the qualities that make your child special, unique, wonderful. Those qualities are there—you only have to look.

CHAPTER 20

Taking Care of You: Building a Support System

It was a moment Richard would never forget. Sometime in the dead of night—his eyes wouldn't focus on the clock's glowing numerals—Richard slowly opened his eyes. It was quiet; what had awakened him? He peered through the darkness of the bedroom and finally saw Gina, his wife, on her hands and knees beside the bed holding a flashlight, tears rolling down her face.

Richard struggled to wake up. "What on earth is wrong, honey?" he said.

Gina turned an anxious face to his. "I had the baby in bed with me and now I can't find him. I thought he might have rolled under the bed."

Richard tried to digest this shocking news. "Gina," he finally said gently, "you know the baby never sleeps with us. I'm sure Brian is in his crib."

Gina blinked slowly at him. "Do you think so? Was I dreaming or something?"

Richard crawled out from under the covers and took his wife's hand. Together they went to look into their three-month-old infant's crib. Brian was sleeping peacefully, one fist jammed into his mouth.

Gina sat down heavily in the rocking chair conveniently placed for night feedings. "I really must be losing it," she said, shaking her head.

Richard smiled. "Gina, the baby wakes up twice a night, every night—you haven't been getting much sleep." But as he led his befuddled wife back to bed and gave her a kiss, Richard wondered whether either of them would survive Brian's infancy. No one had warned them about nights like this!

Raising children—particularly young children—is a demanding, stressful occupation. What other job requires you to be on duty 24 hours a day, seven days a week, 52 weeks a year? What other occupation requires you to be conversant on child development, childhood illness, and proper parenting techniques, as well as be an observant supervisor and tireless dispenser of love and nurturing?

New parents soon discover that infants and toddlers require an astonishing amount of time and attention for such small people—yet other demands of life, such as jobs, laundry, and housework, don't go away. Spouses often find there is too little time for each other, let alone the pleasures and hobbies that amused them "B.C." (Before Children). And what happens if *other* children come along?

Being a parent is a great deal like pouring water from a pitcher: you can only pour out so many glasses of water without refilling the pitcher. And all too often parents and other caregivers suddenly realize they've poured themselves dry for their children—that the pitcher is empty. Effective, loving parenting takes a lot of time and energy. You can't do your best when your pitcher is empty, when you're tired, cranky, stressed out, and overwhelmed. But how do you refill the pitcher?

One of the most important parts of caring for young children is also one of the most easily overlooked. You have to take care of *you*. We know; we can hear your incredulous snorts from here: "You've got to be kidding!" "Where are we supposed to find the time?" That's not an easy question to answer, but it's vitally important to both you and your children that you find a way. Stress and exhaustion lead to resentment and anger, and parents who feel worn out often overreact to their children's demands and misbehaviors; the result can be words and actions that are deeply regretted later.

Taking Care of Mom and Dad

Parents who are contented, healthy, and *relatively* well-rested (being tired seems an unavoidable part of raising young children) are important ingredients in a family that works for all its members. If you are a single parent who must handle it all, there is all the more reason to take special care of yourself. If you have a partner, remember that your relationship is the foundation of your family; invest the time and energy it takes to keep it strong.

It takes time to adjust when a child is added to a marriage or relationship. Before your baby came along, you only had the needs and desires of two people to consider (that's hard enough to do!). Now, suddenly, there are three—and one seems to require an extraordinary amount of attention.

Parents can easily lose sight of each other in their headlong rush to "take care of the baby." Mom nurses the baby; Dad feels left out and a little jealous—and guilty for having those feelings. One parent wants a little snuggling and cuddling; the other is "too tired." One parent is *dying* for dinner and a movie out; the other doesn't trust a baby-sitter or spends the evening phoning home every 15 minutes to make sure everything is okay.

It is important to remember that your decisions and actions teach your child from her earliest days about life and love and relationships. Taking time for each other isn't selfishness or bad parenting—it's wisdom. Your child will learn to respect and value the needs and feelings of others by watching you.

Be sure you leave time each week for activities you enjoy together, whether it's a special dinner after your child is asleep, a "date" night out, or a morning walk (perhaps with the baby along in a backpack or a stroller). Take time to really listen to one another and to talk about all the different parts of your life, not just about the baby!

What About Baby-sitters?

For most parents of young children, finding (and feeling comfortable with) a baby-sitter is a major problem. Perhaps the idea of a night out together does sound wonderful—but how do you find a responsible, trustworthy caregiver for your young child?

You might consider a number of ways:

1. **Ask your friends.** If you have friends or coworkers with young children, ask them for a list of names and phone numbers. Knowing that people you trust recommend someone is probably the best way to feel comfortable when you leave your child with a sitter.

2. **Ask your preschool.** If you have a day care center or preschool, the director may have a list of names. If you don't take your baby or child to day care, a reputable preschool in your neighborhood may still be able to refer you to sitters.

3. **Check with your local church, high school, or youth organization.** Churches, schools, and other organizations often have young people who are willing to baby-sit—and some have even been trained. A few phone calls may get you in touch with a reliable baby-sitter.

4. **Form a baby-sitting coop with other families.** If you know other families with young children, agree to form a coop where you trade child care duties one evening or weekend day each week. If four families form a coop, each couple might have three Friday nights or Saturday afternoons out each month, for example, and one evening or day as the "sitters." A coop can provide you with reliable, free child care—and regular

times to spend as a couple. Keeping track of the hours you watch children and making sure the balance sheet stays even will make things work for everyone.

5. **Include your relatives.** Grandparents, aunts, uncles, and cousins may be more willing than you think to provide child care in exchange for the opportunity to spend time with the youngest members of the family. As long as your relatives know they have the right to say "no" (and as long as you don't wear out your welcome), your extended family may provide you with a great deal of child care, and children can benefit in countless ways from relationships with older members of their family.

No matter who you select to watch your children while you're away, be sure you've talked with him or her enough to feel comfortable—and to be sure that person shares your philosophy of raising children. If your child is old enough to communicate easily with you, check her perceptions occasionally to be sure everything is going well. And always listen to your heart; your instincts will help you know when changes are required.

Learning from the Wisdom of Others

While people seldom agree on every detail of raising infants and children, building a support network, a circle of friends who've "been there," may still provide an invaluable source of information about raising and living with children.

It can be helpful to have people to call when things happen that you weren't expecting. Make an effort to build relationships with folks who have children the same age as yours— or who have recently survived the stage you're going through. Don't be afraid to ask lots of questions; finding out that other people's children have done the same "strange" or "appalling" things can make you feel normal again!

If you can, find a parenting group for parents of young children. Perhaps your parenting group, with dinner out beforehand, can be part of your special time with your partner. Play groups for children of similar ages can also put you in touch with other parents. However you arrange it, having a sympathetic group with whom to discuss problems, ask questions, and explore the world of very young children can make all the difference in the world.

Consult your pediatrician, too. Family doctors see and hear a great deal as they go about the business of helping young patients and parents. They can often provide support as well as practical information and advice.

No matter who you look to for help, however, remember that in the end, you must decide what feels right for you and your child. Gather all the wisdom and advice you can, then listen to your heart before you choose what will work best for you.

Refilling the Pitcher

Taking care of yourself—filling up your pitcher before it runs dry—can take many forms. If you find yourself daydreaming in a quiet moment about all the things you'd like to do, that may be a clue that you should consider ways to take care of yourself.

Here are a few suggestions:

Budget your time wisely.   Most parents find that they must adjust their priorities after the arrival of a child. It can be extremely helpful—and quite a revelation—to keep track for a few days of exactly how you spend your time. Some things, such as work, school, or tasks directly related to raising your children can't be changed much. But we spend much of our time on things other than our true priorities.

For instance, if you're often up during the night with an infant or very young child, make an effort to nap when your child naps. It is tempting to fly around the house doing all the things that "should" get done, but cleaning the bathroom and dusting the furniture will wait for you; you'll be a happier and more effective person if you get enough sleep.

If you can't seem to sleep during the day, list all the things you'd like to do. Then, when your child is napping, spend those precious hours on the most important ones. You might be wise to spend that time on something that nurtures *you,* like curling up with a good book, soaking in the tub, or having a cozy telephone chat with a friend. Time is precious and all too short when you share your life with young children; be sure you're spending the time you *do* have as wisely as you can.

Save time for friendships.   It's amazing how therapeutic a simple cup of tea with a good friend can be. And sometimes a vigorous game of racquetball can restore a positive perspective on life. Conversation with caring adults can refresh you, especially when your world is populated with energetic little people. You and your partner may trade time watching the children so each of you has time for friends, or you may choose to spend special time together with other couples whose company you enjoy. Meeting friends at the park can give both the adults and children time to rest and relax together. Keeping your world wide enough to include people outside your family can help you retain your health and balance.

Do the things you enjoy.   It is important that you find time for the things that make you feel alive and happy, whether it's riding your bicycle, playing softball, singing with a choir, tinkering with machinery, or working in the garden. Hobbies and exercise are important for your mental and emotional health—

and you'll be a far more patient and effective parent if you're investing time and energy in your own well-being.

The following "fairy tale" and information on selfishness illustrates the importance of taking care of yourself:[1]

> Once upon a time there were two fairy princesses, Princess Dew and Princess Bee.
>
> Princess Dew was very busy running around *doing* things for other people—trying to make them happy. Some people loved what Princess Dew did for them, but instead of being happy, they just wanted more. Princess Dew tried hard to do more for them, hoping that someday they would be happy. Other people did not like what she did for them "for their own good," and they wished she would stop interfering.
>
> Princess Dew became worn out, bitter, and frustrated because people did not appreciate all she did for them. She was very unhappy. No one wanted to be around her.
>
> Princess Bee was also very busy—being happy. She enjoyed everything—rainbows and clouds, rainy days, and sunny days. She especially enjoyed people. She loved watching them "be." It never occurred to her to interfere in their "being." People loved being around her. Her happiness was contagious.
>
> . . .
>
> It is popular to have strong negative opinions about selfishness . . . . Selfishness [that originates in] the thought system is based on ego, self-importance, resentment, rebellion, or total disregard for others; selfishness from a natural, happy state of mind is based on feelings of love and the joy of living. With these feelings, we will want to do whatever our inner wisdom leads us to do to enjoy life.

---

1. Nelsen, Jane. *Understanding: Eliminating Stress and Finding Serenity in Life and Relationships.* Rocklin, CA: Prima, pp. 73–76.

One day Mary felt like going for a nice, long walk. She received a message from her thought system: "You should not go for a walk when you have so many other things to do, like cleaning the house and shopping." She went for a walk anyway and enjoyed the beautiful day. Her family came home to a happy wife and mother. They enjoyed being around her and felt her love.

Martha also wanted to go for a walk, but she listened to the "shoulds" from her thought system. She felt depressed and did not get much cleaning done. Her family came home to an unhappy wife and mother.

If you are asking, "How will anything ever get done if we always do what we want instead of doing what really needs to be done?" you have missed the point. The next day Martha went for a walk, but still felt depressed. Mary stayed home and cleaned house, and still felt happy.

From a happy feeling, Mary is able to know what is important for her own well-being and that of her family. From an unhappy feeling, Martha will feel dissatisfied no matter what she does. For example, Martha has trouble getting her children to do their chores, whereas Mary has inspiration for how to win the cooperation of her children. When Mary cleans house, it is because she enjoys a clean house, not because she should do it. When Martha cleans house, she is trying to prove that she is a good wife and mother.

When we enjoy a nice life, we create serenity in ourselves, in our home, and in the world. *Happiness and peace of mind are contagious.*

Yes, having young children can keep you from doing things you want to do as often as you might like—but respecting yourself and your own needs will have the added benefit of teaching your children to respect your needs and, eventually, their own. Remember, parents are important people, too. Your own contentment may be one of your most important parenting tools!

Learn to recognize the symptoms of stress. Clenched teeth and fists, tight muscles, headaches, a sudden desire to burst into tears or lock yourself in the bathroom—these are the symptoms of parental stress and overload. It's important to pay attention to them. Most parents—especially first-time parents— occasionally feel overwhelmed and exhausted, and even angry or resentful.

Kim Parker had just managed to fall asleep when it started: the fretful, whining cry that told her that two-month-old Amanda was awake—again. Kim groaned, thought briefly about burying her head under her pillow, then heaved herself out of bed. Her husband had been out of town on business for more than a week, and this was the second time tonight that Amanda had awakened. Kim was exhausted.

She stumbled into the baby's room and began her night routine without even bothering to turn on the light. Half an hour later Amanda had been fed, changed, and burped, but she was crying more loudly than ever. Kim settled the baby in her arms and began rocking in the old rocking chair, fighting the urge to cry herself. She felt helpless, completely at the mercy of this tiny person who couldn't even tell her what was wrong. She hadn't had time to do the laundry in a week, the house was cluttered, and she would have given her right arm for an hour at the hairdresser's. What had happened? This wasn't what she'd imagined when she was pregnant with Amanda.

Kim looked down at her daughter's face and suddenly saw not a beautiful, beloved baby, but an ugly, demanding, noisy monster who wouldn't even let her get a decent night's sleep. What Kim *really* wanted was to put the baby down and simply leave.

It took almost two hours, but Amanda, soothed by the steady rocking, eventually fell asleep. It took her horrified mother a lot longer to deal with the unexpectedly strong emotions the encounter had created in her.

As we've mentioned before, there's a difference between a feeling and an action. It's not unusual for parents of infants and young children to be frustrated, overwhelmed, and exhausted, and most parents feel terribly guilty for feeling anger and resentment toward their children. The feelings are quite normal—but we need to be careful what we *do* with them.

If you find yourself struggling with anger or resentment, or wanting to snap or lash out at your children, accept those feelings as your cue to do something to care for yourself. Make sure your children are safely occupied and take a few minutes of "time out" (it sometimes works better for parents than for kids!). Better yet, arrange for some time to do something to nurture yourself. Exhaustion and frustration can lead even the best parents to say and do things they later regret; it's far better to invest the time it takes to help yourself feel better.

Teach your children to respect your rights and privacy.
It may come as something of a revelation to you, but parents have rights, too. For example, you can teach your children to knock on your bedroom door before entering (and you can respect them by knocking on *their* door, too). You can help them to understand that Mom's and Dad's things are not theirs to play with, or that while the family room is okay for playing, the living room is not. Remember, respect is a *mutual* thing, and your children will learn best by what they see you do.

Beware of getting into the habit of serving your children. A good rule of thumb is never to do *regularly* for a person what he can do for himself. Your children will quickly learn to get their own cups of juice (if you've taught them first of course— see Chapter 14), to dress themselves, and to do a great many other things as well. You will be teaching your children competence (and sparing yourself a great deal of future resentment and frustration) by helping them to help you.

Teachers Are Important, Too!

Teachers who spend each day in a room with several dozen inquisitive, active toddlers and preschoolers also need to take care of themselves. A wise preschool director will make certain that his or her staff feels contented and appreciated.

If you teach in a preschool or day care center or spend much time caring for young children, consider the following ways teachers can take care of themselves (and each other) and perhaps make some suggestions to your director.

- **Be sure teachers get time off.** Many businesses allow their employees to take "well days" two or three times a year. These days off, which can be taken any time, allow teachers an opportunity to nurture themselves and have a "time out" from work. (Well days can also provide a welcome benefit if wages are lower than desired.) Teachers can also be rewarded with time off when they miss no days of work for a certain period, attend trainings, or perform tasks that are "above and beyond the call of duty."
- **Hold regular staff meetings and make time for encouragement and appreciations.** Holding "family meetings" for your preschool staff can provide a wonderful opportunity to give positive feedback, solve problems, make suggestions, and be sure that no one is overwhelmed or discouraged. You might plan your meetings around a potluck dinner or a night out at an informal restaurant. Be sure the contributions each person makes during the week are noticed and appreciated; extra-special projects, well-decorated classrooms, or handling a delicate situation well merit special attention.
- **Begin a "special angel" program.** Have each staff member draw the name of another to encourage and amuse in special ways. For example, leave notes or flowers, bring in baked goods or candy, or talk to the parents and children and com-

pile a list of their appreciations for the person. Nurturing the team you work with will make caring for your young charges much more pleasant and will create a supportive atmosphere that benefits children and staff alike.

And here's a special note to parents: if you're particularly happy with your child's preschool, teacher, or child care provider, take time to say so. All of us want to feel appreciated, and a little encouragement goes a long, long way. Tell your teacher or the director why you're happy, have your child draw a special picture or make a "thank you" card, or provide a small gift. Finding ways to make those who work for and with your children feel appreciated lets them know you notice what they do—and that may give them the energy to keep on doing it!

Focus on the Joys

Whether you're a parent or a teacher, there will be moments when the task seems thankless and never-ending. That's when it may serve you well to take a deep breath and look (again) in your memory for the face of that sleeping child. Put yourself in touch with the love you feel for your children; remember why you're doing the things that sometimes seem so difficult.

It's one of the things we've said many times, but it's so very important: Take time to enjoy your children and to focus on the pleasures of being with them. Sometimes good parenting (and good teaching) requires that you drop your "shoulds" for a moment and just have fun. Indulge in a game of peek-a-boo or hide-and-seek; curl up together and read a book or watch a favorite video; tickle and laugh and hug, and simply smile at one another. Discover what it means to play.

Children are, at times, a challenge. But they are also one of life's greatest gifts and opportunities. Caring for babies and young children requires tremendous commitment and energy; be sure you make time to refill your own pitcher by taking care of yourself and by remembering to relax and enjoy one another. The hugs and quiet moments of joy will keep you going over the bumpy places.

Conclusion

The years of early childhood are often overwhelming for parents. In those first hectic months, "paradise" is as simple as having time to take a bath or read a novel while the baby naps. Then come the toddler years, when your tiny offspring scoots energetically through your life exploring his new world, often leaving you breathless with laughter—or exhaustion. Each day brings a new discovery and, sometimes, a new crisis. It seems as though the kitchen counter will never be cleared, the laundry will never be done, these years will never end.

But they do. Our job as parents is to make ourselves unnecessary. From the first moments of our children's lives, we steadily lead them toward independence, loving and supporting them when they falter. As they grow and mature, we hover nearby as inconspicuously as we can, holding our breath when they fall, rejoicing when they dust themselves off and go on again.

Yes, the preschool years are busy ones for parents. These years of testing and exploring can sorely try our patience, and we may catch ourselves longing for the day when our child is older and needs us less. But if we are wise, we will take time to enjoy these years that pass so swiftly.

Sometime soon—far sooner than you think—you will look across the room and stare in amazement at the stranger

303

you see. You will suddenly realize that your "baby" has grown up. He's not a toddler anymore; gone is the preschooler with the chronically runny nose. In his place is a grown-up looking child, ready for school and new friendships and new experiences that require your presence less and less frequently.

Our children will face life armed with whatever love, wisdom, and confidence we've had the courage to give them. There will surely be struggles, bumps and bruises, and tears; yet if we've done our job as parents well, our children will know that mistakes are wonderful opportunities to learn and that life is an adventure to be enjoyed.

There is a beautiful fable about two little girls who discovered the value of struggle and perseverance. They found two cocoons hanging from a branch, and as they watched in awe, two tiny butterflies emerged. The little creatures were so damp and fragile that it seemed impossible they could survive, let alone fly.

The girls watched as the butterflies struggled to open their wings. One girl, fearing that the butterflies would not survive, reached for one and gently spread its delicate wings. The second girl offered the other butterfly a twig to cling to; then she carried it to the window ledge, where the sun could warm it.

Both butterflies continued to struggle valiantly, testing their new wings. The one on the ledge eventually opened its wings, paused for a moment in the sun's gentle warmth, then flew gracefully away. But the butterfly whose wings had been pried open never found the strength to fly, and perished without ever taking wing.

It can be painful to watch our young ones struggle, to know that we cannot always save them from trouble and pain no matter how vigilant we are. But wise parents know that, like the butterfly, children gather strength and wisdom from their struggles. It takes a great deal of courage—and a great deal of love—to allow our children to taste life for themselves and learn its lessons.

We can't fight our children's battles. And even the most loving parent can't guarantee that his children will never know pain. But there is a great deal we *can* do.

We can offer our children trust, dignity, and respect. We can have faith in them, and in their ability to learn and grow. We can take time to teach them: about ideas, about people, about the skills they will need to thrive in a challenging world. We can nurture and cultivate their talents and interests, and encourage each small step they take. We can give them the gifts of competence and responsibility.

And best of all, we can love and enjoy them, laugh and play with them. We can steal into their rooms at night and feel again and again that overwhelming tenderness as we gaze on our children's sleeping faces. We can draw on that love and tenderness to give us the wisdom and courage it takes to do what we must as parents.

This book is all about learning from our mistakes and celebrating our successes. As authors and as parents, we hope that you have found it useful. But the ultimate answers will always be found in your own heart and spirit; you will parent best when you parent from the heart.

Take a moment now and then to savor this special time of childhood despite the inevitable hassles and frustrations; *enjoy* your children as much as you possibly can. These are precious, important years, and we can only live them once.

Index

Positive Discipline for Single Parents

by Jane Nelsen, Cheryl Erwin, and Carol Delzer

Being a single parent in this complex world of ours can be both an overwhelming and exhilarating challenge. In *Positive Discipline for Single Parents*, the authors emphasize ways in which single parents can make clear, focused discipline decisions while maintaining positive levels of interaction with their children. Learn how to:

- redefine the parenting role
- set the stage for team-work
- deal with feelings and emotions
- balance your priorities
- understand misbehavior
- create a partnership with your child

The authors also provide re-assuring answers to questions about your own social life, your children's emotional stability, and other pertinent questions that plague parents from time to time.

Positive Discipline A–Z

by Jane Nelsen, Lynn Lott, and H. Stephen Glenn

What should I do when she has a temper
   tantrum in the grocery store?
What should I do when he bites another child?
What should I do when she won't go to bed at night?
What should I do when he won't eat his dinner?

Wouldn't it be nice if there was a book that listed in alphabetical order every child-raising problem parents could imagine? Here it is—from the best-selling parenting experts at CAPABLE PEOPLE ASSOCIATES. This book not only helps parents to solve problem behavior, but also helps children to feel good about themselves, gain self-confidence and self-discipline, learn responsibility, and develop problem-solving skills.

FOR MORE INFORMATION

The authors offer several workshops and seminars on parent education and positive discipline in the classroom for teachers.

Topics include:

> Positive Discipline for Parents of Preschoolers
> Positive Discipline for Single Parents
> Teaching Parenting
> Parenting in Recovery: The Next Step
> Positive Discipline in the Classroom
> Developing Capable People by H. Stephen Glenn

Training is also available for individuals who wish to facilitate their own parent education classes.

Workshops, seminars, and facilitator trainings are scheduled throughout the United States each year. Dates and locations are available by contacting:

Empowering People Associates
P.O. Box 788
Fair Oaks, CA 95628
(916) 961-5551 • Fax: (916) 961-5570

The authors are also available for lectures, teacher in-service training, and conference keynote presentations.

BOOKS BY JANE NELSEN

To: Empowering People Books, Tapes & Videos, Box B, Provo, UT 84603
Phone: 1-800-456-7770

	Price	Quantity	Amount
POSITIVE DISCIPLINE FOR PRESCHOOLERS by Nelsen, Cheryl Erwin, & Roslyn Duffy	$12.95	_____	_____
POSITIVE DISCIPLINE FOR SINGLE PARENTS by Nelsen, Erwin, & Carol Delzer	$10.95	_____	_____
POSITIVE DISCIPLINE A–Z by Nelsen, Lynn Lott, and H. Stephen Glenn	$14.95	_____	_____
POSITIVE DISCIPLINE IN THE CLASSROOM by Nelsen, Lott, & Glenn	$14.95	_____	_____
RAISING SELF-RELIANT CHILDREN IN A SELF-INDULGENT WORLD by Glenn & Nelsen	$10.95	_____	_____
POSITIVE DISCIPLINE FOR TEENAGERS by Nelsen & Lott	$14.95	_____	_____
POSITIVE DISCIPLINE by Nelsen	$9.95	_____	_____
TIME OUT by Nelsen & Glenn	$6.95	_____	_____
UNDERSTANDING: ELIMINATING STRESS . . . by Nelsen	$9.95	_____	_____
CLEAN AND SOBER PARENTING by Nelsen, Riki Intner, & Lott	$10.95	_____	_____
THE FAMILY THAT WORKS TOGETHER by Lott & Intner	$9.95	_____	_____

SUBTOTAL _____

Sales Tax: UT residents add 6.25%; CA residents add 7.25% _____
Shipping & Handling: $2.50 plus 50¢ for each item _____

TOTAL _____

(Prices subject to change without notice.)

METHOD OF PAYMENT (check one):
_____Check made payable to Empowering People Books, Tapes & Video
_____ Mastercard _____ Visa
Card # _____ _____ _____ _____ Expiration _____ / _____
Ship to _____
Address _____
City/State/Zip _____
Daytime Phone _____

For a free newsletter, call toll-free: 1-800-456-7770

About the Authors

Jane Nelsen, Ed.D., is a popular lecturer and author or co-author of the POSITIVE DISCIPLINE SERIES of books. She has appeared on *Oprah!, Sally Jessy Raphael, Twin Cities Live* and was the featured parent expert on the "National Parent Quiz" hosted by Ben Vereen. Jane is the mother of seven children and the grandmother of twelve.

Cheryl Erwin is the parenting education trainer for the Children's Cabinet, a nonprofit family resource center in Reno, Nevada. She graduated from the University of Texas with a degree in journalism and has been writing on parenting issues and teaching parenting classes for six years. Cheryl lives with her ten-year-old son, a cat, and a bird.

Roslyn Duffy is the director and founder of the Better Living Institute in Seattle, Washington. In 1979, Roslyn cofounded the Learning Tree Montessori School, which she still directs. She teaches parenting classes and teacher training programs and lectures nationally. Roslyn lives with her husband and four children.